HOT ICE

THEATRE FOR CLASSICAL AND CHRISTIAN SCHOOLS

LEVEL II: MEDIEVAL AND RENAISSANCE

Student's Edition

EILEEN CUNNINGHAM

MARCEE COSBY

Text Copyright © 2017 Eileen Cunningham and Marcee Cosby

ISBN: 9780692969236

To the community of the

Classical School of Wichita

A special thank you to Ellen Burd for assistance with the manuscript

Table of Contents

INTRODUCTION i
    Purpose i
    Smorgasbord Approach i
    The Title i
    Bible References ii
    Editing ii
    Contact Us ii

MEDIEVAL THEATRE 1
    Introduction 1
    The Aftermath of Roman Theatre 1
    Tropes and Liturgical Drama 2
    Size and Complexity 7
    Prohibitions and Permissions 7
    The Corpus Christi Plays 10
    The Corpus Christi Cycles 11
        The York Cycle 11
        The Wakefield Cycle 11
        The Chester Cycle 11
        The N-Town Cycle 12
        The Role of the Guilds 13
    The Medieval Stage: Pageants 13
        The Stage 14
        The Procession 14
        EXERCISE 1.1: Primary Source 15
        Questions: 16
    Plen an gwari 19
        EXERCISE 1.2: Primary Source 20
        Questions: 21

    Decline and End of Mystery and Morality Plays 22

THE RHETORIC OF MEDIEVAL PLAYS 25

    Introduction 25

    Diction 25

        Meter 25

        Rhythm 26

        Examples 26

    Rhythm and Meter by Era 27

        EXERCISE 2.1: Meter in Mystery Plays 32

        MORE CHALLENGING: 33

    The Sound of Middle English 33

        ACTIVITY A: View and Do: Middle English 35

    Literary Techniques 36

        Débat 36

        EXERCISE 2.2: Analyzing a *Débat* 37

        Alliteration 38

        Allusion 39

        Anachronism 40

        Aphorism 40

        Metaphor 41

        Personification 41

        Rhyme 42

        Simile 43

        EXERCISE 2.3: Diction 44

    Progymnasmata: Expanded Narrative *(Diêgêma)* 44

        Questions: 47

    Progymnasmata: Commonplace *(Koinós Tópos)* 51

        EXERCISE 2.4: Analyzing Commonplace 53

        Approach: Comparison 54

    Question: 54

    Approach: Contrast 54

    Questions: 56

    Approach: Cause 56

    Questions: 56

    Past Life / Profile 57

    Questions: 58

    Approach: Call for Punishment 59

    Question: 59

    Conclusion 60

    Question: 60

MEDIEVAL PLAYS 61

  Introduction 61

  Liturgical Drama 61

  The Term *Mystery Play* 62

  Miracle Plays 62

  Morality Plays 62

    EXERCISE 3.1: Examining a Morality Play 63

    Questions: 66

    ACTIVITY 3.2: Costuming *Everyman* 68

  Comic Elements of the Mystery Plays 69

  Secular Plays 73

    EXERCISE 3.3: Analyzing a Script for a Secular Play 74

    TASKS 75

  Cornish Language Plays 76

MEDIEVAL PLAYWRIGHTS AND PLAYERS 79

  Playwrights 79

    Roswitha of Gandersheim (10th-century Saxony) 79

    Hildegard of Bingen (1098-1179) 81

    Geoffrey de Gorham (12th-century England) 82

    Hilarius (12th-century France) 82

    Schoolboys 84

Fleury (France c. 1200) 84

    EXERCISE 4.1 (ENRICHMENT): Translating Latin Dialogue 85

    BACKGROUND A: 85

    BACKGROUND B 86

    The Wakefield Master (c. 1460-65) 88

Players 89

    Guildsmen 89

    EXERCISE 4.2: Primary Source 89

    Servants 92

    Women 93

    Children 94

    Troupes 95

SPECTACLE ON THE MEDIEVAL STAGE 97

Introduction 97

Costumes and Props 97

Sets 100

Earthquakes and Storms 101

Ascending and Descending 102

Dismemberment and Substitution 104

Vanishing and Going Dark 104

Crucifixion Scenes 105

Blood 107

    EXERCISE 5.1: Outfitting a Mystery Play 108

    COSTUMES 110

    ACTIVITY 5.A: Creating Special Effects 111

Animals 112

EXERCISE 5.2: Analyzing the Use of Animals on Stage 114

Questions: 116

ACTIVITY 5.B: Improvisation with Animals 117

SCENE 1: A hill in England 118

SCENE 2: Mak's cottage 118

SCENE 3: The hill 119

SCENE 4: The cottage 119

SCENE 5: A crooked thorn 119

SCENE 6: The cottage 119

SCENE 7: The hill 120

SCENE 8: A stable in Bethlehem 120

Instructions for Improvisation: 120

ACTIVITY 5.C: Projects in Medieval Spectacle 121

MORE CHALLENGING #1: 121

MORE CHALLENGING #2: 123

MORE CHALLENGING #3: 123

MEDIEVAL THEATRE TIDBITS FROM PRIMARY SOURCES 125

Introduction 125

Richard II and the London Procession 125

ACTIVITY 6.A: Determining the Pageantry Route 127

John Wycliffe, Morality Plays, and the English Language 130

THE THEATRE IN THE RENAISSANCE AND REFORMATION 133

Introduction 133

What Was the Renaissance? 133

Italian City-States 133

Fifteenth-Century Theatre in England 134

Status of "Players" in Tudor England 135

Patronage in Elizabethan England 135

Sumptuary Laws and Livery 137

ACTIVITY 7.A: Tudor Costume 138

Theatres and Stages 139

    Permanent Theatres 140

    The Globe 140

    The Elizabethan Stage 142

How Did the Reformation Affect the Theatre? 144

    Henry VIII: The Demand for Religious Conformity 144

    Protestant Reformers: Doctrine 145

    EXERCISE 7.1: Comparing Traditional and Reformed Scripts 145

    Elizabeth I: The Threat of Political Turmoil 147

    London City Council: Crime and Public Health 148

    Puritans: The Moral Dimension 148

ELIZABETHAN PLAYWRIGHTS 151

Introduction 151

Playwrights 151

    Christopher Marlowe 151

    EXERCISE 8.1: Scriptural Connection *(Doctor Faustus)* 154

    Questions: 158

    MORE CHALLENGING 160

    Thomas Kyd 160

    Ben Jonson 162

    William Shakespeare 164

Social Status of Playwrights 166

ELIZABETHAN PLAYERS 169

Introduction 169

Comic Actors 169

    Richard Tarlton 169

    Will Kempe 172

    ACTIVITY 9.A: Freeze Tag Improvisation 174

- Tragic Actors 175
  - Edward Alleyn 175
  - Richard Burbage 177
  - EXERCISE 9.1: Analyzing Acting Style 180

ELIZABETHAN AND JACOBEAN PLAYS 183
- Introduction 183
- Tragedy 183
  - Definition 183
  - Plot in Tragedy 184
  - Characters in Tragedy 184
  - Catharsis 185
- Comedy 186
  - Aristotle's Definition 186
  - Comic Characters 186
  - Types of Comedy 187
- Tragicomedy 188
- Masques 188
- Witch Plays 189
- The Sound of Elizabethan Plays 191
  - Present-Day British English 191
  - ACTIVITY 10.A: Practicing an English Accent 192
  - The Early Modern Accent 192
  - ACTIVITY 10.B: The Sound of Shakespeare's English 194

WHY SHAKESPEARE? 197
- Introduction 197
- Action (or Plot) 197
  - Character 198
- Idea 198
- Diction 198

Song 202
Spectacle 202
Psychology 202
    Emotions 203
    Borderline Personality Disorder (BPD) 203
    Depression 203
    Schizophrenia 204
    Ophelia Syndrome 205
    Obsessive-Compulsive Disorders 206
    Paranoia 206
Sociology 207
    The Soldiers' Bond 207
    Civil Factions 207
    Influence 207
    Leaders and Followers 207
    The Accused and the Courts 208
    Racial and Ethnic Groups 208
    Parents and Children 209
Health 209
    Perceptions of Body Types 210
    Aging 210
    Substance Abuse 210
    Reactions to Deformity 210
    Infirmity 211
    Laughter and Health 212
    Summing Up 212

SUBTEXT 213
Introduction 213
Subtext via Body Language and Facial Expression 213

- ACTIVITY 12.A: Perceiving Subtext 214
- Subtext and Intonation 214
  - ACTIVITY 12.B: Subtext and Intonation 215
- Subtext in Shakespeare 215
  - ACTIVITY 12.C: Detecting Subtext in *Julius Caesar* 218
- Subtext and Early Modern Pronouns *(Thou* vs. *You)* 218
- Pronoun Chart for Early Modern English 218
  - Singular vs. Plural 219
  - Case in Second-person Pronouns 220
  - Cultural Use of Second-person Pronouns 222
  - ACTIVITY 12.D: Delivering Lines with Second-person Pronouns 227
  - Questions: 230
  - EXERCISE 12.1: Subtext in a Seventeenth-century Witch's Play 231
  - Example: 231
- SPECTACLE ON THE ELIZABETHAN STAGE 233
  - Introduction 233
  - Stagecraft 233
  - Spectacle and Special Effects 234
    - EXERCISE 13.1: Special Effects Analysis 235
    - Weapons 239
    - ACTIVITY 13.A: Special Effects with Stage Weapons 241
    - ACTIVITY 13.B: View and Do: Stage Combat from *Robin Hood* 242
    - ACTIVITY 13.C: View and Do: Stage Combat in *Romeo and Juliet* ... 243
    - Decapitation 244
    - Smoke and Fire 245
    - Optical Illusions 245
    - Music and Sound Effects 246
    - Flying 247
    - EXERCISE 13.2: Special Effects Platt Sheet 249

RHETORIC IN RENAISSANCE PLAYS 251
   Introduction 251
      EXERCISE 14.1: Examining a Shakespearean Encomium 253
      Questions: 254
   Modes of Persuasion 256
      ACTIVITY 14.A: Listening to Marc Antony's Oration 259
      EXERCISE 14.2: Identifying Rhetorical Appeals 259

RENAISSANCE THEATRE TIDBITS FROM PRIMARY SOURCES 263
   Introduction 263
   The *Macbeth* Curse 263

APPENDIX A: Robin Hood Fragment in Modern English A-1
APPENDIX B: Translation of St. Nicholas Excerpt B-1
APPENDIX C: Excerpt from The Conversion of St. Paul C-1
APPENDIX D: TEXTS A and B of the Norwich Grocers' Play D-1
APPENDIX E: Figures of Speech from Shakespeare E-1
APPENDIX F: Excerpt from The Late Lancashire Witches F-1

Image Attribution I-1
Endnotes E-1

INTRODUCTION

Purpose

Though there are textbooks a-plenty for the instruction of drama in middle schools and high schools, we could find little that was written with the curriculum and methodology of classical education in mind. Nor could we find much that reflected the Christian worldview. The purpose of this book, therefore, is to fill the need of students, teachers, and families involved in classical and Christian education. Specifically, the book introduces drama to students in grades 7-12. As a textbook for Christian families, it attempts to explain the sometimes hostile relationship between the stage and the Church and directs students' attention to the moral and ethical responsibilities of the theatre community. It explains why drama is important for students of classical antiquity, and provides focus for young people who wish to turn the talents God has given them back into His service in the form of theatre arts, remembering Colossians 3:17, which says, "And whatever you do, in word or deed, do everything in the name of the Lord Jesus, giving thanks to God the Father through him"

As a textbook for classical education, *Hot Ice* employs primary sources, integrates literature and history, and examines dramatic passages from the perspective of the progymnasmata and other rhetorical techniques. It addresses the classical trivium and, from the quadrivium, discusses music as an aspect of theatre. There are spots in which familiarity with Latin and Greek might be helpful, but exercises involving translation are optional.

Smorgasbord Approach

Teachers should feel free to use a smorgasbord approach to the book. Choose sections, exercises, and activities. as you like. There is much here. If desired, the material can be spread over two academic years—certainly two semesters.

The Title

At the end of *A Midsummer Night's Dream* by William Shakespeare, Bottom and the other "mechanicals" present a play to celebrate the wedding of Duke Theseus. Musing over the oxymorons in the handbill of the play, Theseus speaks.

THESEUS:

[Reading] "A tedious brief scene of young Pyramus
And his love Thisbe; very tragical mirth."
Merry and tragical! tedious and brief!
That is, hot ice and wondrous strange snow.
How shall we find the concord of this discord? (5.1.56-60)

The lines resound with meaning for the lover of literature and of drama, in particular, for they come not just from a play, but from a play within a play, which was written, not by any ordinary playwright, but by the greatest master of the English language ever to set pen to paper. The phrase *hot ice* is particularly apt, as it typifies the wonderful diction of the playwright, calls up the thrill of the stage, and suits, as well, the iconic theatre masks of Comedy and Tragedy. For these reasons, we selected the phrase *Hot Ice* as the title of this book, which we hope will both inform and inspire a new generation of thespians.

Bible References

Unless otherwise noted, all Scripture herein is from the English Standard Version.

Editing

We have taken the liberty of editing material in the public domain for the spelling and conventions of Standard Written English as it is taught in schools in the United States in our times. We confess to tampering with British spellings from public domain materials (e.g., *-our* appears here as *–or*), but we have ardently committed ourselves to the Franco-Britannic *–re* at the end of the word *theatre*. We submit to the charge of snootiness, if need be, but we allow that, like broken clocks, the French and British can be right twice per day—and, besides, seeing the word spelled as *theater* affects us in the same way as squeaky chalk on a blackboard.

Contact Us

If you have questions or comments, please feel free to contact us via our web site: <http://www.writingtheclassicalway.com>.

HISTORICAL TIMELINE	THEATRE TIMELINE

MEDIEVAL PERIOD

476	Fall of Rome	c. 900	*Quem Quaeritis?* is begun.
c. 1350	Turmoil in Italian city-states. Italian Renaissance in art and literature begins		
1453	Fall of Constantinople	1264	Corpus Christi plays begin.
		c. 1440	Nobles begin to establish acting troupes

RENAISSANCE/ REFORMATION

1453	Greek mss. flow into Europe, igniting Renaissance and Reformation		
1485	Henry VII becomes first Tudor king of England		
1517	Martin Luther posts his 95 Theses; Reformation Era begins	1543	Henry VIII makes it a crime for a playwright to contradict the doctrine of the Church of England

ELIZABETHAN ENGLAND

1558	Elizabeth I comes to the throne. Puritans return from exile and exhort the Queen to continue the Reformation in England.	Theatre Builders: Burbage family Playwrights: Jonson, Marlowe, Shakespeare Players: Kempe, Alleyn Theologians: Protestant revisions to plays

JACOBEAN AND CAROLINE ENGLAND

1597	James VI of Scotland publishes a dissertation on witchcraft entitled *Daemonologie*		
1603	James VI of Scotland (a Protestant) becomes James I of England	1606	Witch plays begin with *Macbeth*.
1625	Charles I comes to the throne.		
		1642	Theatres are closed by the Puritans.
1649	Charles I is executed.		

MEDIEVAL THEATRE

Chapter 1

Introduction

Just as the kernel of Greek drama was planted by priests in honor of the god Dionysius in the seventh century BC, so the kernel of medieval drama was planted by Christian priests in the tenth century of the Christian era. This faith-based drama expanded and developed in the thirteenth century after Pope Urban IV established the Feast of Corpus Christi, of which theatre became an integral part. The term *medieval theatre*, then, covers the period from the tenth century through the early sixteenth century, when the Renaissance and Reformation vastly changed the intellectual currents that underlie the arts.

The Aftermath of Roman Theatre

Because of the sordid nature of the Roman stage at the dawning of Christianity, the word theatre became associated with the words pagan and scandalous. In AD 401, the Council of Carthage forbade the performance of plays on Sundays, and later in the fifth century, the Theodosian Code of the Eastern Empire also prohibited *omnis theatorum atque circensium voluptas* (all recreations of the theatre and the circus) on Sundays and other Christian holy days.[1]

The Council of Trullo, meeting in Constantinople in 692, went even further with this ruling:

> Canon 51: This holy and ecumenical synod altogether forbids those who are called "players," and their "spectacles," as well as the exhibition of hunts, and the theatrical dances. If anyone despises the present canon, and gives himself to any of the things which are forbidden, if he be a cleric he shall be deposed, but if a layman let him be cut off.[2]

For these reasons, the theatrical impulse slumbered until the tenth century when certain embellishments were added to the Mass. From that small seed, drama began to reemerge in Europe, this time primarily in service of the Church and its educational mission to an unlettered population.

Tropes and Liturgical Drama

In the tenth century, a churchman on the continent, probably Notker the Stammerer at the Abbey of St. Gall in Switzerland, decided one Easter to "dramatize" the scene recorded in Luke 24, the visit to the sepulchre by the three Marys to anoint the body of the crucified Lord. To do this, he employed a trope, that is, an embellishment to the Scripture for instructional purposes, which could be compared to responsive readings in today's church services.

Notker the Stammerer
c. 840-912

Though other tropes were to follow, the trope for the *Visitatio Sepulchri* (Visit to the Sepulchre) is called the *Quem Quaeritis*, after the first two words in the sequence. Scholars believe the first performance of the trope would have involved two facing choirs, one representing the chorus of angels; the other, the women at the tomb, in an exchange that went like this:

> INTERROGATIO
> *Quem quaeritis in sepulchro, o Christicolae?*
> [Whom do you seek in the tomb, O dwellers in Christ?]
>
> RESPONSIO
> *Ihesum Nazarenum crucifixum, o caelicolae.*
> [The crucified Jesus of Nazareth, O dweller in heaven.]
>
> ANGELI
> *Non est hic; surrexit, sicut praedixerat. Ite, nuntiate quia surrexit de sepulchro.*
> [He is not here; he has risen, as he foretold. Go announce that he has risen from the dead.]

In 973, Aethelwold, Bishop of Winchester, recorded in the *Regularis Concordia* what might be called stage directions for the presentation of the *Quem Quaeritis*, which appear below:

Excerpt from *Regularis Concordia*
By Aethelwold of Winchester

While the third lesson is being read, four of the brothers robe themselves, one of whom, wearing an alb as if for some different purpose, enters and discreetly goes to the place where the sepulchre is and sits there quietly with a palm in his hand. While the third response is being sung, the remaining three come forward, everyone dressed in a cope, carrying thuribles with incense in their hands, and hesitantly, like people seeking something, come to the site of the sepulchre. For these things are performed in imitation of the angel sitting in the tomb, and of the women coming with spices to anoint Jesus' body. Consequently, when the one sitting there sees three nearing him just like people straying about seeking something, he begins to sing sweetly in a moderate voice:

In English and Welsh churches, the Easter Sepulchre is an area in the chancel where the crucifix and holy elements are placed from Good Friday till Easter.

Thurible (censer for dispersing incense)

Quem quaeritis in sepulchro, O Christicolae?
[Whom do you seek in the sepulchre, O dwellers in Christ?]

When this has been sung right through, the three reply in unison:

Ihesum Nazarenum crucifixum, o caelicolae.
[The crucified Jesus of Nazareth, O dweller in heaven.]

He answers them thus:

Non est hic; surrexit, sicut praedixerat. Ite, nuntiate quia surrexit de sepulchro.
[He is not here; he has risen, as he foretold. Go announce that he has risen from the dead.]

At this command, the three turn to the choir saying:

Alleluia, resurrexit Dominus, hodie resurrexit leo fortis, Christus, filius Dei. Deo gratias, dicite eia!

[Alleluia, the Lord has risen, today the strong lion, Christ, the Son of God has risen. Cry joyfully, thanks be to God!]

This being sung, the seated one as if calling them back sings the antiphon:

Venite et videte locum ubi positus erat Dominus, alleluia.
[Come and see the place where the Lord was placed, alleluia.]

Singing these words, he rises and lifts the curtain, and shows them the place with the cross gone but with the linen cloths in which the cross was wrapped lying there. Having seen this, they put down the thuribles which they carried to the sepulchre, and take up the linen, and spread it out in the sight of the clergy, as if making it plain that the Lord has arisen and is not wrapped in the grave-clothes now. They sing this antiphon:

Surrexit Dominus de sepulchro, qui pro nobis pependit in ligno, alleluia.
[The Lord has risen from the tomb, who for our sake hung upon the cross, alleluia.]

And they place the linen upon the altar cloth. When the antiphon is finished, the prior, rejoicing with them in the triumph of our king, who arose, after conquering death, begins the hymn *Te Deum laudamus*. [*We praise thee, O God.*] When this has begun, all the bells peal out together.[3]

Fig. 1 (page 6) shows that the *Quem Quaeritis?* of Bishop Aethelwold could be performed almost entirely in the chancel area of the church. However, as the centuries passed, liturgical drama became more complex, involving multiple scenes and many performers, so it was decided to set up stage mansions (or performing platforms) in the nave of the church so that each scene could be presented in a different locale (these appear with the letter *M* in Fig. 1).

The words *Quem Quaeritus* also began the Christmas trope, but the question was directed to the shepherds:

ANGELS
Quem quaeritis in presepe, pastores, dicite?
[Whom do ye seek in the manger, shepherds, say?]

SHEPHERDS
Salvatorem Christum Dominum, infantem pannis secondum sermonem angelicum.
[The Savior Christ the Lord, the infant wrapped in swaddling clothes, just as the angel said.] [4]

It is interesting to note the addition of music to the Easter trope at Winchester—both vocal (the hymn) and instrumental (the bells), which would have magnified the effect and lifted the hearts of the parishioners. Another Christmas trope called *The Play of the Three Kings* also employed music.

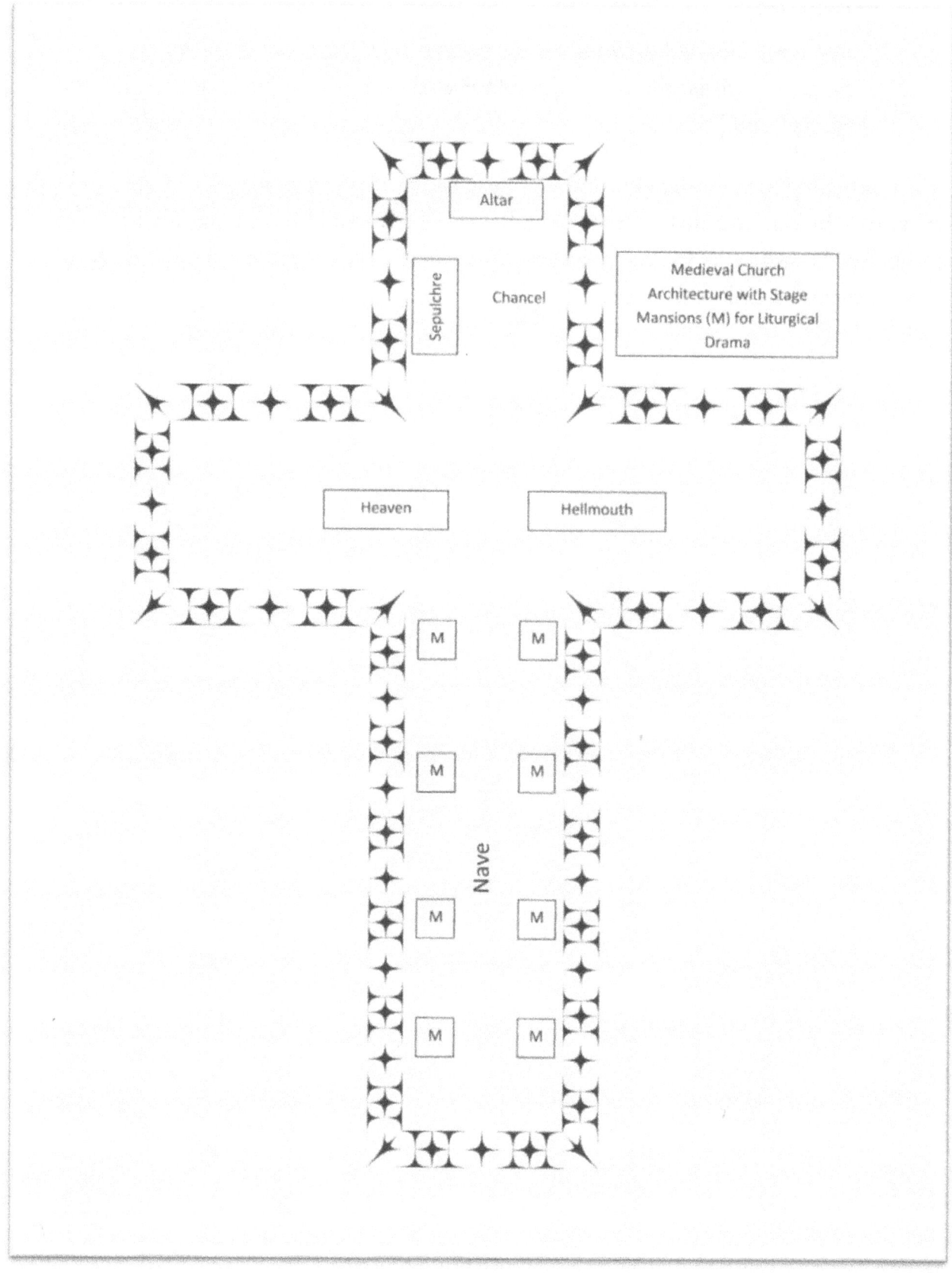

Fig. 1: Arrangement of the chancel area for presentation of the *Quem Quaeritis*?

Size and Complexity

As time passed and dramatic depictions of Bible narratives expanded, they outgrew the chancel of the church. For example, *The Play of Daniel*, which presents the events of Daniel 5 and 6, called for at least six acting spaces:

1. The narrator's mansion
2. King Belshazzar's throne
3. Daniel's quarters
4. King Darius' throne
5. The lion's den
6. Mansion for the angel and Habakkuk (an added character)

Depending on how the person in charge wanted to present the handwriting which needed to appear on a wall, a seventh platform may have been employed as well. In addition, both kings—Belshazzar and Darius—were scripted to have a group of nobles surrounding them, which, of course, increased the number of performers occupying sometimes a quite small space.

A stage mansion for the performance of *The World and the Child*

Because of the turmoil inherent in plays of this size, involving so many platforms and so many players, by the early twelfth century, churches had started performing their liturgical dramas outside in the nearby environs of the church. This innovation marks the end of the first period of medieval European theatre.

Prohibitions and Permissions

It would be nice to say that medieval theatre continued in sinless perfection throughout the Middle Ages, but as with much human activity, folly raised its head. What went wrong?

At issue was an annual event called the Feast of Fools, which is first mentioned in the historical records in 1160. This celebration, which was integrated with New Year festivities, was established by subdeacons in northern France, who felt that, like the deacons and priests, they should have their own feast day. Whether or not the revels associated with the Feast of Fools were originally intended to represent Christian humility, as some have argued, they did not long remain so, as by the end of the century, Church authorities were calling for an end to the revelries.

Considering the meaning of the term *subdeacon* will assist in understanding what went wrong with the subdeacons' idea. *The Catholic Encyclopedia*, which points out that the office of subdeacon has since been abolished, explains:

> The subdiaconate is the lowest of the sacred or major orders in the Latin Church. It is defined as the power by which one ordained as a subdeacon may carry the chalice with wine to the altar, prepare the necessaries for the Eucharist, and read the Epistles before the people.[5]

This definition points to a person with little authority who served as an assistant and was probably young. Like a college student who has a summer internship with a business firm in our times, the subdeacons were old enough to take on some responsibilities, though still essentially learners.

Headlines in our newspapers today will confirm that young people in large groups do not always behave with decorum. They sometimes act up on the beaches during spring break, celebrate a bit too riotously celebrating athletic victories, and allow their parties to get a little out of hand. Such reckless behavior is apparently what happened with the young subdeacons when they established the Feast of Fools. If the idea was to invert the established order—with the subdeacons taking the higher positions and the older men taking subservient positions in order to practice humility—the event quickly lost its emphasis on virtue and became a riotous revel that brought shame on the Church, at least in the eyes of those in charge.

What we know about the ruckus comes mostly from orders delivered to the subdeacons through the chain of command. For example, in 1199, a French cardinal directed a bishop in Paris to tell the subdeacons to cut out some of their shenanigans. One rule was that the bells for first Vespers "are to be rung in the usual way." Apparently, the revelers had been clanging them noisily. Another rule was that there were to be "no *chansons*" (songs) and "no masks."[6] Now, in Latin and in French the word *masque* refers not simply to a facial disguise, but to a short dramatic performance with actors in costume. Probably, at this Feast of Fools, the young men had been putting on plays (or skits) full of silliness and inappropriate jokes entirely unsuited to the serious mission of the Church.

Feast of Fools by Pieter Brueghel, 1559

Perhaps the subdeacons did "sober up" a bit after their reprimand, but just eight years later the rowdiness had flared up again. This time the pope himself, Innocent III, decreed that the subdeacons were to discontinue *larvae* (horrific masks such as those sometimes used on Halloween) and *theatrales ludi* (stage plays). After him, in 1227, another pope, Gregory IX, went so far as to ban all "theatrical spectacles in church,"[7] and, at least in France, even this did not stop the subdeacons. More than two centuries later, in 1445, we find the Paris Theological Faculty writing a letter to the French bishops, describing what they found offensive about the Feast of Fools. Probably more than anything else, this letter reveals exactly what was going on during these revels:

> Priests and clerks may be seen wearing masks and monstrous visages at the hours of office. They dance in the choir dressed as women, panderers or minstrels. They sing wanton songs. They eat black puddings at the horn of the altar while the celebrant is saying Mass. They play at dice there. They cense with stinking smoke from the soles of old shoes. They run and leap through the church, without a blush at their own shame. Finally, they drive about the town and its theatres in shabby traps and carts, and rouse the laughter of their fellows and the bystanders in infamous performances, with indecent gesture and verses scurrilous and unchaste.[8]

This letter finally led the bishops to gain control of the lads, and, from that time on, references to the Feast of Fools in the historical records dwindle and, ultimately, disappear. The end of this festival, of course, was not the end of theatre in the Middle Ages, but it did serve to curb profane tomfoolery inside the churches.

The Corpus Christi Plays

Despite Gregory's prohibition, the theatrical impulse could not be completely suppressed, especially among Christians who realized that, if they kept to the mission of the Church—that is, the spreading of the Gospel—they could turn the theatre into the service of Christ. One such person was an Italian canonist (i.e., an expert in canon law) named Bernard de Bottone, who, in 1263, went back to Innocent's original decretal and scrutinized it to see if he could find some wiggle room. When he did so, he noticed that Innocent had not prohibited all *ecclesiis theatrales*, just those which were *lubricius* (lewd) or *obscoenus* (obscene). As a result, he clarified the matter for interested parties, stating that dramatizations of the Christmas and Easter narratives would certainly still be welcomed in the Church, as would Old Testament stories such as *"Rachel ploravit filios suos"* ("Rachel Crying for Her Children").[9]

Fig. 2. A Corpus Christi procession (late 15th – early 16th century) depicted by an artist known only as The Master of King James IV of Scotland

The following year, Pope Urban IV proposed holding an annual outdoor holy day in honor of the Eucharist (the Lord's Supper) to be known as the Feast of Corpus Christi. The festival was to take place in the spring of the year as the Easter season approached. A look at Fig. 2, which depicts a Corpus Christi celebration, reveals many of the elements which later would become part of medieval theatre: a procession winding through the streets, musicians, a canopy over the priests who are bearing the Eucharist, a bishop being carried on a litter, and, of course, spectators. These features served as the pattern for the next development in medieval theatre: the pageant.

The Corpus Christi Cycles

In England, plays developed in several towns as part of the feast of Corpus Christi. They came to be called the Corpus Christi cycles, primarily because over time each town produced a series, or cycle, of plays. For the most part, each series is known by the name of the town where it developed. A brief description of each cycle follows.

The York Cycle

York is a cathedral town in Yorkshire, which is in the north of England. It was an important city in the Middle Ages because it was the seat of an English archbishop, the only other being at Canterbury.

The plays in the York Cycle were written from the mid-fourteenth century to about 1569 and were performed as part of the Corpus Christi feast on the Thursday after Trinity Sunday, that is, between May 23 and June 24. The cycle eventually came to include forty-eight plays, each presenting a Bible narrative. It started with a play called *The Fall of the Angels* and ended with *The Last Judgment*. In a day before widespread education, the plays were a pleasant way to teach the common folk the Bible story.

The Wakefield Cycle

Wakefield was another Yorkshire town which had a Corpus Christi cycle. It consisted of thirty-two plays (primarily Bible narratives, as in York) and was composed from the late Middle Ages to 1576. They are sometimes called the Towneley plays, after the family who sold them at auction in 1814. Wakefield produced one of the most famous medieval plays, *The Second Shepherd's Play*, more of which later.

The Chester Cycle

Another northern city in England that produced a Corpus Christi cycle was Chester. Municipal records show that plays were already being performed there in 1422, but scholars believe they originated in the fourteenth century (1325 and 1375 have both been offered as possible dates). They remained popular until 1521. The Chester cycle included 25 plays performed over a three-day period, ranging once again from *The Fall of Lucifer* to *The Last Judgment*.

In 1618, Chester antiquarian David Rogers wrote this about the Chester Cycle:

> "Here note that these plays of Chester called the Whitsun plays were the works of one Rondoll [Randle Higden], a monk of the Abbey of St. Warburg in Chester, who reduced the whole history of the Bible into English stories in meter in the English tongue. . . . Then the first mayor of Chester, namely Sir John Arneway,[a] knight, he caused the same to be played."[10]

The N-Town Cycle

The plays in the N-Town Cycle were once called the Hegge Plays, after the seventeenth-century Oxford scholar, Robert Hegge, to whom they once belonged. The story of their name reveals something about the ad campaign that would precede the performances by about a week. The announcement was a nearly 530-line proclamation with three different heralds, the last few lines of which got (finally) to the point:

> THIRD HERALD
> On Sunday next, if that we may,
> At six of the bell we begin our play
> In N-town; wherefore we pray
> That God now be your speed.
> Amen.[11] (525-29)

Latin still holding a place in England, the N stood for *nomen* and was meant to direct the town crier to insert the name of the town where the plays would be acted.

The first play in the N-Town cycle was *The Creation and Fall of Man*, which began with the fall of Lucifer. The last play, as with the others, was *The Last Judgment*, ending a total of twenty-four plays.

---

[a] Sources disagree about the dates of Arneway's mayoralty. Randle Higden may have been a boy during the Arneway period, so the identity of the actual mayor who was coterminous with Higden is uncertain.

The Role of the Guilds

One observation about medieval life that can be drawn from the production of these plays is an awareness of the role (and the wealth) of the guilds in each city, for each guild was in charge of putting on one of the plays. The responsibilities of the guild included financing, building the sets, and even performing the plays. Financing was shared in some cases with the city government or a church.

Depiction of the medieval bakers' guild

One can imagine almost a competitive spirit that went into each presentation, much in the same way campus organizations compete for a prize in the building of a float for a homecoming parade. No doubt, the wealthier guilds were able to produce much more spectacle in their plays than the others.

Interestingly, in the Corpus Christi plays, the Bible narratives were performed by a guild with an associated theme. For example, in York, it was only logical that *The Building of the Ark* would be presented by the shipwrights, and *The Flood* by the fishers and mariners. At Chester, *The Harrowing of Hell* was produced by the cooks, who knew more than a little about fire, and the inn-keepers, though it is hard to say if the inn-keepers were admitting deficiencies in their inns.

The Medieval Stage: Pageants

The grand stone theatres of Greece and Rome were not a part of the medieval stage. The old Roman theatres scattered around England would already have been in disrepair by then, so even in cities like Chester, where the Roman theatre is a tourist attraction yet today, no consideration was given to moving the mystery plays there. Rather, the medieval stage developed naturally out of its own cultural milieu and served its own values. What follows is an explanation of the various directions the theatre took between the thirteenth and sixteenth centuries.

As we have seen, medieval acting began in the churches as part of the liturgy and eventually moved outside. Then, once the Feast of Corpus Christi was initiated, the idea of a procession through the town gave some theatrically minded person the idea that stages could follow the practice of the outdoor procession—if they were made mobile. Thus, was born the medieval pageant.

The Stage

The term *pageant* nowadays most commonly refers to a performance that is presented outside, but in the period we are examining, the pageant was the wagon itself on which was built a stage. Generally speaking, the pageants were moved by horses, as with any medieval carriage.

In earlier times, the pageant would have been fairly simple, perhaps a platform with a curtain so that spectators could not see what was happening "backstage," so to speak. As the decades and centuries rolled by, the pageants became much more sophisticated, involving two yoked wagons, one toting the acting platform and the other, a two-storey structure. From that structure, actors representing God, angels, and kings could be elevated and "speak down" to the less exalted on the platform below. The most elaborate pageants also had a cramped dressing room on the side of the lower storey.

On one side of the stage, the pageants often included a hell-mouth, a structure built to look like a demon with mouth open wide enough for actors to exit or enter, representing demons coming out of hell or condemned souls going in. One has to wonder if some sort of trap door was already being used to give access to the area under the platform, as by Shakespeare's time, the trap door was certainly in use.

The convenience of horse-drawn wagons was not enjoyed in every city where pageants were performed. According to Hugo Albert Rennert, in the Spanish city of Seville, the stage was a *roca:*

> [It was] a kind of platform (*andas*) carried by twelve men and on which were those persons who represented Maria, Jesus, Saints Dominick and Francis, and the four evangelists. There were besides six angels and eight prophets who were playing (*tañendo*); we do not know whether they were upon the *roca*, but rather presume that they went on foot like the devils and the angels who came forth and performed a sort of dance."[12]

The Procession

In the early years, the pageants would follow the procession of the clergy and the Host (the chalice), but as more and more pageants were added, the townspeople would celebrate Corpus Christi Day perhaps a week before the stage productions, which would be performed on Whitsunday (five Sundays after Easter at Pentecost). A public announcement, called the *banns*, would advertise the date of the performances, just as we hear of movie releases via television nowadays.

On the appointed day, the festivities began quite early. In York, in 1415, they began "at the mydhowre betwixt iiijth and vth of the cloke in the mornynge,"[13] which if we reckon from Roman numerals we understand to be 4:30 a.m. This seems very early to us, but York, England, is far enough north that the sun rises on June 2 at 4:39 a.m. In the ages before electric lights, people arose when the cock crowed at daybreak, so 4:30 would not have been a strange hour to them. In 1518, however, the procession was scheduled to begin at 7:00 a.m., allowing enough time to wolf down an English breakfast, which, in the Middle Ages, was "a catch-as-catch-can affair of leftovers" or a little bread dipped in wine.[14]

The guildsmen would arrange their pageants in order, with the first play in the cycle (*The Fall of Lucifer* or *Creation*) being, of course, first in line and the others in historic sequence with *The Final Judgment* appearing last. The stations where the players would perform were marked with banners, with the first station often at a city gate. The actors on the first pageant would perform at the first station and then move on to the second station. The spectators, however, would remain at the first station, and the remaining pageants would draw up, perform, and pass on, each in its turn.until the last pageant pulled away from the last station.

When the Corpus Christi cycle began, there might have been only three pageants: (a) Creation and the Fall; (b) the victory of Christ; and (c) the Final Judgment. But as popularity increased, the processions expanded to as many as twenty-five pageants, as at York, which meant that the performances had to be spread over a period of days, much as a state fair is today.

EXERCISE 1.1: Primary Source

DIRECTIONS: Please read the introduction and the excerpt below. When finished, answer the questions that follow.

INTRODUCTION: *Archdeacon Robert Rogers (d. 1546) of Chester left an eyewitness description of the pageants (i.e., pageant wagons) that he had seen at Whitsun plays in Chester, though one must keep in mind that the pageants he saw would have been the more highly developed wagons since they were being used in the sixteenth century, 200 years after the beginnings of the English mystery plays. Please note that spelling did not become standardized until the eighteenth century, so when reading*

English from this time period, which is called Middle English, one must allow the medievals some grace. Below is the text of the archdeacon's description.

A Medieval Pageant and Procession
By Archdeacon Robert Rogers of Chester

(1) Every Company had his pagint, or parte, which pagints weare a high scaffold with two rowmes [rooms], a higher and a lower, upon four wheeles. (2) In the lower, they apparelld them selves, and in the higher room they played, beinge all open on the tope, that all beholders mighte heare and see them. (3) The places where they played them was in every streets. (4) They began first at the abay [abbey] gates, and when the firste paginate was played it was wheeled to the highe crosse before the mayor, (5) and so every streete had a pagiante playing before them at one time, till all the pagiantes for the day appointed were played; (6) and when one pagint was neere ended: words was brought from streete to streete, that soe they mighte come in place thereof exceeding orderlye; (7) and all the streets have theire pagiantes afore them all at one time playing together; (8) to se [see] which playes was greate resorte [entertainment], (9) and also scafoldes and stages made in the streets in those places where they determined to play theire pagiants.[15]

Questions:

1. Sentence 1:

   a. What is meant by the phrase *every Company*?

   b. How is the stage described in Sentence 1?

2. Sentence 2:

   a. What was the purpose of the lower storey on the pageant Rogers saw?

   b. Rogers states the upper level was "all open on the tope" and then gives a reason. What exactly do you think he means by this? If you like, you can sketch what you understand him to be describing.

   c. In early June the sun sets at around 9:30 p.m. in Chester. From Rogers' statement, do you think the performances might have gone on past 5:00? Explain your answer.

3. Sentence 4

   Sentence 4 refers to the abbey gate (below left) and the high cross in Chester (below right), which appear in recent photos below. Why would these areas be considered particularly good stations?

4. Sentence 5

   a. Were these plays performed in one day or over several days? What phrase from Rogers suggests your answer?

5. Sentence 6

   In order to move forward to the next station at the right time, how did the folks at one pageant wagon know when the group ahead of them was finished?

6. Sentence 9

   a. Rogers begins Sentence 9 with the transition *and also*. What additional type of stage is then introduced.

   b. If you were putting such stages together, what would you use to elevate the playing area so that spectators could see?

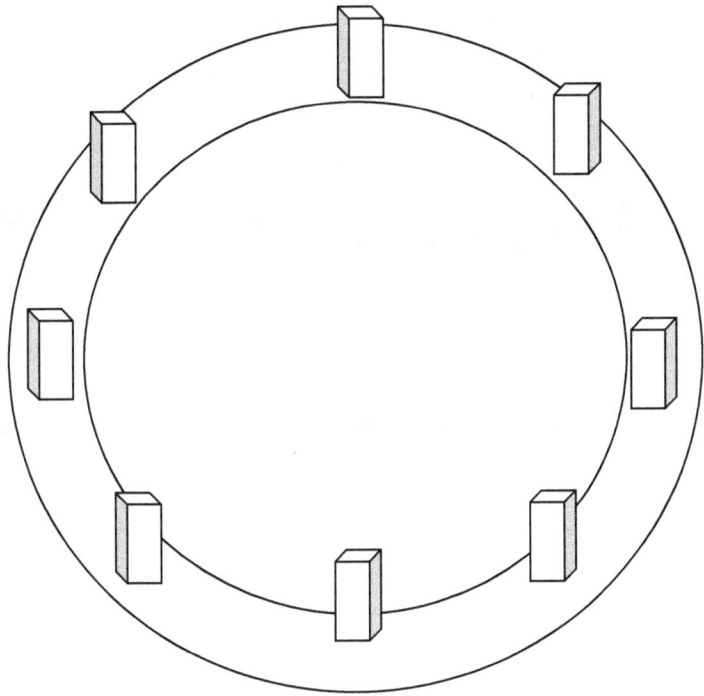

Fig. 3: Layout of a Cornish *plen an gwari* with eight performance stations

Plen an gwari

The procession arising from the Feast of Corpus Christi was customary not only in England, but also in Scotland, Spain, France, Italy, Germany, and many other parts of Christendom. However, recent scholarship has shown that in Cornwall, the southwest tip of England, a completely different notion prevailed.

In several locations around Cornwall, there are traces of earthen structures which, from a bird's-eye-view, show a circular field surrounded by an embankment. The embankment had depressions at the 12:00 and 6:00 positions, which allowed both players and spectators to enter the performance area. In Cornish, this kind of theatre is called a *plen an gwari*, or "playing place."

Around the perimeter of the inner circle were performing stations, or pavilions, where various Biblical narratives would be played out (see Fig. 3). A centuries-old drawing that has survived labels the various pavilions as Heaven, Torturers, Hell, Pharaoh, King David, and so on, what researcher Will Coleman calls "all major locations or characters in the action."[16]

A Cornish *plen an gwari* called St. Pirian's Round, located near Goonhavern in Cornwall

Photo by Alan Simkins

In these playing places, the pavilions remained fixed, and the spectators moved around in the grassy area of the inner circle in much the same way that visitors to a state fair move from booth to booth. Such a venue may have resulted in improved acting and better special effects, as the players were basically in competition with each other. After all, who wants an audience to stray away half-way through the play?

EXERCISE 1.2: Primary Source

DIRECTIONS: Please read the introduction and the excerpt from Richard Carew's book. Then answer the questions that follow.

INTRODUCTION: *In 1602, a Cornishman named Richard Carew described the* plen an gwari *for English readers. However, with the wit of a Celt, Mr. Carew could not resist describing a prank that a "conceited" actor once played on a director/prompter, whom he calls an Ordinary.*

Excerpt from *A Survey of Cornwall* By Richard Carew

(1) The Guary miracle, in English, a miracle-play, is a kinde of Enterlude[a], compiled in Cornish out of some scripture history. . . . For representing it, they raise an earthen Amphitheatre, in some open field, having the Diameter of his enclosed playne some 40 or 50 foot.

(2) The Country people flock from all sides, many miles off, to hear and see it, for they [the plays] have therein devils and devices, to delight as well the eye as the eare.

---

[a] The word *interlude* is sometimes used to refer to plays that appeared between the medieval miracle plays, as well as the more secular plays of Elizabethan times. Here Carew spells the word *Enterlude* and simply means *play*.

(3) The players conne[a] not their parts without booke, but are prompted by one called the Ordinary, who followeth at their back with the booke in his hand, and telleth them softly what they must pronounce aloud. Which maner once gave occasion to a pleasant conceyted gentleman, of practicing a mery pranke: for the undertaking (perhaps of set purpose) an Actors roome, was accordingly lessoned (before-hand) by the Ordinary, that [what] he must say after him. His turne came: quoth the Ordinary, 'Go forth man and shew thy selfe.' The gentleman steps out upon the stage, and like a bad Clarke[b] in scripture matters, cleaving more to the letter than the sense, pronounced those [same] words aloud. 'Oh,' says the fellowe [the Ordinary] softly in his eare, 'you mar all the play.' And with this his passion, the Actor makes the audience in like sort acquainted. Hereon the prompter falls to flat rayling & cursing in the bitterest termes he could devise: which the Gentleman with a set gesture and countenance still soberly related until the Ordinary, driven at last into a madde rage, was faine to give over all.[c] Which trousse [loppings] though it brake off the Enterlude, yet defrauded not the beholders, but dismissed them with a great deale more sport and laughter, than 20 such Guaries could have afforded.[17]

Questions:

1. In Section 1, Carew provides the size of the Cornish *plen an gwari*. What estimates does he give?

2. In Section 2, Carew describes the plays as having "devils and devices, to delight as well the eye as the eare." By *ear*, he probably refers to the poetry of the play, which is supposed to be pleasant to hear. But what do you suppose he means by delighting "the eye"?

---

[a] ken, know
[b] cleric, churchman
[c] happy to give it all up

3. In your own words, summarize the anecdote Carew relates in Section 3.

Decline and End of Mystery and Morality Plays

The mystery and morality plays were started by the Church and were ended by the Church. In 1264, Pope Urban IV, the head of the Roman Catholic Church, had established the Corpus Christi Feast, the environment in which the plays developed and flourished, and, as we have seen, the plays were used to teach Bible narratives and the teachings of the Church. However, once the Protestant Reformation began in the sixteenth century, Roman Catholic teachings which were not compatible with Scripture came under fire, and the reformers began to look askance on plays which communicated what they considered falsehoods to a naïve people. This became a particularly noted trend in England after King Henry VIII had broken away from the Roman Church in 1534, making himself the head of the Church in England. In the ten years following this break, numerous scholars and reformers, such as Martin Luther and John Calvin, were shaking up the religious framework of western Christendom by insisting on a correct reading and understanding of the Bible. These teachings were sometimes in conflict with both the teachings of the Roman Catholic Church and King Henry's Church of England, and religious and political turmoil resulted. Therefore, in 1543, Henry's Parliament passed legislation called *An Act for the Advancement of True Religion and for the Abolishment of the Contrary*. Though the purpose of the act was primarily to prevent what the king considered unorthodox teachings as well as English translations of the Bible, it also touched on the content of the plays:

> It shall be lawful to all and every person and persons to set forth songs, plays and interludes, to be used and exercised within this realm and other [of] the king's dominions, for the rebuking and reproaching of vices and the setting forth of virtue: so [long as] always the said songs, plays or interludes meddle not with interpretations of Scripture, contrary to the doctrine set forth or to be set forth by the King's Majesty.[18]

In other words, the moral dimension of a play was permissible, but any teachings not in accord with the king's interpretation of Scripture were forbidden. Though plays were not banned by the act, as a practical matter it had an effect much like a ban, as the Corpus Christi plays, which had developed over several centuries, would have to be completely rewritten, and, what is more, the persons who did the rewriting would have to be solidly within the king's understanding of Scripture. As a result of Henry's ruling, the mystery and morality plays gradually died out. The last play of the Chester Cycle was performed in 1575; of Coventry in 1575; of Newcastle in 1589; and of York in 1597.

These late sixteenth-century dates, however, comport well with the childhood and adolescent years of Englishmen such as William Shakespeare, born in 1564, who, as a boy, would have seen these mystery and morality plays and perhaps dreamed of ways to improve upon the theatrical experience. This juncture puts one in mind of the words spoken by a dying King Arthur in Alfred, Lord Tennyson's, epic poem, *The Idylls of the King*:

> The old order changeth, yielding place to new,
> And God fulfills himself in many ways,
> Lest one good custom should corrupt the world.[19] (407-409)

THE RHETORIC OF MEDIEVAL PLAYS

Chapter 2

Introduction

Since classical education continued to flourish in medieval Europe, the rhetorical elements defined in antiquity can still be used to examine the rhetoric of medieval plays. What follows, then, is a discussion of the diction of medieval plays as well as an examination of the use of progymnasmata elements in dramatic composition.

Diction

The miracle and morality plays of medieval England are often skipped over as teachers of literature rush from Geoffrey Chaucer of the fourteenth century to William Shakespeare of the sixteenth. Acting companies did what they could in their limited way to create spectacle, but, in terms of the artistry of a play, the words spoken on the stage were paramount. This section focuses on two things: (a) the "sound" of the lines produced by meter, rhythm, and rhyme, and (b) the literary techniques employed by the medieval playwrights.

Meter

Meter is a term that refers to the rhythm of poetry. This is determined by the number of stressed syllables (or beats) in the line:

Stressed Syllables	Name	Pronunciation
Two	Dimeter	DĬM-ĭt-ər
Three	Trimester	TRĬM-ĭt-ər
Four	Tetrameter	tĕ-TRĂM-ĭt-ər
Five	Pentameter	pĕn-TĂM-ĭt-ər

Rhythm

Rhythm is a term that refers to the pattern of syllable stress, that is, the arrangement of unstressed syllables and stressed syllables:

Iambic = one unstressed + one stressed = delay (de – lay)

Trochaic = one stressed + one unstressed = furnace (fur – nace)

Anapestic = two unstressed + one stressed = a delay (a de – lay)

Spondaic = two stressed = Help! Help! (Help! Help!)

Each rhythmic unit is called a foot. Therefore, if there are four iambic feet, we would say the line was in iambic tetrameter.

Examples

Following are some famous lines of poetry which are scanned (marked) to show the underlying rhythm:

Iambic tetrameter (4 iambic units)

Whose woods these are I think I know.[20] (Robert Frost)

Whose woods these are I think I know.

Iambic pentameter (5 iambic units)

Shall I compare thee to a summer's day?²¹ (William Shakespeare)

Shall I com – pare thee to a sum – mer's day?

Trochaic tetrameter (5 trochaic units)

Brethren, join the social measure.²² (Knud Lyne Rahbek)

Breth – ren, join the so – cial meas – ure.

Anapestic trimeter (3 anapestic units)

I am monarch of all I survey.²³ (William Cowper)

I am mon – arch of all I sur – vey.

One last note: Language is slippery. Even Shakespeare was not able to write every single line of a five-act play in unflinching iambic pentameter. Occasionally one finds a line that does not perfectly scan, but the way the actor delivered the line would compensate. How, for example, would you render this 13-syllable line from *Romeo and Juliet* to make it sound like a 10-syllable line in iambic pentameter?

To move is to stir; and to be valiant is to stand.²⁴

Rhythm and Meter by Era

Now comes the question, "Which of these patterns is best for an English play?" The answer, of course, is, "It depends on the time in which the writer lived."

William Shakespeare (1564-1616) is considered the best poet of the English language ever to have lived, and critics tend to compare earlier and later works to his. Let's examine his style first, and then compare them to the style of medieval plays, which he probably heard as a boy growing up in Stratford but later left behind.

Shakespeare used iambic pentameter. This particular meter is quite natural to the English tongue—so much so, in fact, that one can read a line in this meter and not even be aware of the underlying rhythm. Take these lines from *Julius Caesar*, for example, when Caesar tells his friend Antony his impression of Cassius:

> Yond Cassius has a lean and hungry look.
> He thinks too much. Such men are dangerous.[25]

When read in a natural way, the underlying rhythm is not easily detected, but when the lines are scanned, the rhythm becomes more apparent, as seen below:

Yond Cas – sius has a lean and hung – ry look.

He thinks too much; such men are dan – ger – ous.

These lines yield a natural cadence that is suitable for high-minded topics. Conversely, iambic pentameter is rarely, if ever, used in more playful poetry such as nursery rhymes. In children's verse, the lines have a strong rhythm, which employ the faster pace of four beats, that is, iambic tetrameter, shown below in Robert Louis Stevenson's "At the Sea-Side" from *A Child's Garden of Verses*:

> When I was down beside the sea
> A wooden spade they gave to me
> To dig the sandy shore.

In this poem, Stevenson used two lines of iambic tetrameter followed by one of iambic trimeter. Scanned, the lines appear this way:

When I was down be – side the sea

    ⏑   ′   ⏑   ′   ⏑   ′   ⏑   ′
A wood – en spoon they gave to me

    ⏑   ′   ⏑   ′   ⏑   ′
To dig the sand – y shore.[26]

In the next fast-paced nursery rhyme, we encounter iambic dimeter—only two beats per line:

> The cock doth crow
> To let you know,
> If you be wise,
> 'Tis time to rise.[27]

Scanned, the last two lines would like look this:

    ⏑   ′   ⏑   ′
If you be wise,

    ⏑   ′   ⏑   ′
'Tis time to rise.

Such a child-like rhythm, it seems to us, would just not do for medieval playwrights presenting a message as serious as the Gospel. From children's poetry, our ear has been conditioned to accept such simple measures for the simple world of children, but, as adults, it is hard to listen to entire plays that would sound so juvenile to the ear. Still, tetrameter and trimeter are the two most common meters in the medieval morality plays. For example, the following excerpt from *Cain and Abel*, a play from the N-town cycle, uses a mixture of the two:

> CAIN
> Alas, in woe I now am wound,
> Accursed of God as man unkind;
> Of any man if I be found,
> He shall me slay. I have no friend,
> Alas and welaway![28]

When scanned, the last two lines appear thus:

◡ ′ ◡ ′ ◡ ′ ◡ ′

Tetrameter: He shall me slay. I have no friend,

◡ ′ ◡ ′ ◡ ′

Trimeter: A - las and wel – a - way!

Of course, for the most part, the townsmen and peasants standing around the stage on a medieval street would not be aware of such niceties of English verse and, never having known the excellent poetry of Greece and Rome, they would not have missed it. Still, the writers would have been educated and would have known the famous seven-beat line of Latin heptameter, so why did they write the great message of Scripture in such a childish way?

Perhaps the answer lies in the actor's delivery of the line. Could they have read their lines in such a way as to slow them down to allow them more impact on the ear. And could they have drawn on native English poetry to guide them?

Certainly Old English poetry had employed a *caesura* [sē ZHŬR ə] (pause) in the middle of a line, which slowed the presentation down and rendered the lines in a more solemn manner. Below, for example, are the openings of the Anglo-Saxon poem called "The Battle of Brunanburh" displayed in both Old and Modern English.

Old English:

Her Aethelstan cyning,   eorla dryhten,
beorna beag-giefa,   and his brothor eac,
Eadmund aetheling,   ealdor-langetir
geslogon aet saecce   sweorda ecgum
ymbe Brunanburh.

Modern English:

In this year, King Aethelstan, Lord of warriors,
ring-giver to men, and his brother also,
Prince Edmund, won eternal glory

in battle with sword edges
around Brunanburh.[29]

In Old English, the tetrameter (four-beat) line is quite apparent, as shown below:

    Her   Ae – thel - stan cyn – ing,   e – or - la   dryh - ten,

    be – or – na be - ag – gief - a,   and   his   broth - or eac . . . .

Why is it that no one accuses Anglo-Saxon tetrameter of being childish and "sing-songy"? It is likely because the *caesura* in the middle of the line slows the speaker down, allowing a more majestic cadence better suited to grand themes. If, then, one imposes a *caesura* in a line of poetry in Middle English, it follows that the Middle English will sound less childish as well.

Try reading Cain's lines once again, this time inserting a *caesura* in each line to see if doing so improves the sound of the lines:

> CAIN
> Alas, in woe   I now am wound,
> Accursed of God   as man unkind;
> Of any man   if I be found,
> He shall me slay.   I have no friend,
> Alas and welaway!

It is important to point out that the lines in "The Battle of Brunanburh" are not iambic; they are simply expressed in tetrameter. Poets would use whatever meter they deemed appropriate on either side of the *caesura*. This flexibility may account for the fact that in the medieval mystery plays, the rhythm is variable (as in Old English), while the meter generally remains the same. Look, for example, at these words from Cain and Abel, which appear below first without a visible *caesura*, and then with one.

> ABEL
> Almighty God and God full of might,
> By whom all thing is made of nought,

> To thee my heart is ready dight
> For upon thee is all my thought.[30]
>
> ABEL
> Almighty God   and God full of might,
> By whom all thing   is made of nought,
> To thee my heart   is ready dight
> For upon thee   is all my thought.

Now add one more detail: lengthen the vowel in the stressed words, drawing them out but not changing the sound of the vowel. For example, *Gooooooood* would still sound like *God*, not like *good*.

> ABEL
> Almighty Gooooooood   and God fuuuuuuul of miiiiiiiight,
> By whoooooooom all thiiiiiiing   is made of nooooooought,
> To thee my heaaaaaaaart   is ready diiiiiiight
> For upon theeeeeee   is all my thooooooought.

It's not Shakespeare, of course, but it gets the reader much closer to the familiar sound of Old English and disposes of the notion that the rhythmic pattern of the medieval play is juvenile.

EXERCISE 2.1: Meter in Mystery Plays

DIRECTIONS: Place the symbols for stressed (ˊ) and unstressed (˘) syllables above each syllable in the line. Then determine which type of rhythm and meter applies (e.g., iambic tetrameter, trochaic dimeter, etc.)

1. JOSEPH (from *Joseph's Trouble about Mary*)

   I was never ere so light.[31]

   Rhythm and meter:

2. HEROD (from *Herod and the Magi*)

   Go beat yon boy and bring him down.[32]

Rhythm and meter:

3. KING (from *Christ before Herod*)

Oh, my heart hops for joy[33]

Rhythm and meter:

MORE CHALLENGING:

4. THIRD SOLDIER (from *The Crucifixion*; the Third Soldier working with another soldier, raises up the cross heavy with the weight of Christ's body)

Oh, lift![34]

Rhythm and meter:

The Sound of Middle English

Students of Latin will recall that, although Latin vowels appear to be the same as English vowels, their pronunciation was quite different. The Latin *a, e, i, o, u* sounded more like *ä, ā, ē, ō, ū*, vowel qualities which are still found in other European languages today. Now, English also is a European language, and it is important to remember that long ago English vowels had the same qualities as those of Latin.

How did vowel pronunciation change in England? An explanation of the Great Vowel Shift is beyond the scope of this textbook, but perhaps a word would be helpful here. To raise awareness of what your tongue is doing when you speak, pronounce these three words (in order) and pay attention to the shift in tongue position in your mouth:

my ➡ may ➡ me

Notice that in the first word (*my*), the tongue is on the floor of the mouth and the sound is coming from the back of the mouth. In *may*, the tongue is arched upward in the middle of the mouth chamber, and in *me*, it is high, forward, and touching the back of the teeth. For reasons that linguists still debate, in the medieval period the pronunciation of the English long vowels in English changed. To put it in linguistic terms, each vowel moved forward one position in the mouth, and the most high and front vowel /ē/ dropped to the back of the mouth, just as volleyball players rotate in a match. When it did so, it created a diphthong (a glide), so that, to be specific, /ē/ dropped to the back of the mouth and then glided to the front, creating /ä-ē/. (In the International Phonetic Alphabet, it is rendered as /aɪ/.) Therefore, whereas the word *eye* was once pronounced as /ē-ə/, it shifted to the sound we use today /ä-ē/ (or, /aɪ/).

This change can be noted in two lines from the opening of Chaucer's *Canterbury Tales*, in which the author positioned the words *melody* and *eye* at the end of their respective lines, intending them to rhyme. Let's look at them first in present-day English:

> And small fowls make melody,
> That sleep all night with open eye.

Notice how, with Middle English spelling, the last two letters of each line are written the same, *ye*:

> And smale foweles maken melodye,
> That slepen al the nyght with open ye.

This rendering is not just a quaint way of looking at older English. It was written to create the sound that was actually used in the fourteenth century, when they were written. Such spelling is called *pronunciation spelling*, and is still used by authors who wish to capture a certain dialect on the written page (as Mark Twain did in *Huckleberry Finn*).

Using Chaucer's spelling as a guide then, we can make a rather good educated guess that the lines probably sounded like this:

> And small-uh fool-us mahk-en mel-o-dee-uh
> That slayp-ən all the nĭcht with open ee-uh

Now, in addition to the change in the vowel sounds, these lines illustrate another aspect of Middle English that still persisted, at least in part, in Shakespeare's time: the articulation of every syllable, as in Latin. Note, for example, that Chaucer spelled the word *small* as *smale* because he intended the *-e* to be pronounced as /ə/ (or *uh*), which partly explains why Chaucer's line is in iambic pentameter if read with his pronunciation. In present-day pronunciation, the line does not scan. Similarly, readers today might be tempted to pronounce *foweles* as *fowls* or possibly /fōlz/, but Chaucer would have pronounced it as /fūl-əs/: two syllables and a variant vowel quality.

Applying this information to the pronunciation of the medieval mystery plays, we would conclude that the second and fourth lines excerpted from the *Fall of Man* (York) did rhyme, both having the sound of /ē/:

SATAN	SATAN
The kynde of man he thoght to take	The kind of man he thought to take
And theratt hadde I grete envye,	And thereat had I great envy,
But he has made to hym a make,	But he has made to him a make,
And harde to her I wol me hye	And hard to her I will me hie.[35]

Today, however, the word *hie*, meaning *go*, is pronounced as /hä-ē/ (or, /haI /). Why did the sound of *envy* not change as well? The best answer is that the Great Vowel Shift was not absolutely consistent. Some words, for whatever reason, did not submit to change. Another factor might be that in *envy*, the last syllable is not stressed.

ACTIVITY A: View and Do: Middle English

DIRECTIONS: Locate on *YouTube* the reading of the Lord's Prayer from the Wycliffe Bible. As you listen, pay attention to the quality of the vowels and the pronunciation of all syllables. After listening, try to recite the prayer with the sound system of Middle English. URL: <https://www.youtube.com/watch?v=FM2THezuzlI>

The Lord's Prayer from the Wycliffe Bible (14th Century)
Preier of Oure Lord

And thus ye schulen preye
Oure fadir that art in heuenes,
Halewid be thi name;
Thi kyngdoom come to;
Be thi wille don, in erthe as in heuene.
Yyue to vs this dai oure breed ouer othir substaunce,
and foryyue to vs oure dettis, as we foryyuen to oure dettouris;
and lede vs not in to temptacioun, but delyuere vs fro yuel. (Mt. 6:9-14)

Literary Techniques

Though the medieval mystery plays have never received the kind of acclaim given to Greek, Roman, and Shakespearean plays, their authors were classically educated and had studied the great literature of the Greeks and Romans. It should not be surprising, therefore, to find literary gems that add a pleasant dimension to the plays. Some of their techniques are outlined in this section.

Débat

Débat [DĀ-bä] is a literary genre of the Middle Ages in which two or more allegorical characters engage in debate. One finds *débat* of more than one type in *The Castle of Perseverance*. For example, there are debates between Good and Evil Angels as well as between allegorical figures such as Mercy and Justice.

Mercy (with Peace as an ally) and Justice (with Truth as an ally) debate whether God should dispense mercy on humankind, or, on the other hand, dispense Justice, giving sinners their just deserts. After a brief debate amongst themselves, they take their case before God:

> MISERICORDIA (MERCY)
> Therefore, my sisters Righteousness,
> Peace, and Truth, to you I tell:
> When man crieth "Mercy," and will not cease,
> Mercy shall be his washing well—
> Witness of holy kirk[a]
> For, the least drop of blood
> That God bled on the rood,[b]
> It would have been satisfaction good
> For all Mankind's works.[c]
>
> JUSTITIA (JUSTICE)
> Sister, ye sey me a good skil[d]
> That mercy surpasses man's misdeeds;

Figures representing Justice and Mercy by Alexander Mylne (1637)

---

[a] church
[b] cross
[c] deeds
[d] speak truly

> But, take mercy whoso will,
> He must it ask with love and dread.
> And every man that will fulfill
> The Deadly Sins, and follow misdeeds,
> To grant him mercy, me thinketh it no skil.[a]
> And therefore, sister, you I rede[b]
> Let him abye[c] his misdeed.
> For though he lie in hell and stink,
> It shall me never overthink,
> As he hath brewed, so let him drink!
> The devil shall give him his mede.[d] 36

EXERCISE 2.2: Analyzing a *Débat*

DIRECTIONS: In the space below, paraphrase (express in your own words) what each allegorical figure is arguing.

1. What point is Mercy making about how God should handle sinners who desire to enter Heaven? Why?

2. What point is Justice making about the fate of the sinner? Why?

3. Which character best presents the Gospel message? What New Testament verse can you cite to support your answer? (HINT: Re-read Romans 1-8 to inform your

---

[a] not sound
[b] advise
[c] pay for
[d] reward

THE RHETORIC OF MEDIEVAL PLAYS

decision. You may wish to discuss the seemingly different messages of Romans 2 and 3.)[37]

4. Below is God's decision in the case, which he announces to Peace, Mercy, Justice, and Truth.

> FATHER
> Well spoken, Peace, my daughter dear!
> On thee I think, and on Mercy.
> Since you all be accorded here,
> After your will shall my judgment be—
> Not after his deserving, nor as he fears,
> Not damning Man to torment. See,—
> Bring him to my bliss full clear,
> In heaven to dwell endlessly.[38]

Does the playwright's view accord with Scripture or not? Cite a verse to support your position. Discuss your answer with your classmates.

Alliteration

Alliteration is the repetition of a consonant, especially within the same line of poetry. An example appears in *Christ before Pilate (2): The Judgement*:

1ST SOLDIER O man, thy mind is full mad, In our clutches to be clouted and clapped And closed.	
2ND SOLDIER Thou art lashed, lushed and lapped.	
1ST SOLDIER Yea, routed, rushed and rapped; Thus thy name with noy shall be noised.[39]	

Practice: In the boxes on the right, jot down the consonants that are alliterated.

Allusion

An allusion is a brief reference to a person or thing of cultural, political, literary, or historical significance. Its purpose is to transfer the feelings associated with the reference to something at hand. The classically educated writers of the plays would easily have turned to the myths of Greece and Rome to make a point. One example appears in *Herod and the Magi* (York Cycle), where Herod boasts that all the gods are under his authority.

HEROD
The clouds clapped in clearness that these climates enclose—
Jupiter and Jove, Mars and Mercury amid—
Raiking over my royalty on row me rejoices,
Blundering their blasts to blow when I bid.
Saturn my subject, that subtly is hid,
Lists at my liking and lays him full low

. . . .
Venus his voice to me owes. . . .[40]

Herod on His Throne, by Theophilé Lybaert, 1880

Practice: In this space, write the words that are allusions.

Anachronism

An anachronism is a statement that places a thing or a person in the wrong time period. For example, in *The Slaughter of the Innocents* (York Cycle), we read:

> HEROD
> Who hereto is not boun [prepared],
> By almighty Mahound,
> To death I shall him drive.
> So bold look no man be
> For to ask help nor held [favor]
> But of Mahound and me,
> That has this world in wield . . . .[41]

Practice: What word in this passage is an anachronism?

Aphorism

An aphorism is a concise wise saying, such as a proverb or maxim.

> 3RD SHEPHERD
> Seldom lies the devil dead by the gate.[42]
>
> *The Second Shepherd's Play* (Wakefield)

> CAIAPHAS
> It is no bourd[a] to beat beasts that are bound.[43]
>
> *Christ before Annas and Caiaphas* (York)

Practice: In the space provided, explain what point each author is trying to make in his aphorism.

The Second Shepherd's Play:

---

[a] sport

Christ before Annas and Caiaphas:

Metaphor

A metaphor is a comparison that does not use *like* or *as*. In this example, the citizens of Jerusalem welcome Jesus on Palm Sunday, using metaphors to describe his attributes.

> 2ND CITIZEN
> Hail, flourishing flower that never shall fade.
> Hail, violet vernant with sweet odor,
> Hail, mark of mirth, our medicine made . . . .[44]
>
> *The Entry into Jerusalem* (York)

Practice: In the space provided, indicate what Jesus is being compared to in this passage.

Personification

Giving human attributes or abilities to animals or elements is called personification.

> DEUS
> *(speaking to Cain)*
> From earth to heaven vengeance cries.[45]
>
> *The Killing of Abel* (Wakefield)

Allegory can also be considered a kind of personification.

> EVERYMAN
> For my Goods sharply did tell me
> That he bringeth many into hell.[46]
>
> *Everyman*

Practice: In the space provided, indicate what is personified in each excerpt.

The Killing of Abel:

Everyman:

Rhyme

One way to employ rhyme in poetry is to construct the lines so that every other line rhymes, a pattern called ABAB, meaning the first and third lines rhyme (A) and the second and fourth lines rhyme (B).

> 2ND KING
> All-wielding God that all has wrought,
> I worship thee as is worthy,
> That with thy brightness has me brought
> Out of my realm, rich Arabie.[47]

Herod and the Magi (York)

Practice: Mark the rhymed lines with A's and B's.

However, the Master of Wakefield developed a more elaborate rhyme scheme—the *Wakefield Stanza*. It consisted of nine lines arranged this way:

> 4 rhymed lines (called a *quatrain*): AAAA
>
> 5 lines in which the middle three would rhyme, and the first would rhyme with the last (called a *tercet* with rhymed *cauda*): BCCCB

Below is an example from *Noah* by the Wakefield Master:

> NOAH
>
> Above all hills together the water is risen late
> Cubits fifteen. But in a higher state
> It may not be, I ween[a], for this will I wait:

Depiction of Noah from the Roman catacombs, c. AD 2-4, suggesting possible theatrical posture

---

[a] know

This forty days has rain been; it will therefore abate
Full lele.^a
This water in hast
Eft will I tast:^b
Now am I agast^c—
It is waned a great deal!⁴⁸

Noah (Wakefield)

Practice: Place A's in the quatrain and B's and C's in the tercet and cauda.

Simile

Medieval playwrights certainly included artistic touches such as the simile (comparisons with *like* or *as*). Look at these examples:

GOD
As a spark of fire in the sea,
My mercy is sin-quenching.⁴⁹

The Castle of Perseverance

Practice: What is sin compared to?

Practice: What is God's mercy compared to?

WOMAN
[Of Peter as he denies Christ] He looks lurking, like an ape.⁵⁰

Christ before Annas and Caiaphas (York)

Practice: Peter is compared to what?

---

^a full well
^b lower a plumb line
^c amazed

EXERCISE 2.3: Diction

DIRECTIONS: Read each excerpt below and determine which literary technique is employed. Then, in the blank provided, place the letter of the appropriate technique.

    A. Alliteration   D. Metaphor

    B. Allusion   E. Personification

    C. Aphorism   F. Simile

___ 1. EVERYMAN: Where dwelleth that holy man, Confession?[51]

(*Everyman*, l. 539)

___ 2. BAD ANGEL: As flat as a fox, I fall before your face.[52]

(*Mary Magdalene*, l. 730)

___ 3. SATAN: The snares that I will set were never set at Troy.[53]

(*Mary Magdalene*, l. 368)

___ 4. EMPEROR: Lord and lad to my law doth lowte.[a][54]

(*Mary Magdalene*, l. 43)

___ 5. MERCY: Sin not in hope of mercy.[55]

(*Mankind*, l. 845)

___ 6. CURIOSITY: Ah, dear duchess, my daisy's eye![56]

(*Mary Magdalene*, l. 515)

Progymnasmata: Expanded Narrative *(Dlêgêma)*

DIRECTIONS: Please begin by reading the introduction and the passage from The *Fall of the Angels*, a mystery play from the York Corpus Christi Cycle composed in the 1470s. (The excerpt has been rendered in modern spelling and grammar by J. S. Purvus.) In order to assess the quality of the Expanded Narrative, read the associated Bible passages named below and answer the questions which follow.

INTRODUCTION: *The plays that make up the Corpus Christi Cycle would be classified in the progymnasmata as Expanded Narratives. That is, the narrative is based on an original text (the Bible) but has been embellished by the script writer with dialogue. Anytime writers perform a transfer of this type, they must be careful to stay faithful to the source, but when presenting an Expanded Narrative*

---

[a] bow

based on the words of God, one must proceed with great caution. Some in the Judeo-Christian tradition strongly oppose putting words into God's mouth, even if the meaning is consistent with the message of the Bible; others are not categorically opposed, but are nonetheless scrupulous about making the dialogue consistent with Scriptural teachings.

Since the medieval miracle plays were intended to teach about God's work from Creation to the Final Judgment, the question then arises, "Are the plays faithful to Scripture?" To answer the question, read the excerpt about the fall of Lucifer and the angels. The questions that follow allow you to compare the lines of the play to relevant passages in Genesis, Ezekiel, and Isaiah, which are generally believed to describe the deeds and fall of Lucifer.

Excerpt from *The Fall of the Angels*
York Corpus Christi Cycle

After God has created the nine orders of angels, he addresses them, thus:

GOD
[Addressing all] All that wealth shall wield shall dwell in this hall;
This grant I you, ministers mine,
While steadfast in thought ye remain;
And also all them that are nought
Shall pine in hell-prison in pain.
[Addressing Lucifer] Of all mights I have made most near after me,
I make thee as master and mirror of my might;
I set thee here by me in bliss for to be,
And name thee now, Lucifer, as bearer of light.[57]

FIRST SERAPHIM:
Ah, merciful maker, full mickle is thy might,
That all this world at a word worthily hast wrought.
Aye loved be that lovely lord for his light,
That thus us mighty has made, who now were right nought.
In bliss for to bide in his blessing,
Everlasting in love let us lout[a] him,

---

[a] bow to, show reverence to

Who sets us thus closely about him,
Of mirth nevermore to have missing.[58]

FIRST ANGEL LUCIFER

All the mirth that is made is marked in me.
The beams of my brilliance are burning so bright,
And so seemly in sight myself I now see.
Like a lord am I lifted to dwell in this light.
More fairer by far I appear;
In me is no point to impair;
I feel me well favoured and fair;
My power is passing my peers.[59]

FIRST CHERUB

[Addressing God] Lord, with a lasting love we love thee alone,
You mightiful maker that marked us and made us,
And wrought us thus worthily to dwell as thy own
Where never feeling of filth may foul us nor fade us.
All bliss is here biding about us,
The while we are stable of thought
In the worship of him that us wrought;
Of dread need we never more doubt us.[60]

FIRST ANGEL LUCIFER

Oh what! I am favoured and fair and figured full fit;
The form of all fairness upon me is fast.
All wealth I am wielding, so wise is my wit;
The beams of my brightness are built with the best
My showing is shimmering and shining,
So bigly to bliss am I brought;
I need to annoy me right nought;
Here shall never pain bring me pining.[61]

FIRST SERAPHIM

[Addressing Lucifer] With all the wit that we wield we worship thy will,
Thou glorious God that is ground of all grace.
Aye with steadfast sound let us stand still,
Lord, to be fed with the food of thy fair face.

In life that is truly aye-lasting,
Thy dole, Lord, is aye daintily dealing;
And whoso that food may be feeling,
To see thy fair face, is not fasting.[62]

LUCIFER THE DEVIL
Oh sure, what!
I am worthily wrought with worship, I wis;
For in a glorious glee my glittering it gleams.
I am so mightily made my mirth may not miss;
Aye shall I bide in this bliss through brightness of beams.
I need no annoyance to name;
All wealth at my will am I wielding;
Above all yet shall I dwell in fame,
On height in the highest of heaven.
There shall I set myself, full seemly to sight,
To receive my reverence through right of renown.
I shall be like unto him that is highest on height!
Oh what! I am perfect and proud. . . .
Out, deuce! All goes down!
My might and my main are all marring.
Help, fellows! In faith, I am falling.[63]

. . . .

GOD
And all that me worship shall dwell here, I wis.[64]

Wood engraving of the fall of Lucifer, c. 1455, suggesting possible theatrical depiction with heaven above and hellmouth below

Questions:

Genesis 3:1-24

1. Genesis does not reveal the creation of the angels. However, in 3:1, what angel is usually referred to as "the serpent"?

2. Is there any mention of the seraphim in this excerpt? If so, indicate the verse.

3. Is there any mention of the cherubim in this excerpt? If so, indicate the verse.

4. In the play, which order of angels stays true to God—the seraphim or the cherubim?

Isaiah 6:1-7

5. The only passage in the Bible that mentions the seraphim is the sixth chapter of Isaiah. Do those verses support the play's idea that the seraphim were cast out with Lucifer? Explain your answer.

Ezekiel 28:1-10

6. a. Who describes Lucifer in the play?
   b. Who describes Lucifer in the Bible?
   c. Why do you suppose the dramatist made the switch?

7. Below are some passages from the play. In the space provided, write words or phrases from Ezekiel 28:1-19 that express or suggest the idea in the excerpt. The first one serves as an example.

   a. Passage 1

   LUCIFER
   Oh what! I am favoured and fair and figured full fit;
   The form of all fairness upon me is fast.

Words from Ezekiel:

b. Passage 2

    LUCIFER
    The beams of my brightness are built with the best
    My showing is shimmering and shining . . . .

    Words from Ezekiel:

c. Passage 3

    LUCIFER
    All wealth I am wielding, so wise is my wit.

    Words from Ezekiel:

d. Passage 4

    LUCIFER
    Oh what! I am perfect. . . .

    Words from Ezekiel:

e. Passage 5

    LUCIFER
    Oh what! I am . . . proud.

Words from Ezekiel:

f. Passage 6

GOD
These fools from their fairness in fantasies fell.

Words from Ezekiel:

Isaiah 14:3-32

8. In the space provided, write words or phrases from Isaiah 14:3-32 that express or suggest the idea in the excerpt.

   a. Passage 1

   LUCIFER
   Above all yet shall I dwell in fame,
   On height in the highest of heaven.
   There shall I set myself, full seemly to sight,
   To receive my reverence through right of renown.
   I shall be like unto him that is highest on height!

   Words from Isaiah:

   b. Passage 2

   LUCIFER:
   Help, fellows! In faith, I am falling.

   Words from Isaiah:

8. Is there any speech in the play that cannot be connected to Scripture? If so, make a note of it here.

Progymnasmata: Commonplace (Koinós Tópos)

The purpose of a Commonplace is to praise a virtue or to assail a vice. For example, one might hear a sermon about the virtue of faithfulness or about the viciousness of racism. In either case, the pastor would be using the features of a Commonplace to compose his sermon.

There are five components of a Commonplace, though, in the case of a praise type, one would only use the first four. They are as follows:

1. **Contrast:** Here one makes a statement about the opposite of the virtue or vice.

   For a virtue: The opposite of honesty is dishonesty.

   For a vice: The opposite of laziness is hard work.

2. **Comparison:** Here one compares the virtue or vice to one that is even greater.

   For a virtue: Being honest in paying a library fine could be compared to being honest in paying one's taxes.

   For a vice: Cheating on a test could be compared to one author's plagiarizing the work of another author.

3. **Cause:** Here one explains why someone would engage in the virtue or vice.

   For a virtue: A soldier who demonstrates courage may have been inspired by narratives of the 300 Spartans.

   For a vice: A man who kills someone may well have a selfish motive, such as greed or jealousy.

4. **Past Life or Profile:** Here one gives an example of the virtue or vice from history, or provide a profile of the type of person who would exhibit the virtue or vice.

    For a virtue: An example of honesty could be the story of young Abraham Lincoln, who walked six miles to return a few cents. This could be followed by a statement about how the honesty he cultivated as a boy benefited the entire country when he was a man.

    For a vice: An example of jealousy might be the story of Cain and Abel. This could be followed by a statement about the consequence of Cain's sin.

5. **Rejection of pity:** Here, when writing about a vice, one requests that persons who practice the vice be punished. It is not necessary to use all the approaches below, but such a plea is normally based on one or two of the following:

    - **Description:** Describe the effects of the vice. For example, one could describe the ruins of a church destroyed by an arsonist.
    - **Illegality:** Discuss in terms of the law. For example, the law sets out punishment for identity theft.
    - **Justice:** Argue that the most severe punishment possible be applied. For example, there are more severe punishments for murder than for manslaughter.
    - **Expediency:** Show that things will be better the sooner the vice is eliminated. For example, people whose homes are destroyed by a tornado will be happier the sooner the city authorities quit dilly-dallying and start the clean-up.
    - **Honor:** Show how those who eliminate the vice will receive honor. For example, the detective who solves the case of a serial killer will achieve recognition in his or her city.
    - **Practicality:** Argue that the public desires retribution. For example, twenty-four students who do their own work might wish that the one student who cheats would be punished.
    - **Immediacy:** Argue that swift punishment will deter others. For example, if a school bully is punished immediately for an offense, other students may not engage in bullying.

Of course, these are the features laid out for orators. For dramatists, they would need to be modified because the virtue or vice would be exhibited by the characters in the play. The elements would appear in dialogue and would, therefore, become more personal.

One play from the Middle Ages which is founded on Commonplace is *Gallicanus* [găl-Ĭ-kĭn-əs] by Roswitha of Gandersheim. The play focuses on the life and conversion of St. Gallicanus, a Roman general who was executed by the emperor Julian the Apostate in Egypt in AD 363. Written in the tenth century, Roswitha's play is divided into two parts, or, as we would say today, it is a two-act play. Part 1 tells the story of Gallicanus' conversion and baptism during the reign of the Christian emperor Constantine. Part 2 tells of his martyrdom under the emperor Julian, who is called the Apostate because he left the Christian faith and became a persecutor of Christians.

Actually, both parts of *Gallicanus* exhibit Roswitha's familiarity with Commonplace, and the exercise which follows explores this feature of her play.

EXERCISE 2.4: Analyzing Commonplace

DIRECTIONS: Begin by reading the introduction, which summarizes the play. Then read the excerpts from *Gallicanus* which follow. (They are presented in the order in which they appear in the play.) In order to identify and examine the Commonplace approaches in the play, answer the questions which follow each excerpt.

INTRODUCTION: *In Part 1 of* Gallicanus, *a pagan Roman general, desires to marry a Christian woman who has taken a vow of chastity. When he departs for the war, she asks two Christian counselors (John and Paul) to accompany him, and in the course of time, Gallicanus accepts their teaching, becomes a Christian, and honors the vow of chastity.*

In Part 2, we leave the reign of Constantine and enter the time of Julian the Apostate, who, though once a Christian, has become a persecutor of Christians. Failing to persuade Gallicanus to return to the pagan gods, Julian orders his execution. Then the two Christians who helped bring Gallicanus to Christ, John and Paul, are murdered on Julian's command at the hand of a pagan named Terentianus. Almost immediately, Terentianus' son becomes possessed by a devil, but as soon as he confesses that his father was responsible, the demon is cast out. The lad then praises the martyrs, and both he and his father become Christians and are baptized.

Excerpt from *Gallicanus*
A Commonplace against the Worship of False Gods
By Roswitha of Gandersheim

Approach: Comparison

Part 1, Scene 11

Here Gallicanus returns to Rome. He left as a pagan and has returned as a Christian. He stops at a church to pray. The Emperor Constantine, the first Christian emperor of Rome, has asked him about this change.

> GALLICANUS
> Most Sacred Emperor, I confess I visited the temples on my departure, as you have said, and humbly sought the help of gods and demons.
>
> CONSTANTINE
> According to the old Roman custom.
>
> GALLICANUS
> To my thinking, a bad custom.
>
> CONSTANTINE
> I am of the same mind.[65]

Question:

1. In this passage, false gods are compared to what?

Approach: Contrast

Part 2, Scene 5

After the death of Constantine and two other Christian emperors, Julian the Apostate has become emperor. Having executed Gallicanus, Julian now tries to persuade the Christians John and Paul to continue their service to the emperor. They say they cannot do so because he is not like Constantine.

> JULIAN
> How do I differ from my predecessors?

1

JOHN
In your religion and your virtue.

JULIAN
What do you mean?

PAUL
We mean that those most famous and glorious princes,
Constantine, Constantius, and Constance, whom we served, 5
were very Christian rulers who were zealous in the service of God.

JULIAN
I know, but in this I do not choose to follow their example.

PAUL
You follow worse examples. They frequented the churches and, laying their diadems on the ground, adored Jesus Christ on their knees.

JULIAN
And you think that I should imitate them? 10

JOHN
You are not made of the same stuff.

PAUL
By doing homage to the Creator, they elevated the Imperial dignity—yes, they transfigured it with the splendor of their virtue and their holy lives. So they deserved the success which crowned their enterprises.

JULIAN
As I do. 15

JOHN
In a very different way, for the divine grace was with them.

JULIAN
Absurd! Once I too was fool enough to believe in these meaningless practices. I was a priest of your Church.

> JOHN
> Do you hear, Paul? How do you like this priest?
>
> PAUL
> Very well—as the devil's chaplain.[66] 20

Questions:

2. In Line 2, John contrasts Julian to his predecessors. In what two ways does John say Julian differs from them?

3. In Lines 4-6, Paul makes the contrast more specific. How does he refine John's contrast?

4. In Line 20, Paul says Julian is the devil's chaplain, which implies a comparison with John and Paul. By inference, what do they consider themselves?

Approach: Cause

Immediately after the contrast, Roswitha moves the conversation toward the element of cause with these lines from Julian.

> JULIAN
> But when I found that there was nothing to be gained from it [Christianity], I turned to the worship of the true Roman gods, thanks to whom I have been raised to the highest pinnacle of power.[67]

Questions:

5. What reason does Julian give for leaving Christianity?

6. What syllogism underlies Julian's statement?

   MAJOR PREMISE:

   MINOR PREMISE:

   CONCLUSION:

7. In your Bible, review I Peter 1:4-8. How does that passage help to reveal an error in the underlying syllogism?

Past Life / Profile

Part 2, Scene 8

Julian has ordered a man named Terentianus to execute John and Paul. Almost immediately after the execution, Terentianus' son is possessed by demons. Terentianus puts questions to some Christians nearby:

> TERENTIANUS
> Christians, Christians, what ails my son? 1
>
> CHRISTIANS
> He grinds his teeth, foams at the mouth, and rolls his eyes like a madman.
> He is surely possessed by a devil.
>
> TERENTIANUS
> Woe to his father! Where was he stricken?
>
> CHRISTIANS
> Before the tomb of the martyrs John and Paul. He writhes on the ground 5
> and cries out that they are the cause of his torments.
>
> TERENTIANUS
> Mine the fault! Mine the crime! It was at my command that the wretched
> boy laid his impious hands on those holy martyrs.

CHRISTIANS
Since you were the partner of his guilt, it is right that you should share his sufferings.   10

TERENTIANUS
I did but obey the wicked commands of my master, the Emperor Julian.

CHRISTIANS
He himself has been struck down by the divine wrath.[68]

Questions:

8. There are actually three "past life" experiences that are mentioned in this passage.

   a. In Lines 7-8, what past action does Terentianus blame for his son's condition?

   b. In Line 11, what further past action does Terentianus blame?

   c. In Line 12, what was the consequence of Julian's past action—ordering the executions of the Christians?

9. The tendency of underlings to blame their superiors for their actions is a common one, especially notable since the end of World War II when the Nazis claimed they were only acting on Hitler's orders and were not personally responsible for the Holocaust. The Geneva Convention and the United States Military Code of Justice (USMJ) both address this issue. Specifically, the USMJ states the following in Section 892, Article 92: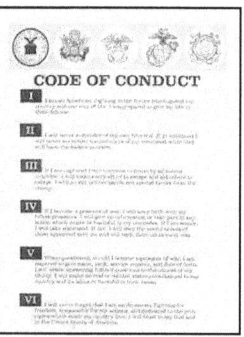

   Any person subject to this chapter who—

   (1) violates or fails to obey any lawful general order or regulation;

(2) having knowledge of any other lawful order issued by a member of the armed forces, which it is his duty to obey, fails to obey the order; or

(3) is derelict in the performance of his duties shall be punished as a court-martial may direct.[69]

Would Terentianus' excuse be acceptable under this law? Explain your answer. It might be helpful to discuss this issue in class.

Approach: Call for Punishment

Part 2, Scene 8

> TERENTIANUS
> I know [that Julian has died], and am the more terrified. I see that no enemy of those servants of God can escape punishment.[70]

Question:

10. In this play, punishment was applied by God without a human appeal. However, Terentianus seems to understand the need for punishment. Of the following seven appeals, which one underlies Terentianus' statement about punishment?

    ___ **Description:** He described the effects of the vice.

    ___ **Illegality:** He discussed punishment in terms of the law.

    ___ **Justice:** He argued that severe punishment was just.

    ___ **Expediency:** He showed that things would be better the sooner the vice was eliminated.

    ___ **Honor:** He showed how those who eliminated the vice would receive honor.

    ___ **Practicality:** He argued that the public desired retribution.

    ___ **Immediacy:** He argued that swift punishment would deter others.

Conclusion

Part 2, Scene 8

After acknowledging his sin and the justice of God's punishment, Terentianus asks the Christians a question and receives an answer:

> TERENTIANUS
> What if in expiation of my crime, I threw myself on my knees before the holy tombs?
>
> CHRISTIANS
> You would win pardon if you were cleansed by baptism.[71]

Question:

11. A Commonplace addresses the issues of Comparison, Contrast, and Cause; surveys the offender's Past Life or the Profile of an offender; and normally ends with a Call for Punishment. In this exchange from Part 2, Scene 8, what two things does Roswitha add as important components of a Christian Commonplace against a vice?

12. Is Roswitha's conclusion Biblical? Explain your answer.

MEDIEVAL PLAYS

Chapter 3

Introduction

Medieval plays can be divided into two types: religious and secular. The religious plays can be subdivided into liturgical drama and the mystery and morality plays. In addition, there is a sixteenth-century Cornish play that is a curious mixture of the religious and the secular. The purpose of this chapter is to explore these variations.

Liturgical Drama

Liturgical plays are so called because they developed as part of the Church liturgy (the worship service). As we have seen, these plays began with the *Quem Quaeritis?* and the *Visitatio Sepulchrum*, which depicted the Easter story. In the eleventh and twelfth centuries, monks began to write Christmas tropes as well. Interestingly, the Christmas trope begins in the same way as the Easter trope: *Quem Quaeritis?* However, this time it is the shepherds who are asked, "Whom do you seek?" Quite short, the St. Gall version of the trope went this way:

> **On the Nativity of the Lord at Mass let there be ready two deacons having on dalmatics,[a] behind the altar, saying:**
>
> *Quem quaeritis in praesepe, pastores, dicite?*
> [Whom seek ye in the manger, say, ye shepherds?]
>
> **Let two cantors in the choir answer:**
>
> *Salvatorem Christum Dominum, infantem pannis involutum, secundum sermonem angelicum.*
> [The Saviour, Christ the Lord, a child wrapped in swaddling clothes, according to the angelic word.]

---

[a] loose vestments

And the deacons:

Adest hic parvulus cum Maria, matre sua, de qua, vaticinando, Isaias Propheta: ecce virgo concipiet et pariet filium; et nuntiantes dicite quia natus est.
[Present here is the little one with Mary, His Mother, of whom Isaiah the prophet foretold: Behold, a virgin shall conceive, and shall bring forth a son; and do ye say and announce that He is born.]

Then let the cantor lift up his voice and say:

Alleluia, alleluia, jam vere scimus Christum natum in terris, de quo canite, omnes, cum Propheta dicentes: Puer natus est!
[Alleluia, alleluia. Now we know indeed that Christ is born on earth, of whom sing ye all, saying with the Prophet: Unto us a child is born.][72]

The Term *Mystery Play*

These outdoor performances, a part of the mission of the Church, are known as *mystery plays*. The term *mystery*, as it is used here, has been the subject of some debate among scholars. One explanation is that, since the plays presented religious topics, the term reflected the sacred mysteries of the faith, but the more likely explanation is that the word *mystery*, when used to describe medieval plays, derives from the Latin word *misterium*, which translates into English as *guild*. This is because the funding, preparation, and presentation of the plays were the responsibilities of the various guilds in a medieval town—the bakers, the shipbuilders, and the makers of armor, to name just a few.

Miracle Plays

One type of mystery play is the miracle play, which emerged during the twelfth and thirteenth centuries. Like the liturgical dramas, the theme of the miracle play was religious in nature. Miracle plays included Bible narratives (such as Creation, the Fall, and the Flood) and lives of the saints, with a special emphasis on conversion experiences (such as *The Play of the Conversion of St. Paul*).

Morality Plays

Morality plays, which appeared much later, were largely allegories, that is, plays in which the protagonist encounters various vices, such as Greed, Lust, and Sin, and various virtues such as Love, Kindness, and Generosity. In the course of the play, the vices try to derail the Christian, and, conversely, the virtues try to keep him or her on the true path. The morality play—which has perhaps had the longest run and still has a place in literature textbooks—is *Everyman*, which depicts the struggle every person has in trying to walk "the straight and narrow."

EXERCISE 3.1: Examining a Morality Play

DIRECTIONS: Please begin by reading the introduction. Then read the excerpt from *Everyman* and answer the questions that follow.

INTRODUCTION: *The protagonist in the story is called* Everyman, *because he represents all of humankind. At the beginning of the play, God appoints Death to tell Everyman that he is going to die. Everyman resists but is told that Death spares no man. Feeling sorry for himself, Everyman seeks out Fellowship and Kindred (or Cousin), but they decline to journey with him—Fellowship because he fears it would cause him pain; Cousin because he has his own reckoning to make. Recalling that his riches have always comforted him, Everyman calls upon his old friend, Goods.*

Excerpt from *Everyman*

EVERYMAN
[To himself] If that my Goods now help me might,
He would make my heart full light;
I will speak to him in this distress,
Where art thou, my Goods and Riches?

GOODS
Who calleth me? Everyman? What has thou haste? 5
I lie here in corners trussed and piled so high,
And in chests I am locked so fast,
Also sacked in bags, thou mayst see with thine eye,
I cannot stir; in packs, low I lie.
What would ye have? Lightly [to] me say. 10

EVERYMAN
Come hither, Goods, in all the haste thou may,
For of counsel I must desire thee.

GOODS
Sir, and [if] ye in the world have sorrow or adversity,
 That can I help you to remedy shortly.

EVERYMAN
It is another disease that grieveth me; 15
In this world it is not, I tell thee so,
I am sent for another way to go,
To give a straight account general
Before the highest Jupiter of all.
And all my life I have had joy and pleasure in thee. 20
Therefore I pray thee go with me:
For, paraventure[a] thou mayst before God almighty
My reckoning help to clean and purify,
For it is said ever among,
That money maketh all right that is wrong. 25

GOODS
Nay, Everyman, I sing another song;
I follow no man on such voyages,
For, and [if] I went with thee,
Thou shouldst fare much the worse for me:
For because on me thou did set thy mind, 30
Thy reckoning I have made blotted and blind,
That thine account thou cannot make truly;
And that hast thou for the love of me.

EVERYMAN
That would grieve me full sore,
When I should come to that fearful answer. 35
Up, let us go thither together!

GOODS
Nay, not so; I am too brittle. I may not endure:
I will follow no man one foot, be ye sure.

---

[a] perhaps

EVERYMAN
Alas! I have thee loved, and had great pleasure
All my life's days on goods and treasure.   40

GOODS
That is to thy condemnation without lesing,[a]
For my love is contrary to the love everlasting;
But if thou had me loved moderately during,
As to the poor given part of me,
Then shouldst thou not in this dolor[b] be,   45
Nor in this great sorrow and care.

EVERYMAN
Lo, now was I deceived ere I was aware,
And all I may wite[c] my spending of time.

GOODS
What—thinkest thou I am thine?

EVERYMAN
I had thought so.   50

GOODS
Nay, Everyman, I say no:
As for a while I was lent thee;
A season thou has had me in prosperity;
My condition is man's soul to kill,
If I save one, a thousand I do spill.   55
Thinkest thou that I will follow thee?
Nay, from this world not verily.

EVERYMAN
I had thought otherwise.

---

[a] releasing
[b] pain
[c] blame

GOODS
Therefore, to thy soul Goods is a thief,
For when thou art dead, this is my gyse,[a]   60
Another to deceive in the same wise
As I have done thee, and all to his soul's reprefe.[b]

EVERYMAN
O false Goods, cursed thou be,
Thou traitor to God that hast deceived me
And caught me in thy snare.   65

GOODS
By Mary! Thou brought thyself in care,
Whereof I am glad:
I must needs laugh, I cannot be sad.

EVERYMAN
Ah, Goods, thou hast had long my hearty love;
I gave thee that which should be the Lord's above;   70
But wilt thou not go with me indeed?
I pray [for you] the truth to say.

GOODS
No, so God me speed!
Therefore, farewell and have good day.

EVERYMAN
O! to whom shall I make my mone[c]   75
For to go with me in that heavy journey?[73]

Questions:

DIRECTIONS: Examine this passage from *Everyman* by using Aristotle's categories.

---

[a] custom
[b] reproof
[c] complaint

1. CHARACTER

   a. Explain how the characters in this play are allegorical?

   b. Goods reveals some facts about himself that Everyman had never seen before. What are they?

2. THOUGHT

   a. This exchange between Everyman and Goods is from a morality play. What lesson is being taught?

   b. Is the lesson (or idea) of this excerpt Biblical? If so, cite a Bible verse that teaches the same thing. If not, cite one that teaches the opposite.

3. DICTION

   a. An **aphorism** is a terse statement that makes a point. One example in the excerpt can be seen in Lines 24-25.

   What seems to be the meaning of the aphorism?

   Does the author seem to set this belief out as a true or a false belief?

b. A **classical allusion** is a reference to a person, place, or figure from the myths of Greece or Rome. Line 19 contains an allusion to Jupiter.

Who is Jupiter?

Why does it seem perhaps an odd choice for the author to use Jupiter in this play?

What reason might one give to explain this choice?

4. SPECTACLE

   a. The first time Goods speaks (Lines 5-10), he describes his situation. If you were to perform this scene, how would you set the stage to help convey the meaning?

ACTIVITY 3.2: Costuming *Everyman*

DIRECTIONS: The purpose of the activity that follows is to become familiar with medieval costume and the options available to players in the medieval period.

- Divide into groups of two or three. Your teacher will assign each group one of the characters—Everyman, Death, or Goods. If you are adventurous, you might try Fellowship (i.e., Friends) and Kindred/Cousin as well.
- Your group's task is to discuss how to costume the allegorical figure you have been assigned.
- To generate ideas about medieval dress, consult a book or web site on the history of costume.
- Consider colors, material, shape, headwear, shoes, gloves, and/or jewelry.

- Select a symbolic prop for your figure to carry.
- When finished, share your ideas with the class. (If you have artistic talent, perhaps you could draw a picture of your concept on the board.)

Comic Elements of the Mystery Plays

The liturgical plays of the early period were entirely sacred in nature, and no comedy was employed. However, the mystery plays were performed on the streets in a more raucous setting, and a bit of buffoonery was probably considered a sure way to keep the attention of a generally uneducated audience, including children. Therefore, it is not surprising to find comedy as a feature of the mystery plays.

It is important to note, however, that the slapstick scenes are generally associated with the fallen condition of humankind. One of the most famous examples of such a scene occurs in the play entitled *Noah* from the Wakefield Cycle, believed to have been the work of the Wakefield Master, more of whom later. In this play, the author has expanded the Biblical narrative of Noah and the ark by characterizing Noah's wife as a bit of a shrew, a true "daughter of Eve," if you will. Such a theme was not uncommon in the Middle Ages. The age-old battle of the sexes, as it is called, erupts when Noah's wife (called *Uxor*, the Latin word for *wife*) refuses to board the ark, preferring to get some more spinning done. The two argue and then begin to hit each other in a slapstick, comic way, as Noah urges his disobedient wife to go aboard.

As Professor David Bevington has written:

> Like every other aspect of the Noah story, this comic war of the sexes took on typological [symbolic] meaning for a medieval audience. The ark represents the true Church, and those like the wife who refuse to come aboard are recalcitrant sinners. Even when faced with the imminent prospect of death, the sinner perversely refuses to acknowledge that salvation is possible only through the Church.[74]

In the excerpt below, after Noah has threatened her three times, Uxor "breaks the fourth wall" by directly addressing the women in the audience, and Noah, not to be outdone, directly addresses the men. Then the ruckus ensues. (Note: The text is in Middle English with a gloss in Modern English appearing in smaller font.)

Noah
By the Wakefield Master

[The wife appeals to the women in the audience.]

UXOR
Lord, I were at ese, and hertely full hoylle,
Might I onys have a measse of wedows coyll.
For thy saull, without lese, shuld I dele penny doyll.
So wold mo, no frese, that I se on this sole
Of wifys that ar here,
For the life that they leyd,
Wold thar husbandys were dede.
For, as ever ete I brede,
So wold I oure sire were!

Lord [Husband], I'd be at ease and sound in heart, if I might just once enjoy the widow's lot. For thy soul, without loss, I would give a penny for the mass for your dead soul. The wives that are here, due to the life that they lead, wish their husbands were dead. For, as truly as I eat bread, so I wish our sire [my husband] were!

[Noah appeals to the men in the audience.]

NOE
Yee men that has wifys, whilst thay ar yong,
If ye luf youre lifys, chastice thare tong.
Me think my hert rifys, both levyr and long,
To se sich strifys wedmen emong.
Bot I,
As have I blis,
Shall chastise this.

You men that have wives, while they are young, if you love your lives, chastise their tongue. I think my heart breaks, both liver and lung, to see such strife among wedded men. But, as I hope to be saved, I will chastise this.

[[He strikes out at her again.]]

UXOR
Yit may ye mis,
Nicholl Nedy!ᵃ

You still can't hit me, Nicholl Nedy!

NOE
I shall make thee still as stone, beginnar of blunder!
I shall bete thee bak and bone, and breke all in sonder.

I will make thee still as a stone, beginner of blunder [Eve]! I shall beat thee, back and bone, and break all asunder.

[They fight.]

UXOR
Out, alas, I am gone! Oute apon thee, mans wonder!

Get out! Darn it, I'm done! Get out, you monster!

[[As they fight, they fall to the floor and begin to roll across the stage, the wife ending up on top of Noah, beating him.]]

NOE
Se how she can grone, and I lig under!
Bot, wife,
In this hast let us ho,
For my bak is nere in two.

See how she can groan—and I'm lying under her! But, wife, let us stop this violence, for my back is nearly broken in two.

UXOR
And I am bet so blo
That I may not thrife.

And I am beaten so black and blue that I may not win.

ᵃ You dolt!

[Then their children intervene, begging them to cease fighting. Now both Noah and his wife see their danger and appeal to God, as shown in this exchange]:

NOE

We will do as ye bid us; we will no more be wroth,
Dere barnes,
Now to the helme will I hent,
And to my ship tent.

We will do as you children bid us; we will no more be angry, dear bairnes.[a]
Now, I will lay hold of the helm and attend to my ship.

UXOR

I se on the firmament,
Me think, the seven starnes.

I think I see the seven planets in the sky.

NOE

This is a grete flood, wife, take hede.

This is a great flood, wife. Take heed!

UXOR

So me thoght, as I strode. We ar in grete drede;
Thise wawghes ar so wode.

So I was thinking, as I was walking. We are in great dread.
These waves are so wild!

NOE

Help, God, in this nede!
As thou art stere-man good, and best, as I rede,
Of all,
Thou rewle us in this rase,
As thou me behete hase.

---

[a] children

Help us, God, in this need! As thou art the steersman—and the best one of all, as I reckon. Rule us in this rush of water as you have promised me.

UXOR

This is a perlous case.
Help, God, when we call![75]

This is a perilous case. Help, God, when we call!

Secular Plays

The second type of play concerned not the matters of the Church, but the matters of the world. Since in Christian Latin, the word *saeculum* was translated as *world*, the plays about worldly matters are called secular plays. Examples include plays about the traditional English heroes Robin Hood and St. George.[a] It would be a mistake, however, to think that these plays were completely divorced from Christian culture, because they were performed primarily at parish ales, festivities where fermented drinks were sold to raise money for church furnishings or renovations. These plays were performed for "paying customers," so to speak, much in the same way that tickets are sold in theatres today.[76]

The dragon advances in a production of *St. George and the Dragon* by the St. Albans Mummers, 2015.

Ale, of course, was a fermented drink (such as beer) and, though it may seem odd to us that ale was sold to help the church, it is important to remember that the ale of the Middle Ages was not strong enough to cause intoxication. Rather, it contained only enough alcohol to kill bacteria in the water and to preserve the hops, a grain used in the production of the beverage. Since ale was the most common drink at the medieval table—even for children—all families needed this staple, and in the spring of the year, parish churches would sell ale as a fundraiser.

To attract a crowd, the parish-ales would include entertainment, and church budget records show that theatrical elements were included. For example, at St. Cuthbert's parish in Wells, dancers and a procession were included, and in nearby Croscombe,

---

[a] In one sense, plays about St. George might be considered miracle plays, but since they would have involved the slaying of a dragon, they would have been an attraction for younger members of the community, who might imagine themselves engaging in worldly heroics, like St. George, with sword in hand.

costumes were provided for the characters of a Robin Hood play. Though the miracle and morality plays made up most theatrical entertainment in the Middle Ages, these parish plays have been considered the first plays to involve money-making.[77]

EXERCISE 3.3: Analyzing a Script for a Secular Play

DIRECTIONS: In this exercise, you will examine the text of a medieval play about Robin Hood. Please begin by reading the introduction as well as the information about the various scenes. The play is written in Middle English with definitions of archaic words provided in footnotes. If necessary, you may consult the transliteration into the spelling of Modern English which appears in Appendix A at the end of the book. When finished reading, please perform the tasks that follow.

The Robin Hood Memorial in Nottingham

INTRODUCTION: The only surviving script of a medieval play about Robin Hood has survived in a fragment of only twenty-one lines and is believed to have been written around 1475. Its contents reveal that in this period Robin Hood *was not a children's story (see especially Lines 11-12). The script presents the lines the players are to deliver, but it does not indicate who is to speak what lines. Matters are further complicated by the fact that there is no punctuation and no indentions for new speakers. One line simply flows into another. Various scholars have tried their hand at determining which character is speaking which lines, and certainly there is more than one logical solution. Your task will be to decide (with a partner) the best dialogue scheme (i.e., who speaks what).*

A Fragment of *Robin Hood and the Sheriff* (c. 1475)

SCENES

- Scene 1: The sheriff and a knight come to an agreement.
- Scene 2: Robin and the knight compete twice, followed by a grisly ending.
- Scene 3: Two men (perhaps members of Robin's band) encounter each other, and one asks the other if he has heard anything about Robin. There is some discussion, and then a resolution is made.
- Scene 4: Friar Tuck and two others (perhaps the two from the previous scene) are arrested.

SCRIPT

    Syr sheryffe for thy sake / Robyn Hode wull y take
    I wyll the gyffe golde and fee / This be heste[a] thou holde me
    Robyn Hode ffayre and fre / Undre this lynde[b] shote we
    With the shote y wyll / Alle thy lustes to full fyll
    Have at the pryke[c] / And y cleve[d] the styke[e]   5
    Late us caste the stone / I graunte well be Seynt John
    Late us caste the exaltre[f] / Have a foote before the
    Syr knight ye have a falle / And I the Robyn qwyte shall
    Owte on the I blowe myn horne / Hit ware better be un borne
    Lat us fight at ottraunce / He that fleth god gyfe hym myschaunce   10
    Now I have the maystrey here / Off I smite this sory swyre[g]
    This knyghtys clothis wolle I were / And in my hode his hede woll bere
    Welle mete[h] felowe myn / What herst thou of gode Robyn
    Robin Hode and his menye[i] / With the sheryffe takyn be
    Sette on foote with gode wyll / And the sheryffe wull we kyll   15
    Be holde wele ffrere Tuke / Howe he dothe his bowe pluke
    Yeld yow syrs to the sheryffe / Or ells shall your bowes clyffe
    Now we be bownden alle in same / ffrere (T)uke this is no game
    Come thou forth thou fals outlawe / Thou shall (be) hangyde and y drawe
    Now allas what shall we doo / we (m)oste to the prysone goo   20
    Opyn the yatis[j] faste anon / An(d la)te theis thevys ynne gon[78]

TASKS

- Work with a partner to try to determine who is speaking each line, using Appendix A, if needed. There are probably several logical options.
- Make a list of props that would be needed with special attention to Scene 2.

---

[a] be heste = promise
[b] linden tree
[c] sharp point, point of a sword
[d] cleave, split
[e] stick, branch
[f] axletree, a wooden axle
[g] neck
[h] well met = hello
[i] meinie, retinue (the "merry band")
[j] gates

- Decide, as the director would, on the best blocking for Scene 2.
- Share and discuss your decisions with your classmates.

Cornish Language Plays

In 2000, a previously unknown sixteenth-century play was discovered among some papers bequeathed to the National Library of Wales. Written in the Cornish language, it shows a mixing of the miracle play with the secular play, and, as a primary source document, it also reveals the lingering hatred of the Cornish people for the Tudor kings of England—Henry VII, Henry VIII, and the Protectorate of the boy-king Edward VI, in particular.

The play is called *Bewnans Kea* [KĀ] *(The Life of St. Kea)*. The first part of the manuscript is a miracle play about the fifth-century figure St. Kea, but the second, and longer part, is a secular play about the legendary King Arthur. What ties these seemingly unconnected subjects together is that the villain in both parts of the play is an "emperor" called *Teudar*, which is not only a homophone for *Tudor*, but also the Cornish word for *fat*.

For half a century, Cornwall defied the Tudor kings. First, in 1497, they violently protested Henry VII's burdensome tax increases on the poor people of Cornwall. Then, during the Protestant Reformation of the next century, the people of Cornwall, who generally wished to remain Roman Catholic, opposed the changes King Henry VIII was making in Church governance and theology, as well as the dissolution of the Cornish abbeys, which were the centers of Cornish literature. Last, in 1549, after the distribution of the English-language Book of Common Prayer, which was to be used throughout the kingdom, the Cornish demanded the book be translated into their own language.

Each of these protests ended with a Tudor king ruthlessly crushing the Cornish. Their leaders were beheaded, and thousands of oppositional Cornishmen were killed in open battle. Understandably, these conflicts generated a hatred for the Tudor dynasty, and it has been argued that the Cornish play *Bewnans Kea* was a thinly veiled satirical stab at these oppressive kings.[79]

Professor John Mills, who serves on the Research Panel of the *Akademi Kernewek* [Cornish Academy], has pointed to several features of this play and others that point to the author's anti-Tudor sentiment. One of the most obvious is the use of language. To be specific, the heroes speak in Cornish, while the villains speak in English, a technique

Mills calls *code-switching*. One example from *Bewnans Kea* occurs when St. Kea comes to Cornwall for the first time and is brought as a prisoner before King Teudar, who speaks to him first in Cornish (shown here in italics), then "code-switches" to English, to reveal Teudar's true colors, so to speak:

TEUDAR	TEUDAR
Te javal ew henna gwyr	You scoundrel, is this true
labar heb gaw	Don't lie! From whence
A bele eta then tyr	Do you come to the region?
menek the bow	Declare your country
What hath thy man	and further your domain.
Ho ys thy lord tel me that![80]	Who is your lord? Tell me that![81]

Mills also identifies other Cornish mystery plays in which English is the language of the villains, including Lucifer, Lucifer's angel, Pontius Pilate, Caiaphas, and Christ's torturers.

As in ancient Greece, the playwrights of the Middle Ages—at least those in Cornwall—found ways to insert political commentary in their plays, though, as in ancient Rome, they had to find subtle ways to do so, in the absence of freedom of speech.

MEDIEVAL PLAYWRIGHTS AND PLAYERS

Chapter 4

Playwrights

Few medieval playwrights are known to us by name, but profiles appear below for those writers whose names have come down to us, as well as some anonymous writers whose distinct style has made them memorable. Centers of playwriting will also be explored.

Roswitha of Gandersheim (10th-century Saxony)

One of the few medieval playwrights who is known to us by name is Roswitha of Gandersheim, a Benedictine canoness at Gandersheim Abbey in what is now Bad Gandersheim, Lower Saxony. She is believed to have been born in about AD 935, and because of the high quality of her education, her family is thought to have been in the Saxon nobility. Roswitha would have had a classical education with early instruction in the grammar stage of the liberal arts provided by a teacher named Rikkardis. Then she was introduced to the classical authors and the writings of the

Roswitha of Gandersheim
935-1002

Church Fathers by Abbess Gerberga II. This famed abbess was the daughter of Henry I of Bavaria and the niece of the Holy Roman Emperor, Otto I, and probably received her own education at the Abbey of St. Emmeran in Regensburg, the center of Bavarian culture.[82] One cannot imagine a better teacher for young Roswitha.

The spelling *Roswitha* is an Anglicized rendering of a Saxon name, which is variously spelled as *Hrosvitha, Hrostvitha,* and *Hrotsuit*. As a sobriquet, Roswitha referred to herself as *"clamor validis Gandeshemensis"* ("the strong voice of Gandersheim"), which has given linguistic scholars some etymological fun. Jacob Grimm, of the famous Brothers Grimm of children's literature, for example, observed in 1838 that this Latin moniker was actually a pun on the name *Roswitha*, which is based on two words from Old Saxon: *hruot* (strong) and *suid* (voice).[83] So, both by birth and by name, this playwright was a "strong voice for the Lord."

By means of Gerberga's instruction, Roswitha became familiar with the works of the great Roman authors such as Horace, Ovid, Boethius, Terence, and Virgil, and also became well-acquainted with the writings of some of the great churchmen, such as Jerome, Alcuin of England, the Venerable Bede, Notker, and others. Roswitha respected the high quality of plays by the pagan author Terence, whose works, you will recall, were popular throughout the Middle Ages as vehicles for the teaching of Latin. In an effort to explain her decision to use Terence as a model for great writing, she wrote in the preface to her works:

> I, the strong voice of Gandersheim, have not hesitated to imitate in my writings a poet [Terence] whose works are so widely read, my object being to glorify, within the limits of my poor talent, the laudable chastity of Christian virgins in that self-same form of composition which has been used to describe the shameless acts of licentious women.[84]

As a canoness, a status similar to that of a nun, Roswitha was committed to a life of chastity, and it should come as no surprise that four of her six plays deal with this theme. For example, in the play *Callimachus* [kə-LĬM-ə-kəs], Drusiana is so determined to remain chaste, despite the threat of Callimachus to use all his "strength and skill" to trap her, that she renders this prayer in the form of a soliloquy:

> DRUSIANA
> O Lord Jesus, what use is my vow of chastity? My beauty has all the same made this man love me. Pity my fears, O Lord. Pity the grief which has seized me. I know not what to do. If I tell anyone what has happened, there will be disorder in the city on my account; if I keep silence, only Thy grace can protect me from falling into the net spread for me. O Christ, take me to Thyself. Let me die swiftly. Save me from being the ruin of a soul.[85]

The last line of this soliloquy indicates that Roswitha was not simply concerned with Drusiana's safety, but also with the spiritual condition of Callimachus—a detail that indicates Roswitha had thought deeply about how the sin of unchastity affects victim and perpetrator alike.

Scholars disagree as to whether Roswitha's plays were intended to be read or performed, but since she wrote stage directions here and there, it is fair to conclude that perhaps she at least desired them to be performed. If, indeed, they were performed, it is fun to imagine the nuns memorizing their lines, getting up their costumes, and actually performing the play within the confines of the Abbey.

Roswitha died in about 1002 but her name lives on in the German theatrical community to this day. Since 1975, it has been the custom of the city of Bad Gandersheim to award the Roswitha Ring to the actress with the best performance in the city's annual dramatic festival, the *Gandersheimer Domfestspiele*. In addition, in 1906, when August Kopff discovered an asteroid and named it the "615 Roswitha," he made a lasting tribute to the star power of the strong voice of Gandersheim.

Hildegard of Bingen (1098-1179)

Hildegard of Bingen (left) in a medieval manuscript

Hildegard of Bingen is another of the few playwrights whose name is known to us. Her parents, who were of the free lower nobility in the Holy Roman Empire, gave her as an aspiring nun to Jutta of Spanheim, the prioress of a cell of nuns affiliated with the monastery of Disibodenber near Bingen. Hildegard is said to have experienced mystical visions in which she saw flames of fire reaching down to her from heaven, and these became the substance of her book *Scivias*. She also became an accomplished poet, musician, and playwright.

Her Latin liturgical play entitled *Ordo virtutem (The Play of the Virtues)* is, like *Everyman*, an allegory. It involves a contest between *Virtutes* (Virtues) and *Diabolus* (Devil), as they struggle to win *Anima* (Soul), who, in this play, is clearly female. A total of twenty-one characters, including these three, have a role to play, including such virtues as *Scientia Dei* (Knowledge-of-God), *Timor Dei* (Fear-of-God), *Contemptus Mundi* (Contempt-for-the-World), and *Amor Celestis* (Heavenly Love).

For one who is not considered to have had much formal education, Hildegard shows remarkable literary talent,[86] as in this passage where Chastity employs a metaphor to explain her protection to Soul:

> CHASTITY
> Gentle maiden, you will never know the shadow over the falling flower!

Then the main character steps in with additional metaphors:

> VIRTUES
>
> The flower of the fields fails in the wind, the rain splashes it. But you, Virginity, remain in the symphonies of heavenly habitants: you are the tender flower that will never grow dry.[87]

Geoffrey de Gorham (12th-century England)

Another writer known to us by name is Geoffrey de Gorham (d. 1146). Though known in history as Geoffrey of Dunstable or Geoffrey of St. Albans, he was actually a native of the Norman province of Maine. Because he gained a reputation as a learned cleric, he was invited to England, which by this time had been under French-speaking Norman kingship for eighty years, to take charge of the abbey school in St. Albans. However, because he delayed in coming, the position was filled by the time he arrived, so he was given a place at Dunstable.

It was during his time there that Geoffrey wrote a miracle play about St. Katharine, perhaps to please King Henry II, who was devoted to the saint. It was probably performed either by Geoffrey's students or by the local weavers' guild, who had chosen Katharine as their patron saint.

Two medieval men in choir copes

To costume his play, Geoffrey had borrowed the choir copes of St. Albans, but disaster befell him when, on the night after the play's performance, fire destroyed his house, his books, and the costly copes. Distressed by what he perceived as a sin against the saint, the abbot, and God, Geoffrey decided the best recompense would be to dedicate himself to God by becoming a monk of St. Albans. He eventually rose to become the abbot there, and it is said that he always made it his special concern to make sure the abbey was provided with excellent choir copes![88]

Hilarius (12th-century France)

Hilarius [hĭ-LÄ-rē-əs] (sometimes Anglicized as *Hilary*), who lived in the twelfth century, is thought to have been an Englishman, though his works were composed in France, where he was first a student of the famous teacher Pierre Abelard and then a resident of Angers [Ä-zhē], the capital of Anjou [än-ZHŪ]. Hilarius wrote in rhymed Latin intermixed with refrains in French, and is important in the history of the theatre in that he was the first to make mention of a stage outside the church door.[89]

Hilarius wrote three plays: *The Raising of Lazarus*, *The Play of Daniel*, and *The Icon of St. Nicholas*. St. Nicholas was a particularly popular subject for medieval saints' plays, but one mustn't conceive of him as the St. Nick of an American Christmas. Rather, the stories involve the Greek bishop of Myra (AD 270-343) who lived in what is now Turkey and who is honored as a saint in the Greek Orthodox, Roman Catholic, Lutheran, and Anglican traditions.

Statue of St. Nicholas of Myra

The Icon of St. Nicholas tells the story of a man named Barbarus, a name which conjures up the image of a heathen barbarian. In the play, Barbarus is, in fact, a non-Christian, who is nevertheless attracted to the figure of St. Nicholas because of the saint's reputation for honesty. When Barbarus must go abroad, he places his riches in front of an icon (image or statue) of St. Nicholas, trusting in the saint so much that he does not even lock the doors of his house. In his absence, thieves break in and steal the treasure, causing Barbarus, upon his return, to become enraged and approach the image of the saint with a whip in hand, crying out:

BARBARUS	BARBARUS
Tuum testor deum:	I call thy god to witness
Te, ni reddas meum,	Unless thou return my property
Flagellabo reum.	I shall scourge thee, culprit!
Hore ten ci,	Now I've got you here,
Quare me rent ma chose que gei mis ci.	So return to me my property which I placed here.[90]

At this point, the statue comes to life, and Nicholas begins his search for the thieves. Once they are found, he threatens them with hanging if they do not return the treasure, and when Barbarus receives back his property, he joyously falls to his knees and extols Nicholas, who tells him that he should thank God instead. Barbarus then renounces his heathen past and becomes a Christian.[91]

Schoolboys

It is certain that students at the monastery schools wrote (and possibly performed) plays as school exercises. Examples include the twelfth-century St. Nicholas plays in the Loire Valley (France), the play of Daniel in the cathedral school at Beauvais (France) c. 1140, the play of St. Catherine in the abbey school at St. Albans (England) in 1110, and the feast day plays composed in the cathedral school at Augsburg (Germany) in 1119.[92]

Education in the Middle Ages was normally continued only to age fourteen. Did schoolboys of this age have the skills to write such plays? As students receiving a classical education, they would certainly have been prepared to include progymnasmata elements such as historical narrative, invective, encomium, and speech-in-character in their plays. Though it is not known who wrote the Cornish play *Bewnans Kea*, the second part, which concerns King Arthur, commences with a series of *encomia* both by Arthur's followers to Arthur and by Teudar's followers to Teudar—almost to the point of boredom for the listener/spectator. One has to wonder if these *encomia* were schoolboy exercises solicited by a monk/teacher/writer who then inserted them into his play. That is speculation, of course, but it would certainly be reasonable to say that the students in medieval monasteries and cathedrals had the ability to compose them.

Fleury (France c. 1200)

At Fleury Abbey in St. Benoit-sur-Loir [sānt bĕn-WÄ sər lə-WÄR], France, a monk (or group of monks) assembled a collection of plays in what is called today the *Fleury Playbook*. These plays are written primarily in Latin and date from the twelfth century.

Fleury Abbey at St. Benoît-sur-Loire

Professor C. Clifford Flanigan of the University of Indiana regarded this collection as highly significant in the history of theatre in western Europe. Since little had been done theatrically in Europe since the debased form of drama that emerged in the late Empire, the Fleury collector "helped create and enforce an understanding of a literary form that had been absent from the consciousness of Europe for almost a millennium [sic]."[93] The plays were not liturgical in nature, nor were they meant as plays simply to be read as school exercises. Rather, the scriptwriters often inserted phrases to the effect that plays were intended to be *videtur a populo* (i.e., to be seen by the people) and could be performed almost anywhere as stand-alone performances in their own right. As

Flanigan put it, the Fleury monk had a clear sense of the art of theatre, that is, "mimetic activity for the sake of affecting an audience by means of physical enactment."[94]

The playbook contains ten plays: two Christmas plays, two Easter plays, a play about the raising of Lazarus, a play about the conversion of St. Paul, and four plays about Saint Nicholas. The number of plays about St. Nicholas may seem disproportionate until one recalls that Nicholas was the patron saint of school children, and since a number of medieval plays were created for and performed by monastery students, the reason for choosing Nicholas becomes more apparent. Of the St. Nicholas plays, one of them *Tres Filiae (The Three Daughters)* contains the seed of the Christmas stocking custom, which is still a part of Christmas celebrations to this day.

The Dowry for the Three Virgins by Gentile da Fabriano

EXERCISE 4.1 (ENRICHMENT): Translating Latin Dialogue

DIRECTIONS: Below is an excerpt from the *Fleury Playbook* entitled *How Saint Nicholas Freed the Son of Getron*. It was originally written in medieval Latin. Working alone or with a partner, translate the excerpt into English. Please notice that the bold-faced words are glossed to provide assistance. When finished, you can check your work by consulting Appendix B.

Excerpts from *How Saint Nicholas Freed the Son of Getron*
A Fleury Play

BACKGROUND A: The son of a Christian man named Getron has been captured by the pagan king, Marmorinus. The king tries to persuade the boy to abandon God and follow Apollo, but the boy is steadfast. Meanwhile, the boy's parents are understandably distraught and see hope in the approaching festival of St. Nicholas:

GETRON

In crastino erit festivitas
Nicholai, **quen** Christianitas
Tota debet ***devote colere,***
Venerari et benedicere.
Audi ergo mea consilia   5
Adeamus eius ***sollemnia;***
Conlaudenus eius ***magnalia;***
Deprecemur eius ***suffragia.***[95]

Line	Latin word	Comments
1	in crastino	tomorrow
2	Nicholai	genitive of *Nicholas*
	uen	medieval spelling of *quem*
3	devote	adverbial form of *devotus, -a, -um*
	colere	infinitive of *colo*, to worship or honor
5	audi	singular imperative of *audio*
6	adeamus	let us go; 1st plural present active subjunctive of *adeo*
	sollemnia	sacred festivals
7	conlaudenus	let us praise; 1st plural present active subjunctive of *conlaudo*; note the medieval spelling which replaces *m* with *n*
	magnalia	wonderful works, mighty deeds
8	deprecemus	let us ask for, pray for; 1st plural present deponent subjunctive of *deprecor*
	suffragia	In medieval Latin, this word meant *intercession.*

BACKGROUND B: They do attend the festival and pray; then the wife returns home. The scene shifts back to the boy and the king, and the boy laments that a full year has passed since his abduction. Then we see stage directions (shown here in brackets) followed by dialogue between CIVIS and PUER:

[Intrea veniat aliquis in similitudine Nicholai;
Pueram, scyphum cum recentario tententem,
Op[p]rehendat, ap[p]rehensumque ante fores
Componat, et quasi non compertus, recedat.
Tunc vero unus de civibus ad puerum dicat.] 5

CIVIS:
Puer, quis es, et quo vis peregere?

. . . .

PUER:
Huc venio, non ibo longius;
Sum Getronis unicus filius.
Nicholao sit laus et Gloria,
Cuius hic me reduxit gratia.[96] 10

Line	Latin	Comments
1	*intrea*	contraction of *interea*
	In similitudine	In the likeness (i.e., dressed up as Nicholas)
2	*pueram*	*puerum*
	scyphum	goblet
	recentario	container of new wine
	tententem	adj. from verb *teneo*, describing *puer*
3	*op[p]rehendat*	Let him grab; 3rd singular present active subjunctive of *apprehendo*; note the medieval spelling which replaces *o* with *a*
	ap[p]rehensum	the captured boy
4	*componat*	Let him place, arrange; 3rd singular present active subjunctive of *compono*
	compertus	certain
	recedat	Let him go away, depart; 3rd singular present active subjunctive of *recedo*
5	*de*	With cardinal numerals, *de* means *of*
	dicat	Let him speak; 3rd singular present active subjunctive of *dico*
6	*peregere*	infinitive of *perago*
7	*longius*	further
8	*Getronis*	*Getron* is a third declension noun, so this is the genitive form
	unicus	only, only-begotten

The Wakefield Master (c. 1460-65)

The plays in the Wakefield cycle (Yorkshire) emerged gradually in the first half of the fifteenth century. However, some of the Wakefield plays (also called the Towneley plays) contain evidence that a more masterful playwright was producing scripts between 1460 and 1465. Since his name is unknown, he has come to be called the Wakefield Master.

Representing the workplace of the Wakefield Master.

Five plays are attributed to the Wakefield Master: *Noah, The First Shepherds' Play, The Second Shepherds' Play, Herod the Great,* and *The Buffeting of Christ*. These plays are artfully written in the complex pattern called the Wakefield Stanza, which was introduced in Chapter 2. The stanzas are typically nine lines long divided into a quatrain (four lines) rhymed AAAA, and a tercet (five lines) containing a *cauda* (i.e., a tail, or last line, that rhymes with the first line, BCCCB.) Below is an example from the Wakefield play:

NOAH:
Above all hillys bedeyn the water is risen late	A
Cubettys fifteyn. Bot in a higher state	A
It may not be, I wen, for this well I wate:	A
This fourty dayes has rain beyn; it will therefor abate	A
Full lele.	B
This water is hast	C
Eft will I tast:	C
Now am I agast--	C
It is wanyd a great dele!97	B

Note the presence of internal rhymes as well: *bedeyn/fifteyn; wen/beyn*. Because of this feature, the Wakefield Stanza can also be laid out as a 13-line, thus:

Above all hillys bedeyn	A
The water is risen late	B
Cubettys fifteyn	A
Bot in a higher state	B
It may not be, I wen,	A
For this well I wate:	B
This fourty dayes has rain beyn;	A

It will therefor abate	B
Full lele.	C
This water is hast	D
Eft will I tast	D
Now am I agast—	D
It is wanyed a great dele!	C

Since these plays show a certain sophistication, it is believed that the Wakefield Master was a local cleric or a monk from a nearby monastery.

Players

Who acted in the medieval plays? Were the actors professionals? Were they independent of each other, or were there traveling troupes of actors? These are some of the questions scholars have tried to answer primarily by digging around in the financial records of towns, abbeys, nobles, and kings to find evidence of names and payment, and they have discovered more variety than one would assume.

Guildsmen

What is known is that the guildsmen who built the pageant wagons also acted in the plays. Shakespeare, as a boy, would no doubt have seen morality plays performed by guildsmen, and they made enough of an impression on him that he later used them as comic figures in *A Midsummer Night's Dream*, where the "mechanicals" rehearse and perform *Pyramus and Thisbe* for the duke of Athens at his wedding. He called them Bottom, the weaver; Flute, the bellows-mender; Quince, the carpenter; Snug, a joiner; and Starveling, the tailor. That he makes them out to be not the most accomplished of thespians is obvious, but his humor is gentle, and the sincerity of the players is apparent.

EXERCISE 4.2: Primary Source

DIRECTIONS: The ordinance book for the city of York in 1476 contained a regulation regarding the players who would perform in the city's Corpus Christi play. The purpose of this exercise is to examine this source to determine what towns did to put on these plays. Please begin by reading the ordinance, and then answer the questions that follow.

1476 Ordinance of the City of York

Yearly in the time of Lent there shall be called afore the Mayor for the time being four of the most cunning,[a] discrete, and able players within this city to search here and examine all the players and plays and pageants throughout all the artificers belonging to the Corpus Christi play, and all such as they shall find sufficient in person and cunning[b] to the honor of the city and worship[c] of the said crafts for to admit and [en]able and all other insufficient persons either in cunning, voice, or person to discharge, remove, and avoid.[d] [98]

1. Does it appear there were auditions for the medieval morality plays? Explain your answer.

2. Who selected the players "for the time being"?

3. a. When were the actors selected?

   b. In your opinion, for what reason were actors selected then?

   c. From these facts, can you estimate how much time they had to prepare for the plays?

---

[a] skilled
[b] skill
[c] honor, reputation
[d] dismiss

4. In Line 2 of the ordinance, we are told the city authorities searched out actors who were "cunning, discrete, and able." In Middle English, the word *discrete* meant *separate*. What would it probably mean to search out "separate actors"?

5. In Line 4:

   a. What is meant by the word *artificers*?

   b. To whom do you think the writer was referring?

6. In Lines 5-6:

   a. Why do you think the city council wanted to hire persons who would bring "honor" to themselves and the guilds (crafts)?

   b. Does it suggest anything that might have happened before this ordinance was passed which made this qualification important?

8. In Line 7, we read they were looking for people who were sufficient in "voice and person."

   a. Why would the first quality be important?

   b. What do you think the second quality refers to?

Unlike Greeks and Romans, who benefitted from the special talents of actors like Roscius, the medievals have left us no names of famous actors. However, occasionally the names of individual actors were recorded in the city's payroll, and for those of us who have an instinct for history, hearing the names of persons who loved the same things we do, albeit hundreds of years ago, can strike a chord of affection. Here are some of the examples of theatrical persons whose names have come down to us:

Coins of Edward IV

- "Rhyngold's man Thomas," who played Pilate's wife for the smiths' guild in Coventry, Warwickshire, 1476.[99]
- Robert Crow, who was paid 3 sh. 4 d. in Coventry to play "God's part" in 1566.[100]
- "Wylliam Clark and his players," who were paid 10 d. for "rehersyng" for the "paujand" by the Mercers [Merchants] Guild in York in 1467.[101]

Names of other individuals involved in the production of the play also appear:

- **Wheelwrights:** In 1448, the Mercers of York also paid "Iohn Catryck" 13 sh. 3 d. "for a newe Whele to our pageand."[102]
- **Playwrights:** In 1506, John Burgess was paid for writing a play about Mary Magdalene at Magdalene [MŎD-lĭn] College, Cambridge.[103]
- **Costumers:** In 1491-92, John Soper was paid 10 d. for making costumes for plays in Ashburton, Devon.[104]
- **Seamstresses:** At Chester, "Widow Ellis" was paid for supplying three yards of fringe for a banner.[105]
- **Carpenters:** In 1501, the York Mercers paid Thomas Drawswerd eight marks to "mak the pagiant of the dome belonging to the merchauntes newe . . . for the warkemanship and Stuff of the same."[106]

Servants

From the commoners of England, not only guildsmen but also servants of the gentry sometimes became players. At least one particular servant, whose name survives as T. Platting, is known to us from the survival of the letters of the Paston family of

Norfolk. In this message, Sir John Paston lodged the following complaint about Platting:

> No more but I have been and am troubled with mine over large and courteous dealing with my servant and now with their unkindness. Platting, your man, would this day bid me farewell, to to-morrow, at Dover, notwithstanding Thryston, your other man, is [away] from me, and John Myryel, and W. Woode which promised you and Daubeney, God have his soul, at Caister, that if ye would take him in to be again with me, that then he would never go from me; and thereupon I have kept him this three years to play Saint George, and Robin Hood, and the sheriff of Nottingham, and now when I would have good horse, he is gone into Bernysdale,[a] and I without a keeper.
>
> Written at Canterbury, to Calais ward, on Tuesday, and hap be upon Good Friday, the 16th day of April, in the 13th year of Edward IV [1474]
>
> Your JOHN PASTON knight[107]

Women

As in Greece and Rome, the parts of women were primarily played by young men who did not "have a beard coming on."[108] However, Paul Kuritz has pointed out, "In 1468, a glazier's daughter played the part of St. Catherine in Metz. And in 1547 Jeanette Caralieu played the Virgin at Valenciennes."[109] Furthermore, there are records showing that nuns performed in plays at their convents. From the thirteenth century, we find this interesting note in the records of Barking Abbey in London:

> [S]ince the congregation of the people in these times seemed to freeze in devotion, and human torpor greatly increasing, the worthy lady, Lady Katharine of Sutton [the Abbess] then being responsible for their pastoral care, desiring to get rid of the said torpor completely and the more to excite the devotion of the faithful to such a renowned celebration instituted the performance of the *Visitatio*.[110]

---

[a] Barnsdale in Yorkshire

The choice of the *Visitatio* is particularly appropriate for women to perform, as it concerns the visit of the three Marys to the tomb of Jesus. Luke, who recorded the scene, noted that "two men stood by them in dazzling apparel" (24:4). This statement has long been considered a reference to angels, who were all identified as males in the Bible. Whether the nuns also appeared as these male angels is not known.

Artistic rendering of the *Visitatio Sepulchri* with the three Marys and an angel

The issue of nuns presenting male characters also arises in the case of the Saxon canoness Roswitha, whose plays generally had numerous male roles—both villainous and charitable. As mentioned above, it is uncertain if her plays were performed, but the stage directions frequently suggest that the nuns were moving about in a playing space such as the chapterhouse.

Children

Children were also asked to perform certain roles, according to town and guild records. For example, in a pre-Elizabethan Tudor play called *The Play of the Weather*, playwright John Heywood called for "a boy, the least that can play."[111] By *least*, the author means *youngest*, and since grammar school students ranged in age from eight to twelve, we can conclude the youngest were eight. Whoever he was, this lad had a good number of lines to memorize as he appears throughout the play.

Three-dimensional representation of the *Killing of the Innocents* in medieval costume

Another play that probably involved children was a play about Herod the Great called *The Killing of the Innocents*. As in the Bible narrative, Herod, in the play, directs that all boys up to the age of two are to be killed. It is hard to imagine two-year-old children moving about freely on the scaffold, but they could have been carried on, as suggested by the stage direction, "Then shall come in the women of Israel with young children in their arms."[112]

Other stage directions in that play suggest children did some "acting." For example, in Scene 3, when the mothers are pleading with the soldiers not to kill their children, we read the stage direction, *"Hic occident pueros.* (Here the boys are killed.)" One of the mothers then laments:

> Alas, alas, good gossips, this is a sorrowful pain,
> To see our dear children that be so young,
> With these caitiffs suddenly to be slain.[113]

This line certainly suggests that the women "see" their children slain before them, and there is no stage direction or dialogue to suggest otherwise.

Town records show that the money earned by child actors was normally paid to their mothers. At Coventry, for example, twelve pence was paid "for the angelles and the women for the child." The coopers' guild in Coventry paid both in cash and in kind (i.e., with gifts), as we learn that they gave "a perre of gloves to the childe yat caryede the arms and a quarte of wyne to his mother and for the makynge of his cloke xi d."[114]

Troupes

For the most part, there were few, if any, wandering actors or troupes of actors in England in thirteenth, fourteenth, and early fifteenth centuries—probably because of the sumptuary laws, that is, laws which decreed what kind of clothing could be worn by persons of various social ranks.

Shoes with pikes, worn by nobles

Though it seems strange to us today, acts of Parliament actually dictated the color and type of clothing each rank could (or could not) wear, as well as the use of furs, fabrics, and trim. For example, the Act of Apparel of 1464 forbade shoemakers from making "any shoes or boots having pikes (i.e., lengthened toes) more than two inches long for anyone lower in rank than a lord."[115]

Such laws, of course, prevented actors from using such items of clothing for their costumes, but once the great lords began to support acting troupes in their households, the nobles applied enough political pressure that exceptions were granted to "minstrels" and "players of interludes."[116]

Medieval Court Entertainment

One of the first nobles on record to have supported such a troupe was Humphrey, Duke of Gloucester, who is known to have had an acting company in the 1440s. Others followed suit in the latter half of the fifteenth century, after exceptions were made to the sumptuary laws,[117] and household account books show the rise of "professional" troupes maintained by numerous nobles. Examples include the following:

- William Fitz Alan, 16th Earl of Arundel (1417–1487), sponsored touring players in Kent, when he served as hereditary royal butler to Richard III and Henry VII in the 1480s.
- In the last quarter of the fifteenth century, several troupes were sponsored by the gentry (such as the Pastons).
- Henry Bouchier, Earl of Essex (d. 1483), maintained a group of actors.
- Richard, Duke of Gloucester (later King Richard III, d. 1485), supported a company of players, who, along with those of the Earl of Essex, performed for John, Lord Howard of Stoke-by-Nayland, Suffolk in 1482 and 1483.

SPECTACLE ON THE MEDIEVAL STAGE

Chapter 5

Introduction

In the medieval mystery plays, mere mortals purposed to present, before the eyes of an audience standing close in, the spiritual realms and the actions of supernatural beings—heaven, hell, God, the Holy Spirit, angels, demons, and Satan. Thus, one must ask how these mere mortals brought about, on a small stage, the sense of wonder  associated with many of the Bible narratives: Satan's fall from heaven, the burning bush, the appearance of angels, the fire of hell, the vanishings of Christ, Paul's encounter on the Road to Damascus, and the ascension of Christ into heaven. In addition to miracles, the plays also had to depict acts of human depravity, such as the beheading of John the Baptist, the scourging of Christ, and the crucifixion? How were these miracles and atrocities to be presented on a small stage and with the limited resources available to the denizens of the medieval towns? The purpose of this chapter is to shed light on this question.

Costumes and Props

To begin, let us focus on the costuming and stage properties which would have enhanced the "spectacle" of the stage, as Aristotle termed it. Unlike the Greeks and Romans who devoted more attention to masks than to costume, the medievals, who had smaller stages with up-close audiences, devoted greater attention to costuming. Masks were used, but of a much different type than the ancients had devised, and costumes of Biblical figures needed to approximate the attire of the Near East.

Sidney W. Clarke, historian of theatre and stage magic, provides a list of the "curious and costly" costumes typical of the miracle plays:

- Saints and holy persons appeared with gilt hair and beards.
- Christ wore a long sheep skin.

- Herod was dressed as a Saracen (Muslim) and carried a sword.
- Demons wore hideous masks.
- Angels wore diadems, flowing white surplices, and gilded skins with golden wings fastened to their shoulders.
- The Devil was represented with horns, a tail, and a bright red beard and wore a coat and hose made of rough hair.
- Both Satan and Pilate carried huge clubs made of leather and stuffed with wool.
- God was represented as a pope with a tiara and scepter.
- The leaders of the Jews were costumed as bishops wearing mitres, hoods, and white vestments.
- Adam and Eve were dressed in close-fitting coats of white leather and hose, probably dyed to the color of skin.
- Most of the characters wore gloves and either wore masks or painted their faces.
- Lost souls blackened their faces and wore costumes of black and yellow to represent the flames of Hell.[118]
- Players in France devised a sword with a retractable blade for the suicide of Herod and a statue with movable arms, hands and eyes to represent Mary.[119]

Stained glass window showing medieval concept of Lazarus in a winding sheet

The apostles often appeared carrying a symbol with which they are associated in Scripture. For example, in fourteenth-century France, Moses appeared with tables of stone; David, with a harp; and St. Peter, with keys, presumably representing the keys to Heaven. St. John appeared with a palm branch; John the Baptist carried the Gospels; Aaron, a flower; Daniel, a pike; and Habakkuk, "a wallet full of roots, which he pretends to eat."[120]

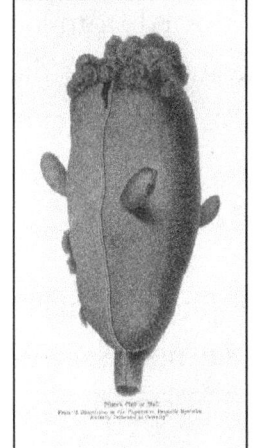

The leather and wool head of Pilate's "club"

At Coventry, Pilate always wore green and came on stage with a club made of leather and wool so that, like a Nerf toy, it would look real but not cause injury. Strangely, he also entered with several leather balls, which may have represented "the insignia of office"—or perhaps were used for juggling during interludes of the play.[121]

Exactly how realistic could the costumes and props be? At least a partial answer to that question can be found in a medieval chronicle which recorded an event of 1205. At that time, Albert, bishop of Riga, was asked to undertake the Christianization of the Livs, a tribe in the Baltic region which had not yet accepted Christianity. This was part of a larger crusade which included twenty-three fleets of soldiers. Now, believing the stage to be an engaging form of communication, Albert arranged to present his message by means of a play. With the hundreds of soldiers in his train, the players found it easy enough to borrow swords, shields, and helmets to be used for costumes and props, but no one anticipated the result. Henry of Lovinia writes, "The subject of this play was most diligently explained to both converts and pagans through an interpreter. When, however, the army of Gideon fought the philistines [sic] the pagans began to take flight, fearing lest they be killed."[122]

Medieval conception of Gideon fighting the Philistines, showing figures in contemporary medieval costume. Prague, c. 1350-75.

What exactly was it that caused the audience to flee? Most scholars think they did not understand that stage combat was merely simulated. Rather, seeing props such as swords and costumes involving breastplates, helmets, and/or shields, the Livs believed they had been lured into an ambush. However, as Shakespeare said, "All's well that ends well," and the chronicler recorded that the spectators were soon "quietly called back" and, as the old saying goes, the show was able to go on. Still, the incident is instructive. In this case, costumes and props had, no doubt, been borrowed from the soldiers who had accompanied Albert to Riga, just as the attire of churchmen was frequently borrowed from local churches. These certainly would have created a realistic effect for the audience, as the reaction of the Livonians proves. (By the way, Albert was eventually successful and completed the building of a cathedral in Riga within the next ten years.)

Sets

Despite the small size of the stage, stage furnishings were often employed, especially when necessary to present a Bible narrative. For example, an apple tree was placed onstage for the Garden of Eden; a throne for Pilate; a pillar for the scourging of Christ; a cross for the crucifixion, and a beam for Judas' suicide. On at least one occasion, the attempt to create realism for the audience nearly ended in tragedy when a chaplain of Metrange, in the role of Judas, was nearly hanged "in good earnest" in the presentation of the suicide.[123]

A medieval Hell-mouth

Indispensable to pageants which portrayed Satan, demons, or lost souls was the Hell-mouth, which Sidney Clarke described, thus:

> It was generally represented as a square, embattled tower, the entrance to which was through a gaping, hideous dragon's head, with glaring eyes, enormous nose, and movable jaws lined with rows of long, projecting teeth.
>
>> An hideous hole all vaste, withouten shape,
>> Of endless depth, orewhelm'd with ragged stone
>> With oughly mouth and griesly jaws doth gape,
>> And to our sight confounds itself in one.[124]

At Mons, the Hell-mouth was described as a huge "mask of a toad face."[125]

> When the jaws opened, fire and smoke, produced by braziers and bellows hidden away behind, were vomited from the mouth and nostrils. Drums were beaten, horns blown, tin cans banged, and amid the wild din, the devil and his imps leapt

in and out of the flaming opening, to drag the wicked characters to limbo, or to stir up the unhappy occupants of the infernal regions.[126]

Guild records reveal the substantial costs of building, maintaining, and storing this staple of the mystery play:

> Item paide for payntyng and makyng new hell hede xij d
> Item payd for mendyng new hell hede vj d
> P'd to John Huyt for payntyng of hell mowthe xvj d
> P'd for makyng hell mouth and cloth for hyt iiij s
> Payde for kepynge hell hede viij d
> Item payd for kepyng of fyer at hell mothe iij d[127]

In plays about Noah, the set was the ark itself. At Chester, for example, a stage direction in *The Flood* indicated: "Then Noah shall go into the ark with all his family, his wife excepted, and the ark must be boarded round about. And on the boards all the beasts and fowls hereafter rehearsed must be painted, so that their words may agree with the pictures."[128] If the word *all* was intended literally, then the painters would have had quite a job, as the subsequent dialogue named forty-four animals and birds, including even such specifics as polecats, bitterns, and rooks.

Earthquakes and Storms

Earthquakes were introduced in the Coventry plays in 1556. We know from account books that barrels were purchased for the purpose, but we can only speculate about how they produced the effect of tremors. One theory is that stone-filled barrels were attached to a pillar with a cylindrical gudgeon, which would have allowed stagehands to turn the barrel around, causing the stones to rumble and make enough noise to create a trembling sensation in the immediate area. However, others believe that a device rotating inside the barrel produced the effect.[129]

Coventry account books also list the purchase of starch "to make a storm" (probably the imitation of a hailstorm) as part of *The Destruction of Jerusalem*.[130] One theory is that "starch was showered down from a concealed perch above the playing area."[131] Another is that, as with the earthquake, a barrel was used, this time filled with gooey starch.[132]

Ascending and Descending

In other plays, we discover the need for a sort of *deus ex machina*, but without the *scaena* of the ancients to support the weight of a winch. Clearly the bi-level stage of the pageant wagon was set up with acting areas for heaven and earth, and certainly scripts survive which include stage directions for ascent and descent. For example, in *The Fall of the Angels* (York), the opening scene would have been performed on the upper level, representing Heaven, so that Satan could "fall" to the lower level, representing Hell. The dialogue tells us what is happening:

> FIRST ANGEL LUCIFER
> Above all yet shall I dwell in fame,
> On height in the highest of heaven.
> There shall I set myself, full seemly to sight,
> To receive my reverence through right of renown.
> I shall be like unto him that is highest on height. 5
> Oh what! I am perfect and proud....[a]
> Out, deuce! All goes down!
> My might and my main are all marring.
> Help, fellows! In faith, I am falling.
>
> SECOND FALLEN ANGEL
> From heaven are we hurled down on all hand. 10
> To woe are we wending, I warrant.
>
> LUCIFER THE DEVIL
> Out, out!
> Haro,[b] helpless! so hot is it here.
> This is a dungeon of dole in which I am dight.
> Where are my kin now, so comely and clear? 15
> Now am I loathliest, alas, that ere was so light.
> My brightness is blackest of hue now.[133]

---

[a] The modern translator added the ellipsis, probably to indicate a momentary pause in the action as the falling sequence begins.
[b] An interjection used when crying outa cry for assistance

From the dialogue, it is apparent that between Lines 6 and 7, the "fall" from the upper to the lower level begins, and three lines of dialogue are presented by the falling Lucifer. The Second Fallen Angel also "falls" and seems to present Lines 9 and 10 while descending. Lines 12-14 indicate that the players are now performing on the lower level, Hell: "So hot is it here," says Lucifer, now called "the Devil." In addition to the lowering of the actors, the special effects here might also have included a change of costume, as Lucifer remarks (Lines 16-17) that, whereas he once had been "so light," he now has become "blackest of hue."[134]

There are also numerous scripts that refer to ascending from the lower to the higher level, as we see in this excerpt from *Christ's Ascension* (Chester Taylors):

> JESUS
> Now to my Father I am going.
> Ye shall have, brethren, my blessing,
> for to heaven I must rise.
> *Tunc adducet discipulos in Bethaniam; et cum pervenerit ad locum,*
> *ascendens dicat Jesus, stans in loco ubi assendit. Dicat Jesus,*
> *Data est mihi omnis potestas in caelo et in terra.*
>
> JESUS
> My sweet brethren leif[a] and dear,
> to me is granted full power
> in heaven and earth, far and near,
> for my Godhead is most.
> To teach all men now go ye
> that in world will fulfilled be
> in the name of my Father and me
> and of the Holy Ghost.
> *Tunc Jesus ascendet, et in ascendendo cantabit Ihesus vt sequitur.*
>
> JESUS
> *Ascendo ad Patrem meum et Patrem vestrum,*
> *Deum meum et Deum vestrum. Alieluya.*[135]

---

[a] beloved

How was the ascending and descending accomplished? The records of the York Mercers Guild provide some clues. For one thing, they noted the need for "a brandreth[a] of iron that God shall sit upon when he shall rise up to heaven with four ropes at four corners."[136] Perhaps, as in later times, the lift was covered by a "cloud," for in the Ascension at York, Mary marvels at the sight:

> Ah, mightful God, aye most of might,
> A wondrous sight is this to see!
> My son thus to be ravished right,
> *In a cloud going up* from me.[137] (Emphasis added.)

Dismemberment and Substitution

Some mystery plays involved decapitation, dismemberment, or even disembowelment. In Angers, France, Jean Michels included a stage direction for his *Passion* in 1486, which stated, "Here Judas bursts at the belly and the guts fall out and the soul comes out."[138] It is quite possible that animal entrails would have been involved in this scene, but for dismemberments it was common to employ fake arms.

Vanishing and Going Dark

Methods for ascending and descending are perhaps easy to figure out, but what about vanishing? The author of *Christ Appears to the Disciples* (Chester), which is based on Luke 24, desired to remain true to Scripture, which records two vanishings of the resurrected body of Christ. Where Scripture says, "And he vanished from their sight" (24:31), the scriptwriter wrote, "*Tunc Jesus evanescet.* [Then Jesus will vanish.]" A few lines later when the resurrected Christ is speaking with the disciples, he wrote, "*Iterum evanescet Ihesus* [Again Jesus vanishes]."

Even today the "vanishing" of characters in the middle of a scene would be tricky to bring off, yet it appears from the stage directions that the Chester artisans found a way.

The Cornish mystery of the crucifixion, of which only the last scene has survived, contains the anguish of Mary, John's comforting words, the taunting of the soldiers, the offer of vinegar, the respectful centurion, and the words of Jesus, "*Eli, Eli, lema*

---

[a] gridiron

sabachthani?" (Mt. 27:46.) Just as in Chester, where the writer desired to stay true to the Scripture, the Cornish writer did not ignore the words of Luke, who records that at the sixth hour, when Jesus died, "there was darkness over the whole land until the ninth hour, while the sun's light failed" (Lk 24:44-45). Amazingly, we find this conclusion to the Cornish script:

> JESUS
> O Father, into thy hands
> I commit my spirit.
> By thy will, take it to thee.
> As thou sent it into the world.
>
> *[Then Jesus shall die. Here the sun is darkened.]*[139]

Crucifixion play in 15th-century Flanders, showing the upright crosses of the two thieves and Jesus carrying his cross

The fact that the stage directions call for the sun to darken supports the notion that the theatre community in Cornwall found a way to re-create this effect of darkness despite the presence of the sun which provided light through either a roofless theatre or an outdoor *plen an gwari*. How did they do that? Of course, audiences at these plays were willing to suspend disbelief in order to make the play "work," so it is possible they contrived a wooden sun on the upper level of the stage along with a black disk that would appear at the right moment and cover the golden sun. Are there other creative ways to devise darkness on a medieval stage?

Crucifixion Scenes

The crucifixion play presents several challenges for anyone performing on a pageant wagon. How can you make a cross heavy enough to hold the weight of a man, yet light enough to be portable from station to station? Do you secure it to the stage, or do you use a stand of some kind, as for a Christmas tree or a flag? Do you make it tall to elevate Christ far above the "ground," as we often see in movies, or, to make it less unwieldy, do you make it just tall enough to raise the actor a few inches above floor level—which is suggested by a stage direction that the cross would be supported by "two angels." At what point in the process is the actor representing Christ placed on the cross? How do you raise the cross up? How are you going to create the effect of nail wounds on the hands or wrists? What will you do for "spotters" so that, if the cross begins to fall, the actors are not injured?

Guild and town records along with stage directions from the manuscripts once again provide some hints about the tricks of their trade, though what was done in one town is not necessarily what was done in all. We know about the size of the cross used in the Towneley play called *The Scourging* from a line spoken by Mary. Unable to bear the sight of her son struggling under the weight of the cross, she begs to carry it for him, but he kindly replies, "This cross is large in length / and also bustus[a] withal" (l. 320).[140]

Because of the size and weight of the cross, it would have been difficult to raise in the short space of time available to the pageant, but various methods were employed. In the records of the Coventry Smiths Guild, who put on the play of the crucifixion, we know they searched out "a cross with a rope to draw it up."[141] In the Towneley play, the cross was dropped into a hole in the ground: "Set we the tree in the mortice / and there will it stand fast" (ll. 213-14).[142] The York Mercers' records refer to "seven great angels holding the passion of God,"[143] which was probably a safety measure so that the cross would not topple.

However, in one of the surviving scripts from York, though there is no mention of angels, we find a well-developed dialogue designed to expose the cruelty of the soldiers. In this crucifixion play, while the cross is on the ground, Jesus lays himself willingly upon it, no doubt to emphasize the sacrificial nature of the crucifixion. But the soldiers who had constructed the cross had botched their job in such a way that the bores were located too far apart. "It fails a foot and more / the sinews are so gone in [shrunken]," notes one of the soldiers (ll. 107-108). To align the limbs of Christ with the pre-cut bores (holes), the soldiers must pull on his arms and legs, a job one of them brags he will do as "snelly[b] as a snail" in order to increase the suffering (ll. 118).[144]

As with the Towneley play, the York rendering of the crucifixion involved a hole dug into the ground, no doubt in advance of the performance. The sadistic soldiers decide to "let him fall in all at once" to inflict a pain that has "no peer," but now they are confronted with a second botched job: the soldier who dug the hole made it too big,

---

[a] heavy, as an oak
[b] quickly

and the cross wobbles. They gather wedges and hammer them in place, concluding, "Now will this cross ful[l] stably stand." It is so secure, in fact, that even if Jesus "rave" (struggle), the wedges will not "rive" (budge) (ll. 247-48).[145]

In the N-Town crucifixion play, a stage direction indicates that after Jesus thanks Pilate's wife for her kindness, "they shall pull him down and lean him along on the cross, and after that they nail him thereon." In opposition to Scripture, the author has the Jews carry out the execution. One of them rejoices that Jesus is "tacked to a tree," and they mock him, saying, "Hail King of Jews, if thou be!" At this point comes a stage direction: "Here shall they leave off and dance about the cross shortly."[a] Mary is overwhelmed with emotion and runs to embrace the cross. The apostle John comforts her and leads her away. At that point, a stage direction reads, "And here shall Pilate come down from his scaffold with Caiaphas and Annas [Ananias] and all their meinie[b] and shall come and look on Christ." The wording here suggests that the cross had been raised in front of the pageant and that the three players came down from the scaffold into the street where the cross had been raised. The next direction provides even more clues:

> Here shall Pilate ask [for] pen and ink, and a table shall be taken [to him], written afore, "*Hic est Jesus Nazarenus, Rex Judeorum.*" And he shall make him to write,[c] and then *goes up on a ladder* and sets the tablet above Christ's head.[146] (Emphasis added.)

This is the only play that references a ladder in connection with the crucifixion. Step ladders were still centuries away, so the one referenced here would have been a ladder of ropes and rungs, yet long enough to be extended to the top of the cross. Whether it was placed in front of, behind, or beside Jesus is, unfortunately, not stated. At any rate, no nailing seems to have taken place here as the tablet is "set" above Christ's head.

Blood

A number of the mystery plays called for blood: the murder of Abel, Abraham's sacrifice of the substituted lamb, the slaughter of the innocents, the scourging of Christ, and the crucifixion. Ever inventive, the guildsmen devised clever ways to fake the

---

[a] briefly
[b] group
[c] act as if he is writing

shedding of blood without actually drawing a player's blood! Readily available in the Middle Ages was paint made from vermilion, a scarlet powder made from cinnabar and readily available from local artists.

This liquid could be soaked up by a sponge which would then release the "blood" when pressed at just the right moment, or whips could be laced with wet paint that would spray out onto the player's back during a simulated scourging.

It was probably not by mere chance that the York play of *The Death of Christ* was put on by the butchers' guild. After all, they would have had easy access to animal entrails or pig's bladders which could be filled with blood and placed under costumes to be pierced at just the right moment, as seems to be suggested in these lines:

> PILATE
> Sir Longinus, step forth in this stead;
> This spear, lo, have hold in thy hand.
> . . . .
> In Jesu's side
> Shove it this tide.
> No longer bide. (ll. 290-98)
>
> *[The action is taken.]*
>
> LONGINUS
> Full spitously[a] spilt is and spent
> Thy blood, Lord, to bring us to bliss
> Full free.[147] (ll. 306-307)

EXERCISE 5.1: Outfitting a Mystery Play

DIRECTIONS: Below is a list of the props and costumes used by the Smiths' Guild at Coventry, who presented the trial, condemnation, and crucifixion of Christ from 1449 to 1585.[148] Your task is to find images that depict each item on the list. To determine what some of these items looked like, you should always keep the time period in mind. For example, medieval buckram and modern buckram are not the same thing. You may want to make use of several resources available on the Internet or at a library:

---

[a] spitefully

a. A dictionary of Middle English

b. Word etymologies (looking for archaic meanings, for example)

c. Sourcebooks or web sites about medieval weapons

d. Sourcebooks or web sites about medieval costume (clothing)

e. Medieval works of art (esp. for headgear)

Bring an image to help explain the term to your classmates.

PROPS

- 4 [medieval] scourges

- Gilding for the pillar and the cross (Check for the archaic meaning *gilding*.)

- 2 pair of gallows (Consult a Middle English dictionary.)

- A staff for the demon

- Falchion for Herod

- Maces

WAGON AND SCENERY

- Fanes to the pageant

- A standard of red [medieval] buckram

- Two red pensiles of cloth painted

- Iron to hold up the streamer

COSTUMES

- 4 jackets of black buckram with nails and dice upon them

  Other 4 gowns with [medieval] damask flowers

- 2 [medieval] jackets party [parti-] red and black for the torturers

- 2 mitres (for Caiaphas and Ananias)

- A rochet for one of the bishops

- Herod's crest of iron

- A tabard

- 3 cheverels

- Hats for the tormentors (Consult medieval art to discover the medieval concept of Roman soldiers' headgear.)
- A hat for Pilate (Consult medieval art to discover the medieval concept of Middle Eastern headpieces; probably a Saracen's headwear)

ACTIVITY 5.A: Creating Special Effects

DIRECTIONS: Below are lists of materials, services, and inventions available to the theatre community of the Middle Ages. With one or two partners, brainstorm ways they could have been employed for stagecraft on medieval pageant wagons.

Cresset

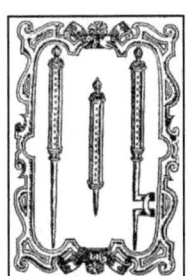

Bodkins

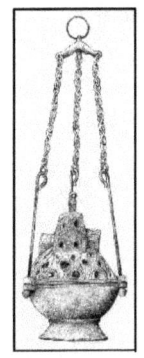

Censer

Services Available in Medieval England

Acrobats
Apothecaries
Carpenters
Dyers

Jugglers (stage magicians)
Plasterers
Seamstresses / tailors
Smiths

Devices and Inventions Available in Medieval England

Cowls (covers for the top of a chimney)
Dummies
Firemasters (firecrackers)
Marionettes
Ovens (including small clay ovens)
Quickmatch (cotton wick coated with gunpowder slurry)
Retractable knives
Rotation devices
Swivels
Trap doors
Wigs

Materials Available in Medieval England

Animal blood, entrails, and internal organs	Mirrors
Axeltrees (axels)	Nails / pins / bodkins
Barrels	Rope
Brimstone (burning sulfur)	Rotten eggs
Candles	Saltpeter (niter)
Carpets	Sea coal
Censers and perfume	Stones
Chains	Torches
Cloth	Vermilion
Cord	Water
Cressets	Wax
Cups of gold and silver	Weapons
Firemasters (fireworks)	Wheels
Fire screens	Wicks
Glass	Winches and pulleys
Gunpowder	Wine
Harnesses	Wire
Horsehair	Wood
Ladders (rope or wooden with rungs)	Wool
Manure	
Metals: iron, tin, lead, silver	

Animals

Animals and birds are mentioned frequently in Bible narratives, so the question before us is whether the medieval guildsmen actually used live animals in their plays. A few examples where the scripts seem to suggest the use of live animals are the following:

- Jesus handed John the Baptist a lamb after the baptism scene, saying:

    By this beast, known thou shall be,
    That thou art John Baptist.[149]

- The surviving manuscript of the Chester play about Herod has a marginal notation about "the boy and pigge."[150]

- In the Chester play about Jesus' entry into Jerusalem, Jesus asks Peter and Phillip to fetch him a donkey and a foal. Then ensues a conversation between the disciples and the farmer, which suggest the presence of a donkey and a foal in front of them. And a few lines later Jesus enters *"sedens . . . super aseliam* [sitting upon the she-ass]."[151]

- In the Chester *Magi and Herod*, after the three kings decide to ride to "Mount Victoryall" in order to follow the star, we find this stage direction: *"Hic descendunt de equis et ibunt in montem* [Here they descend to the horses and go into the mountain]."[152]

- In the Chester Nativity, Mary and Joseph are traveling to Bethlehem, and when they reach the city, Mary says: "Helpe me down, my leeffe fere,[a] for I hope my time be near."[153] It is at least possible that Mary was riding on a donkey here. At the close of *The Slaying of the Innocents* (also from Chester), the dialogue suggests that Joseph is helping Mary get up on the donkey for the journey to Egypt.[154]

- The Wakefield Noah mentions two birds—a raven and a dove. These could have been live creatures that were released to fly over the heads of the spectators in a somewhat dramatic flourish, or, since the dove must return with an olive branch, they may have contrived a "marionette" stand-in instead.

- The Towneley play called *The Killing of Abel* required a team of ten horses, or possibly a mixture of horses and oxen. The opening lines are spoken by a boy named Garcio, who tells Cain he needs to move on and stop making such a ruckus. When Cain cannot get his horses to move, Garcio tries to help him along, and during the process they both call out the horses' names (italicized in the excerpt that follows):

    > CAIN
    > Go forth, *Greenhorn*! And look out, *Grime*!
    > Draw on! God give you an evil time!
    > Ye stand as ye were fallen in swyme[b].

---

[a] beloved companion
[b] dizziness

What! Will ye [go] no further, mare?
Watch out! Let me see how Down will draw.
Git, shrew, git, pull on a thraw[a]!
What! It seems to me ye stand none aw[b]!
I say, Donning, go fare!
A, ha! God give thee sorrow and care!
Lo! Now heard she what I said.
Now yet art thou the worst mare
In plough that ever I had.
How! Pike-harness, no! Come hither alive!

GARCIO
I fend[c], God forbid that ever thou thrive!

CAIN
What, boy, shall I both hold and drive?
Hearest thou not how I cry?

GARCIO
Say, Mall and Stott, will ye not go?
Leming, Morell, White-horn, ho!
Now will ye not see they hie[d]![155]

It is conceivable that live animals were used in this play (and others), for it is known that at Mons in the Low Countries, real animals and fish were used in the Garden of Eden play.[156] Dummies of Greenhorn, Grime, and the others may have been used in the Towneley play, but Garcio's last line indicates the animals do, at last, start to move on at the end of the scene.

EXERCISE 5.2: Analyzing the Use of Animals on Stage

DIRECTIONS: The purpose of this exercise is to determine from the script whether a live animal was used in the staging of this play. Please begin by reading the introduction. Then read the excerpt and answer the question that follows.

_____

[a] carry on
[b] have no awe
[c] defend
[d] go

INTRODUCTION: *The excerpt below is from a fifteenth-century English mystery play, written in the dialect of East Anglia and presenting the events recorded in Genesis 22: Abraham's sacrifice of Isaac. Its author is unknown, but it is referred to as the Brome play because it was found in the nineteenth century on Brome Manor in Suffolk. Interestingly, William Shakespeare is known to have seen this play when he was still "young Will," a lad.[157] The text has been edited for vocabulary and contemporary spelling, while still allowing for the rhyme scheme of the author. Begin by reading the excerpt and then answer the questions that follow.*

Excerpt from *Abraham and Isaac* (Brome)

ABRAHAM
Yon beast shall die here in thy stead
In the worship of our Lord alone.
Go fetch him hither, my child, indeed.   355

ISAIAH
Father, I will go seize him by the head.
And bring yon beast with me anon.
A, sheep, sheep, blessed may thou be
That ever thou were sent down hither.
Thou shall this day die for me   360
In the worship of the Holy Trinity:
Now come fast and go we together
To my father in hie.[a]
Though thou be never so gentle and good,
Yet had I rather thou sheddest thy blood,   365
Rather, sheep, than I.
Lo, father, I have brought here full smart
This gentle sheep, and him you I give.
But Lord, I thank thee with all my heart;
For I am glad that I shall live   370
And kiss once my dear mother.

---

[a] haste

ABRAHAM
Now be right merry, my sweet child,
For this quick[a] beast that is so mild
Here I shall present before all other.[158]

Questions:

1. Between what lines does Isaac seem to move away from Abraham?

2. Why does he move away?

3. To whom is Isaac speaking in Lines 358-66?

4. What stage direction would you write between Lines 366 and 367?

5. Based on this excerpt, would you guess that a live sheep was used in this scene? Give reasons for your answer.

6. For the purpose of the exercise, assume for the moment that a live animal was used. Then read the additional excerpt below, and discuss whether the lamb was actually slaughtered onstage or not. Give reasons for your answer.

    ABRAHAM
    Now Lord God of heaven in Trinity,
    Almighty God omnipotent,
    Mine offering I make in the worship of thee,   385
    And with this quick beast I thee present.

---

[a] living

Lord, receive thou mine intent,
As thou art God and ground of our gree[a].

GOD
Abraham, Abraham, well may thou speed[b],
And Isaac thy young son thee by,   390
Truly, Abraham, for this deed
I shall multiply your bothers' seed
As thick as stars be in the sky,

ACTIVITY 5.B: Improvisation with Animals

DIRECTIONS: Please begin by reading the introduction and summary of the seven scenes of a medieval morality play. Then read the instructions for acting out the play by improvisation.

INTRODUCTION: The Second Shepherd's Play, *which should be understood as the second play about the shepherds, was written by the Wakefield Master between 1400 and 1450. The author's identity is known from the use of the Wakefield stanza, which appears throughout the seven-scene play. As he had done in* Noah, *the Wakefield Master employs humor when representing the foibles of humankind and reverence when representing the sacred. The purpose of the play is to present the Nativity of Christ and the redemption of humankind apparent at his birth. The need for salvation is shown in the first six scenes, which focus on the shady doings of the shepherds. The change in the shepherds becomes apparent in the last scene when, directed by the angel, they visit the stable in Bethlehem. To emphasize the relevance of the redemption story to the fifteenth-century audience, the author set the play in contemporary England, with costuming, no doubt, done in the attire of the simple folk of the day. It was not part of the Corpus Christi Cycle, but was a morality play enacted on two (or possibly three) platforms set up in the city streets. Like* Everyman, *this play is considered a classic of the medieval period and remans a standard in anthologies of English literature and in live performance, one of the more recent being that of the Folger Consort in Washington, DC, in December 2016.*

---

[a] favor, pleasure
[b] prosper

Summary of *The Second Shepherd's Play*
By the Wakefield Master

CHARACTERS
Gill
Angel
Mary
Joseph
First Shepherd
Second Shepherd
Third Shepherd
Mak

SCENE 1: A hill in England

Three shepherds, who make reference to being in England, are with their sheep on a hill. It is raining, and the men complain of the English weather. They are hungry and tired. Mak enters with a cloak covering his tunic. Grouchy and confused, he has been wandering the moors and has stumbled upon the shepherds, who are leery of him since he has a reputation as a sheep stealer. He gets angry ("Fie on you!"), and inflates his importance by claiming to be a messenger of the king. So far, Mak has been faking a London accent, but the shepherds are on to him and guffaw at his pretense. They inquire about his wife, and Mak grumbles that his numerous children are noisy and bothersome. Then, all four decide that they are weary and should lie down to sleep. However, not trusting Mak, they ask him to lie between them, reasoning that, any furtive movement toward the sheep on his part would immediately wake them. They doze off, and Mak sneaks away. He "recites a night spell" (actually Latin, *"Manus tuas commendo, Pontio Pilato,"* demonstrating Mak's misunderstanding of what he has heard in church: *"Pater, in manus tuas commendo spiritum meum"* ("Father, into your hands I commend my spirit") (Lk 23:46). Mak's "magic words" will induce a deep sleep upon the shepherds, giving him time to steal a sheep. Here a fat sheep wanders in, and Mak rejoices that now he and his wife will have "sheep meat" to eat. He swoops the animal up and exits, carrying the sheep.

SCENE 2: Mak's cottage

When Mak arrives at the cottage, his wife Gill (Jill) immediately realizes that he has stolen a sheep and worries that he will be hanged. They fear the shepherds will come looking for the sheep before it can be slaughtered, cooked, and eaten. But what if the sheep bleats and gives it all away? They decide to disguise the sheep as a baby and put it in the cradle. Gill will lie on her bed and moan and groan, as if exhausted by giving birth. If the sheep bleats, they will say it is the baby crying. They arrange the scene for the expected visit by the shepherds, and Mak leaves to return to the hill so that he will be there when they awake.

Gill and the "baby" as performed by the Folger Consort, 2016.
Photo by Brittany Diliberto

SCENE 3: The hill

Mak having rejoined the others, the shepherds wake up first. They try to rouse Mak, who is pretending to be sound asleep. One has dreamed that Mak had disguised himself as a wolf. When Mak awakes, he stretches and complains that his neck hurts because he has been sleeping in the wrong position. Then he excuses himself by saying he needs to get home to his wife as he has dreamed that she is giving birth and needs him. After he exits, the shepherds agree they should count their sheep to see if any are missing.

SCENE 4: The cottage

Mak returns to the cottage. Again, there is sparring between Mak and Gill, who complains that woman's work is never done, so to speak. They wrap the sheep in cloths and lift it into the cradle, and Gill hops onto her bed. She tells Mak that he should sing a lullaby to the "baby," which he begins to do, singing very out of tune.

SCENE 5: A crooked thorn

The shepherds concur that a theft has occurred, and, suspecting Mak, they head toward his cottage.

SCENE 6: The cottage

Approaching the cottage, the shepherds hear Mak singing and joke about the racket he is making. When they enter, Mak offers them food and drink, but they decline, saying they are too upset to eat as one of their sheep has gone missing. They say they suspect that either Mak or his wife is the thief. Feigning outrage, he invites them to search the cottage, which they begin to do. Seeing the shepherds picking through her household goods, Gill becomes agitated, accuses them of thievery, and orders them out. The shepherds fear the sheep has probably been slain by now anyway, so they depart. But once outside, they realize they did not give the baby a gift and return to give him sixpence. Though they want to peek at the baby, Mak tells them, no, the baby is sleeping and they shouldn't wake him. However, at that moment, the sheep bleats. There is much humorous rhyming: "He sleeps." "No, methinks he peeps." "When he wakens, he weeps." When one of the shepherds leans over the cradle to kiss the "baby," he recognizes the sheep by its brand. Angry now, they "swaddle" Mak so that his arms and legs cannot move and then toss him on a canvas blanket to punish him.

SCENE 7: The hill

The shepherds have worn themselves out, so they lie down on the hill to sleep once again. An angel appears singing, *"Gloria in excelsis!"* When they awake, the angel tells them they should go to Bethlehem to see the Christ Child, and the shepherds comment on the angel's beautiful singing, which stands in contrast to Mak's crooning.

SCENE 8: A stable in Bethlehem

The shepherds enter the stable. They extol the "comely" and "hail" condition of the baby and remark on the "mild" maiden who has given him birth. This stands in contrast to Gill's groaning and carrying on. The first shepherd offers the child "a bob of cherries" and kneels before him. The second shepherd gives him a little bird. The third shepherd laments that he has no pennies to give the child but asks him to hold out his hand to receive a small ball that he has made for the child. He tells him to "go to the tennis." Mary prays, thanking God for sending His child, and the shepherds turn to leave, saying to each other that they have been "won" (redeemed) and must sing loudly with joy. They exit, singing.

Instructions for Improvisation:

Take parts and improvise the action of the play, keeping in mind that the first six scenes focus on the foibles of humankind and are, therefore, presented with humor while the last scene, which depicts the Nativity of Christ, focuses on the sacred and is reverent in tone. For the role of the sheep, choose between (a) an obedient dog (perhaps dressed as a sheep), (b) a stuffed toy, or (c) a student disguised as a sheep. Two "beasts" were included in the manger scene in the medieval production.

ACTIVITY 5.C: Projects in Medieval Spectacle

DIRECTIONS: An abridged version of *The Conversion of St. Paul* appears in Appendix C. Please begin by reading the introduction. Then read the play, paying special attention to stage directions. Divide the class into four groups, one each for (1) staging and props, (2) costumes, (3) special effects, and (4) interlude dancing. Each group will then undertake the questions and activities that correspond to their group assignment. Be prepared to present the results of your research to the class.

1. **Staging, Sets, Props:** Make a sketch of your concept of the staging areas and mark the following on the sketch:

    - The acting platforms or scaffolds (Would you need three, or could you get by with two?)
    - The action on each platform
    - Sending of Paul, receiving word of Paul's conversion, and dance of the demons on one platform.
    - Paul's experience on the Damascus Road, with Ananias the Disciple, and with the escape at another.
    - The path of the three horses. The horses would need to be led in to stand in front of the Jerusalem platform in order for the men to mount. Then they need to go "around and out" of the staging area. Consider where the horses will be located during the action at Station 2.
    - At each platform on your sketch, list the props that would be required there.

MORE CHALLENGING #1:

Set up two platforms and furnish each with the necessary props. Act out a scene.

2. **Costumes:** Using a book or a web site on the history of costume, study the clothing that was customary in the time of the apostle Paul (first century Judea) and make

decisions about how you would design costumes for the items listed below. Sketch, print out, or photocopy images to show the class. Excellent resources include:

- **Book:** Hennesy, Kathryn, and Gadi Farfour, eds. *Fashion: The Definitive History of Costume and Style.* Smithsonian. London: DK, 2012.
- **Book:** Kretschmer, Albert, and Karl Rohrbach, eds. *Pictorial Encyclopedia of Historic Costume: 1200 Full-Color Figures.* Mineola, NY: Dover, 2012.
- **Web:** *The History of Costume: Braun & Schneider.* 2007. Web. 19 Apr. 2017. <https://www.siue.edu/COSTUMES/>

a. The Jewish high priests, Caiaphas and Ananias

b. Saul (before the conversion)

c. The Christians (Ananias the Disciple; Saul after the conversion)

d. The knights (Consider anachronistic medieval costumes here.)

e. Belial (Consult medieval art for the medieval concept of Belial.)

f. Mercury (Consult medieval art.)

g. Servant of the high priests

3. **Special Effects:** How would the medievals have created the "flash of lightning" that is required in the scenes on Damascus Road and with the demons? A good online resource, which includes a video demonstration, can be found at this URL:

Medieval pageant with fire cressets on both sides.

- Klein, Becca. "Medieval Mystery Play Staging: Scenery and Fire Effects for Mystery Plays." *Northern Boundary News.* United States Institute for Theatre Technology (USITT). May 2011. Web. 19 Apr. 2017. <http://www.stolaf.edu/nbs/NBS_May_11/Article5/Article5.html>

MORE CHALLENGING #2:

Following the fire safety requirements in your state and city, coordinate with the science teacher at your school to conduct the flash experiment in the science laboratory. Your science teacher may have an alternative method.

4. **Interlude Dancing:** There is little record to shed light on interlude dancing in medieval plays. Since virtually all the plays were religious in nature, it is doubtful that jigs and morris dancing were involved, but one can get some ideas about how typical dances of the period might have been adapted to the stage by watching some online videos. As you view them, give thought to whether these dances would have been suitable as they are, or whether they would have required adaptation. Explain your answer. The following videos might be good starting places:

   - Wellings, Bernard. *Conwy Castle Medieval Dance*. Plantagenet Medieval Society. YouTube. 31 Jan. 2010. Web. 19 Apr. 2017. <https://www.youtube.com/watch?v=JiE17pvisBg>
   - Lady Vivian. *Danze Medievali di Todi. YouTube.* 22 June 2011. Web. 19 Apr. 2017. <https://www.youtube.com/watch?v=n8JDIPKFg7A>

MORE CHALLENGING #3:

Perform a medieval dance for your classmates. For accompaniment, you could use the music from the videos or find another suitable sound track. Keep in mind that these dances, though entertaining, would have been reverent in view of the subject matter of the plays they supported.

MEDIEVAL THEATRE TIDBITS FROM PRIMARY SOURCES

Chapter 6

Introduction

Despite the absence of huge theatres like those of Greece and Rome, the great sweep of history still left its imprint on the stage; or perhaps it was the other way around. The purpose of this chapter is to relate some of those points in time when theatre and the political arena intersected.

Richard II and the London Procession

During the reign of Richard II, a number of political issues had resulted in conflict between the king and the city of London. For Londoners, the proverbial straw that broke the camel's back came in 1392 with Richard's "request" that the city lend him £1,000. The Londoners refused. Angered, King Richard deposed John Hinde, Lord Mayor of London, and other city officials, and imprisoned them in different locations around the country. He then removed his court from London to Nottingham. These actions, and others, were designed to bring the city of London to its knees. However, the Londoners held firm.

Several months later, seeing that his gambit against the city had failed, Richard sought reconciliation with his subjects in London. On August 29, 1393, to demonstrate his good faith, the king sponsored a grand procession through the city streets, in which the theatre community of London seems to have played a role.

A description of the extravagant event, known as the Reconciliation of Richard II with the City of London, has come down to us in the form of a Latin poem composed by the Carmelite friar, Richard of Maidstone, who was an eyewitness to the event. Though originally in the form of a Latin poem, it was summarized in English prose in 1859 by the antiquarian Thomas Wright. Below are excerpts from Wright's summary of Richard of Maidstone's *Concordia facta inter regem et cives Londinia [Reconciliation between the King and the City of London]*, which reveal the theatrical elements of Richard's procession through the city streets.

Excerpts from *Concordia*
By Richard of Maidstone (Trans. Thomas Wright)

I.

Slowly they gained Chepe,[a] the principal street, which was decked out with extraordinary magnificence, and its windows were filled with beautiful women and maidens. The fountains in Chepe ran wine, and in the middle of the street was raised a lofty tower at the top of which were a boy and a beautiful maiden, the first in disguise of an angel and the latter bearing a crown. As the king and queen approached, these two personages descended, as though in a cloud, in a manner which Richard of Maidstone professes not to have understood, the boy, or angel, holding in his hand a cup of gold full of wine and the maiden holding two crowns of gold in her hand. The maiden delivered her two crowns to the guardian, who presented them to the king and queen, and both accepted them gracefully and drank of the cup with a smiling countenance which carried joy to the hearts of the citizens.[159]

II.

Ludgate was the scene of another pageant, from which angels threw flowers and perfumes on the royal party. But the grandest pageant of all was at Temple Bar, on which was represented a forest and desert filled with all kinds of wild beasts. In the middle of it appeared the John the Baptist with the *agnus Dei* [Lamb of God][b]. This subject was cleverly and even artfully contrived. It appears that John the Baptist was King Richard's favourite saint, and as his eyes fell upon this exhibition, he was seized with a sudden feeling of devotion and all traces that may have remained of his irritation against the citizens of London disappeared. Besides John the Baptist, there was an angel at the summit of this pageant, who descended suddenly as the king and queen approached, holding a golden tablet or altar-piece in each hand, which he delivered to the guardian. The latter

---

[a] Cheapside, an important street in central London
[b] John 1:29: *"[A]ltera die videt Iohannes Iesum venientem ad se et ait ecce agnus Dei qui tollit peccatum mundi."* ("The next day John [the Baptist] seeth Jesus coming unto him, and saith, 'Behold the Lamb of God, which taketh away the sin of the world.'")

presented one, on which there was a representation of the crucifixion, to the king, which he touched, declared that he had entirely forgiven the citizens, and invited them to follow him to Westminster to hear his final determination with regard to them.[160]

ACTIVITY 6.A: Determining the Pageantry Route

DIRECTIONS: With your classmates, try to determine the location of some of the stations and the staging that might have been required.

1. Using Fig. 1, locate the three places mentioned in the text and draw a circle around each. (Note: This image depicts London in 1666, but the Tower, the gates, the wall, the streets, and the cathedral would have been the same in the Middle Ages.)

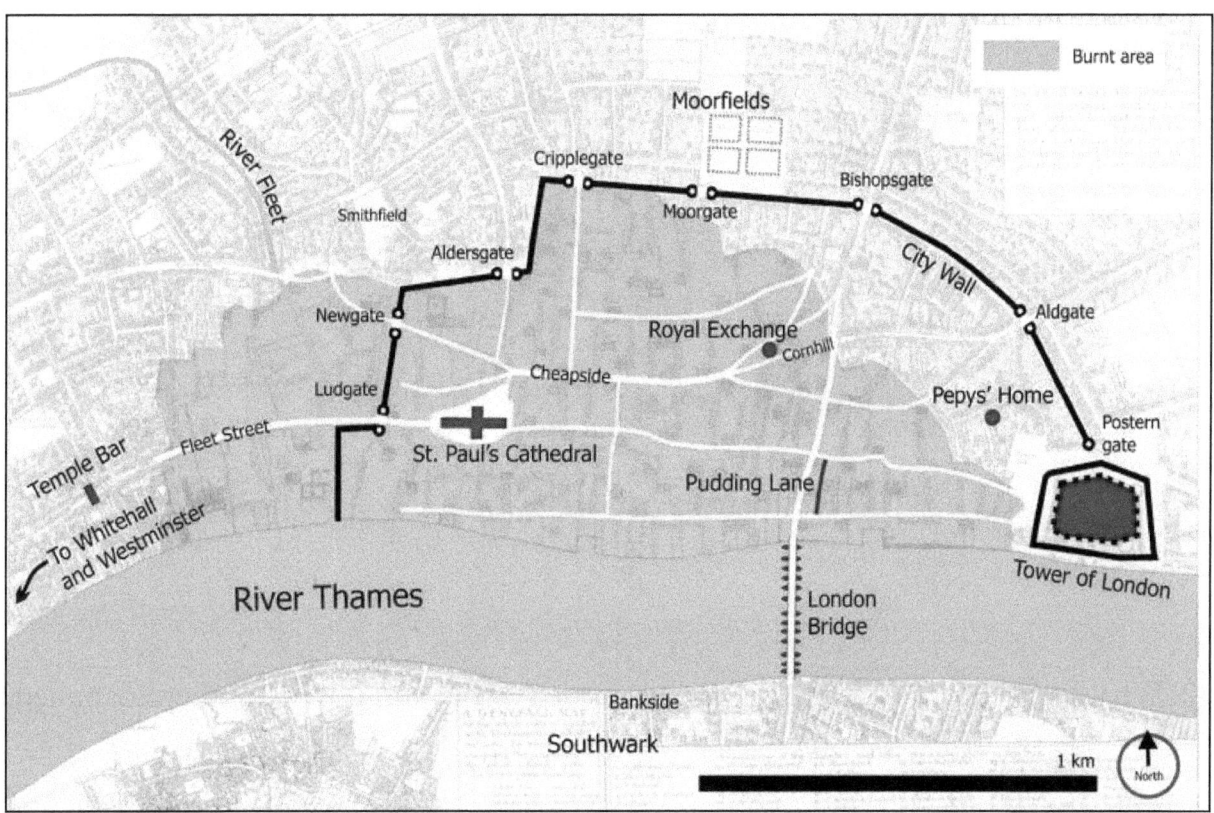

Fig. 1. London

Fig. 2. Cheapside

2. What two performers were at the Cheapside station, and how were they costumed?

3. What props would have been needed?

4. In Fig. 2, use an A to mark the windows where "the beautiful women and maidens" would have stood. Use a B to mark the fountain. Use a C to mark the possible

location of "the tower that was set up" from which the boy (angel) and maiden descended.

5. We read that the performers representing the angel and the maiden "descended as though in a cloud" [from the tower that was set up] in a manner which Richard of Maidstone professes not to have understood. Consider these staging concerns:

   a. Brainstorm possible ways this could have been done in an undetectable way.

   b. What do you imagine the "tower" to have looked like?

Fig. 3. Ludgate

Fig. 4. The gate at Temple Bar did not have the upper extension supporting the sculptures in the 14th century. ©Ray Blythe. Used with permission.

6. The observer reported the tossing of "flowers and perfumes on the royal party" as they passed Ludgate (see Fig. 3). In 1393, the structure above the gate was being used as a prison. Keeping this in mind, what method would you have devised to "toss perfume," had you been in charge of the spectacle?

7. How many performers would have been needed at the Temple Bar station (see Fig. 4)? Identify their characters.

8. How would you create a set representing "a forest and desert filled with all kinds of wild beasts"?

9. Exotic animals (e.g., lions, pelicans) were kept at the Tower of London.

   a. Do you suppose any of the beasts in this scene were actually brought from that menagerie?

   b. If not, how do you imagine the organizers would have made and positioned "wild beasts" on top of Temple Bar?

John Wycliffe, Morality Plays, and the English Language

The emergence of English as the language of government, education, and literature—in place of Latin—occurred in England largely in the fourteenth century. We have seen how the miracle and mystery plays, which were also taking shape at that time, were also written in English instead of Latin, which had been the language of the liturgical plays.

The beginning of the Gospel of John in the Wycliffe Bible

There were many contributing factors to the trend toward English. First, after King John lost Normandy in 1204, England became the primary home of the Plantagenet kings, who also started speaking English regularly for the first time since the Norman Conquest in 1066. Second, since the miracle and morality plays were intended to familiarize the less well-educated with the story of God's plan for salvation, it made sense to perform them in the language of the audience. However, the writers of the plays were normally monks or priests subject to the authority of the pope. To show the difficulty the playwrights were up against in the choice of language for their plays, one has only to look at the story of Randall Higgenet, a Benedictine monk in Chester. When he began to compose miracle plays, he had to make three trips to Rome before receiving permission to compose his plays in English![161] It is believed that his first play, which was the beginning of the Chester Cycle, was performed in English around 1327. Third, in the 1360s, the great poet Geoffrey Chaucer began translating French works into English and, what's more, composing his own works in English, earning him the sobriquet "father of English literature." Last, at about the same time, Parliament voted in 1362 to make English the official language of the courts and Parliament.

But what about the Church? Enter John Wycliffe (c. 1320-1384), Oxford professor and theologian, who fell out of favor with the pope because he argued that some of the practices of the Church were not Biblical. For all to understand exactly what the Bible said, he desired to have the Bible translated into English but was opposed at every turn. Now, Wycliffe was no great supporter of the Corpus Christi plays, which he considered garish and sometimes non-Biblical in their message, but he had noticed their use of the native tongue. Therefore, while advocating for use of the vernacular language in the Church, he used the plays as precedent in his argument:

Excerpt from *De Officio Pastoralis*
By John Wycliffe

[I]t seemeth first that the wit[a] of God's law should be taught in that tongue that is more known, for this wit is God's word. When Christ sayeth in the gospel that both heaven and earth shall pass but his words shall not pass, he understandeth by his words his wit. And thus God's wit is holy writ, that may in no manner be false. Also the Holy Ghost gave to the apostles wit at Whitsunday for to know all manner languages to teach the people God's law thereby; and so God would[b] that the people were taught God's law in diverse tongues; but what man

Wycliffe's Pater Noster

Oure fadir that art in heuenes, halewid be thi name; thi kyndoom come to; be thi wille don in erthe as in heuene: gyue to us this dai oure breed ouer othir substaunce; and forguye to us oure dettis, as we forgyuen to oure gettouris; and lede us not in to temptacioun, but delyuer us fro yuvel. Amen.

---

[a] knowledge
[b] willed

on God's [be]half should reverse God's ordinance and his will? And for this cause Saint Jerome traveled and translated the Bible from diverse tongues into Latin [so] that it might be after[wards] translated to other tongues. And thus Christ and his apostles taught the people in that tongue that was most known to the people; why should not men do now so? And heretofore authors of the new law, that were apostles of Jesus Christ, wrote their gospels in diverse tongues that were more known to the people. Also the worthy realm of France, notwithstanding all lettings, hath translated the Bible and the gospels with other true sentences of doctors[a] out of Latin into French, why should not English men do so? As lords of England have the Bible in French, so it were not against reason that they have the same sentence in English; for thus God's law would be better known and more trowed[b] for onehed[c] of wit and more accord betwixt realms. And friars have taught in England the *pater noster* [Our Father] *in English tongue as men say in the play of York and in many other countries.*[d] (Emphasis added.) Since the *pater noster* is part of Matthew's gospel, as clerics know, why may not all be turned to English truly, as is this part? Especially since all Christian men, learned and lewd, that should be said, must algatis[e] sue[f] Christ and know his lore[g] and his life. But the commons of Englishmen know it best in their mother tongue.[162]

It is of special interest that Wycliffe, a Yorkshire man himself, was quite aware of the mystery plays at York, though he may never have attended one. Due to his reformist views, Wycliffe was eventually expelled from his position at Oxford. In 1382, after his expulsion, he began to devote himself to translating the Latin Vulgate Bible into English—in defiance of the authorities. The end product, now known as the Wycliffe Bible, was published in 1384—written in the English of his day.

---

[a] teachers
[b] believed
[c] unity
[d] counties, shires
[e] in all cases
[f] pursue
[g] workmanship

THE THEATRE IN THE RENAISSANCE AND REFORMATION

Chapter 7

Introduction

What changes the world, changes theatre. This principle became apparent as the mantle of world leadership passed from Greece to Rome, and then again when pagan Rome was replaced by the spread of Christianity in the Roman Empire. We have seen how theatre emerged in the Christian world in the Middle Ages, but, as time passed, subsequent historic movements such as the Renaissance and the Protestant Reformation manifestly affected theatre in a variety of sometimes conflicting ways. Such changes go to show that literature cannot be totally understood without understanding the culture that produced it. Therefore, like a king's edict or a treasonous letter from one noble to another, a work of literature can be seen as a primary source of history. The next few chapters show ways in which religion, politics, and economics converged to shape the theatre from the fourteenth century to the seventeenth.

What Was the Renaissance?

The word *renaissance* means *rebirth*. It was coined in the nineteenth century to describe the rebirth of classical antiquity in terms of art, architecture, philosophy, and literature that began in the fourteenth century in the northern city-states of the Italian peninsula, burgeoned through western Europe, and ended in the seventeenth century.

Lorenzo de'Medici
(1449-1492)

Italian City-States

One of the key Italian city-states of the fourteenth century was Florence, where the Medici [MĚD-ĭ-chē] family, Europe's first bankers, rose to prominence and sought to promote the fame and prestige of their family—and their city—by fostering works of great beauty. One of the names most strongly associated with the Italian Renaissance is that of Lorenzo de Medici (1449-1492), who is known by the sobriquet "Lorenzo the Magnificent" due to the many works of art produced under his patronage.

As time passed, the Renaissance spread to other countries in Europe, notably France, Spain, and England, and, like all the humanities, the dramatic arts benefited and flourished in the new environment where wealthy patrons sought out the most talented people to glorify their names, their cities, and their nations.

Constantinople under attack by the leader of the Ottoman Turks, Sultan Mehmed II, 1453

But the stimulus for the Renaissance was not limited to the vanity of the rich. It was also set in motion by the horrors of war. Though the Crusades were long over by this time, Greek Christians in Constantinople were still struggling to survive against the Muslim pursuit of an expanded caliphate driven by the Ottoman Empire. When Constantinople finally fell in 1453, these Christians fled to the west for safety, bringing with them priceless Greek manuscripts which had not been seen in the west for centuries. This triggered a re-birth (or, *renaissance*) of classical culture.

Suddenly all things Greek were the hottest items of the day. Part of this necessarily included a resurgence of interest in the Greek language as scholars scrambled to delve into these precious gems from antiquity—including, of course, Greek plays. The persons who undertook the study of these great works came to be called humanists, not because they believed that man should replace God as the primary object of study (as it means today), but because they studied the humanities—that is, works of human culture such as art, music, architecture, philosophy, religion, and literature. And from these Renaissance humanists flowed a cascade of changes to the way Europeans "did drama"—some of which will be outlined in this chapter.

Fifteenth-Century Theatre in England

Just as the Medici family of Florence supported great artists to enhance the way they were seen by rival families and city-states of Italy, so the households of the nobles and the monarchs of England supported dramatists and acting troupes. We saw in an earlier chapter that Humphrey, Duke of Gloucester, was one of the first to do so, and it is no surprise that he has gone down in history as one of the early figures of the Renaissance in England. The problem in England was that throughout the fifteenth century, when the Renaissance was gaining steam elsewhere, England was embroiled in a struggle for the English crown, and it was not until the Wars of the Roses came to an end in 1485 that the acting companies truly became an established feature of aristocratic life. The first Tudor king, Henry VII, and his sons, Prince Arthur and Prince Henry (later Henry VIII), served as patrons for three royal acting companies, which performed at eleven different state events. We know details of a few of them.

In 1494, Henry's four-man troupe called the Royal Interluders was led by an actor named John English. A joiner by occupation, he must have had exceptional theatrical talent, as he and his company were invited to accompany the king's daughter Margaret, as she journeyed north to Scotland for her marriage to James IV. English's men performed a traditional morality play for the royal couple on August 13, 1503.

Status of "Players" in Tudor England

As troupes of traveling actors began to roam around the countryside in England, they encountered a problem stemming from the customs of the day. People rarely moved from one town to another. They lived and died, just as their ancestors had done before them and their children would do after them—in the same community. As a result, strangers were regarded with suspicion, and sometimes rightfully so, as shady characters might be more likely than local denizens to pilfer and cause trouble.

To gain control of these wanderers, King Henry VIII issued a proclamation in 1546 requiring "all such ruffians, vagabonds, masteries men, *common players* and evil disposed persons" to face punishment as forced laborers in the galleys of his war ships.[163] (Emphasis added.) The fact that "common players" are included in the king's list goes some way toward showing the attitude of the people toward actors in that time. The closest equivalent with our own time would be in lumping touring rock bands together with roaming biker gangs. The players needed a way to enhance their esteem, and, to accomplish this, they sought the support of noble patrons. The hope was that the prestige associated with the duke, earl, king, or queen would rub off on the actors, elevating their status and providing legal protection.

Patronage in Elizabethan England

Although the patronage of the nobles and royals began in the fifteenth century, the nobles became much more serious about their troupes in the sixteenth century and even competed for the best players and playwrights. Some of the more famous of these troupes include the following:

The Earl of Leicester's Men: Robert Dudley, 1st Earl of Leicester (LĔS-tər) formed the first Elizabethan acting troupe in 1559. Since Leicester was a favorite of Queen Elizabeth I, his acting company enjoyed great success from 1570 to 1583, when Elizabeth organized her own company.

The Lord Chamberlain's Men with Shakespeare in the center

The Queen's Men: Formed in 1583, this troupe was supported by Queen Elizabeth, who, it is true, was a theatre enthusiast, though her primary purpose for keeping an acting company close to her was probably political (more on this to come).

The Chamberlain's Men: The chief official of the royal household was called the *Lord Chamberlain*. In the time of Queen Elizabeth I, when Shakespeare was growing in fame, a father and son held the office, one after another: Henry Carey, 1st Baron Hunsdon (1524-1596), and his son George Carey, 2nd Baron Hunsdon (1597-1603). They supported a stellar group of actors and playwrights, including arguably the best playwright of all time, William Shakespeare.

The Admiral's Men: Because Charles Howard, 1st Earl of Nottingham, was appointed Lord High Admiral in 1585, his acting company came to be called the Admiral's Men. His company included Philip Henslowe, a wheeler-dealer in the theatrical business whose diary has left us many insights into Elizabethan theatre management.

The King's Men: When King James VI of Scotland became James I of England in 1603, the new king took over the Chamberlain's Men, who from that time, became known as the King's Men. Shakespeare remained with the company until the end of his career. After the death of James I, the company continued under James's son, King Charles I.

Because the nobles and royals were financially supporting the companies, medieval theatre—with guildsmen playing their parts and then re-donning their work aprons—had given way to professional acting troupes associated with rich and powerful persons. This is not to say that actors from the period were beloved by all people, as they most certainly were not, but the profession of acting itself had taken a major step forward.

Sumptuary Laws and Livery

We hear a lot today about government "over-regulation," but the Elizabethans may have had it even worse. Whereas we are still free to run to the mall and buy whatever clothing we might want or need, the Elizabethans were restricted by the sumptuary laws—those laws that regulated what one could and could not wear. However, servants and retainers of a nobleman were permitted to wear the noble's livery, that is, the distinctive uniform and colors which served to express identity and loyalty to their lord (just as school colors express loyalty today). Generally, this privilege was extended to the nobles' players as well, which was a plus for folks classified by law in the rank of "rogues and vagabonds."

The sons of Edward IV in the livery of the House of York

Now, in 1571, amidst the religious turmoil of Elizabethan England, some of the queen's Roman Catholic enemies had begun dressing their spies in the liveries normally worn by their retainers. This led the Protestant queen, Elizabeth, to issue a proclamation in January 1572, stating that the nobles could only give such a privilege to their household "servants." So, since actors were not servants, Elizabeth had stripped the players of the protection afforded by association with the nobles.

Enter James Burbage, an actor in the Earl of Leicester's Men, who was destined to become instrumental in the establishment of theatre in Elizabethan England. Burbage, with the support of some of his fellow actors, penned a letter to the Earl, one of the most influential nobles in the realm. Beginning with a summary of the new law regarding the retainers, he wrote:

> We, therefore, your humble servants and daily orators, your players, for avoiding all inconveniences that may grow by reason of the said statute are bold to trouble your lordship with this our suit, humbly desiring your honor that (as you have always been our good lord and master) you will now vouchsafe to retain us at this present [time] as your household servants and daily waiters, not that we mean to crave any further stipend or benefit at your lordship's hands, but our liveries, as we have had, and also your honor's license to certify that we are your

household servants when we shall have occasion to travel amongst our friends, as we do usually once a year and as other noblemen's players do.[164]

Note sub-title touting performances by the "Lord Chamberlain his servants."

And so, ironically, actors came to have a more prominent social status by costuming themselves as servants, but one more detail remains. In 1574, the queen updated the sumptuary laws. By this time, the Earl of Leicester was a favorite of the queen, who had also become enamored of his players and had given them a special license to perform. In doing so, she made it clear that "the meaning of this order is not to prohibit a servant from wearing any cognizance of his master, or henchmen, heralds, pursuivants at arms; runners at jousts, tourneys, or such martial feats, and such as wear apparel given them by the Queen, and *such as shall have license from the Queen* for the same."[165] (Emphasis added.) The pronoun *such* included the players..

ACTIVITY 7.A: Tudor Costume

DIRECTIONS: The purpose of this activity is to familiarize you with issues of fashion, theatrical costume, and social class in the reigns of Henry VIII and his daughter Elizabeth I (1509-1603). Please complete the following steps and share your results with the class.

1. Take a picture of yourself (a head shot may be easier to work with, but include the neck), scan it into a computer, and print it out. Glue it at the top center of a piece of construction paper or 9" x 12" poster board Then in the search bar of your Internet navigator, enter a phrase such as *Elizabethan fashion*. Alternate terms would be *Tudor fashion, Elizabethan costume, Tudor costume, 16th-century fashion, 16th-century costume,* and so on. (NOTE: The plural form *costumes* will bring up costumes for sale

on the Internet, whereas the singular *costume* is more likely to bring up drawings, art work, or photographs.)

2. Search for an example for each of the various classifications of clothing. Choose at least four, but each should represent a different class of person.

   a. king or queen

   b. nobleman or noblewoman

   c. man or woman in livery

   d. middle class man or woman

   e. peasant or lower-class underling (man or woman)

   f. Puritan man or woman

3. Cut and paste the image, and print it out in a size suitable to fit the head-shot of yourself. Trim it as you would a paper doll, and place it with the head so that it appears you are wearing the costume. If for some reason your technology is not available, simply cut out the head shot and the costumes, and glue them onto poster board.

4. Share your results with the class and discuss what the sumptuary laws reveal about Tudor society. Why did the monarch care so much about this matter that he or she enshrined it into law?

Theatres and Stages

As the era of the medieval pageants was coming to an end in the late sixteenth century, players in London performed not on the old pageant wagons of the previous century, but in royal palaces, private homes of members of the nobility, or—in the case of the more common folk—the courtyards of inns. An example of such an inn is the George Inn in Southwark (see image), which was built in a U-shape with a cobbled courtyard where platforms could be set up for the players. Playgoers would either stand in the galleries or, as in medieval times, around the stage. When permanent theatres were built in London, they followed this same basic pattern but with an enclosed courtyard, as will be seen below.

Permanent Theatres

The first person to establish a permanent theatre in the City of London was James Burbage (1567-1619), the actor who had helped players gain the right to wear the livery of their patron. His first venture was in 1567 when he and his brother-in-law opened the Red Lion in Whitechapel just outside the city wall. Sadly, due to shoddy construction, this theatre lasted only long enough for one performance, but Burbage tried again in 1576, borrowing money from his father-in-law to build the first permanent theatre in London, called simply The Theatre, which was built on leased land in Shoreditch. Other playhouses followed: The Rose (1587), The Swan, (1594); and Blackfriars, the first roofed theatre (1599).

When Burbage died, his sons Cuthbert and Richard (more of whom to come) took over the family business, and by means of their ingenuity, Shakespeare's famous theatre came to be. It happened, thus: When threatened with a law suit over their lease in 1599, the theatre owners hatched a plan to escape the long arm of the law. To be specific, under the cover of night, the Burbage brothers, along with their friend Will Shakespeare and others, dismantled The Theatre board by board and hauled the lumber across the Thames into Southwark [SŬTH-ərk], a rather rough district where unsavory attractions like bear-baiting and cockfights were drawing crowds. Despite its low reputation, Southwark had the advantage of being outside the city limits and, therefore, not subject to the sometimes smothering regulations of the London City Council. This new theatre, destined to become the very symbol of Elizabethan London, they dubbed the Globe.

The Globe

Though Shakespeare referred to the theatre as "the wooden O"—and, indeed, it was depicted as round on Wenceslas Hollar's sketch of 1647—the Globe was actually polygonal in shape, having perhaps eighteen to twenty sides. Traditionally, the Globe

was thought to have been 100 feet in diameter, but recent archaeological excavations at its site in London indicate that it was probably 85 feet wide. The modern reconstruction of the Globe, however, is 102 feet wide.[166]

Like all London theatres before it, the Globe was open to the sky so that the performances could be lighted by the sun. A flag would be placed on top of the theatre to announce the performance of a play, and apprentices and students from the Inns of Court would sometimes slip away to watch the afternoon plays.

Three stories high, the Globe could seat about 3,000 spectators. Nobles, gentry, and other prosperous folk would sit in the upper galleries, while the ordinary folk stood around the stage, just as they had done in the courtyard inns. In fact, the area around the stage continued to be called "the yard." Those who stood in that area earned the moniker of *groundlings* since, of course, they stood on the ground.

Groundlings were charged only a penny to watch a play (at a time when there were 240 pennies in £1). A wooden bench in the lower galleries went for two pennies—three, for those who desired a cushion. The wealthiest members of the audience sat in what were called the Lord's Rooms, which were immediately above the tiring house. Those in the Lord's Rooms could not see the stage well but, being closer to the stage, could hear better, overcoming the poor acoustics of an open-air theatre. You will recall that in this period the theatre-goers would refer to "hearing a play" more frequently than to "seeing" one, so perhaps seats in the Lord's Room might not have been as undesirable as we would think today.

Latin Link-Up

Have you ever wondered why theatre-goers are normally referred to as the *audience* while circus attendees and sports fans are normally called *spectators*? Latin word origins will provide the answer: the word *audience* is derived from *audire* ("to hear"), while *spectator* is derived from *spectare* ("to watch").

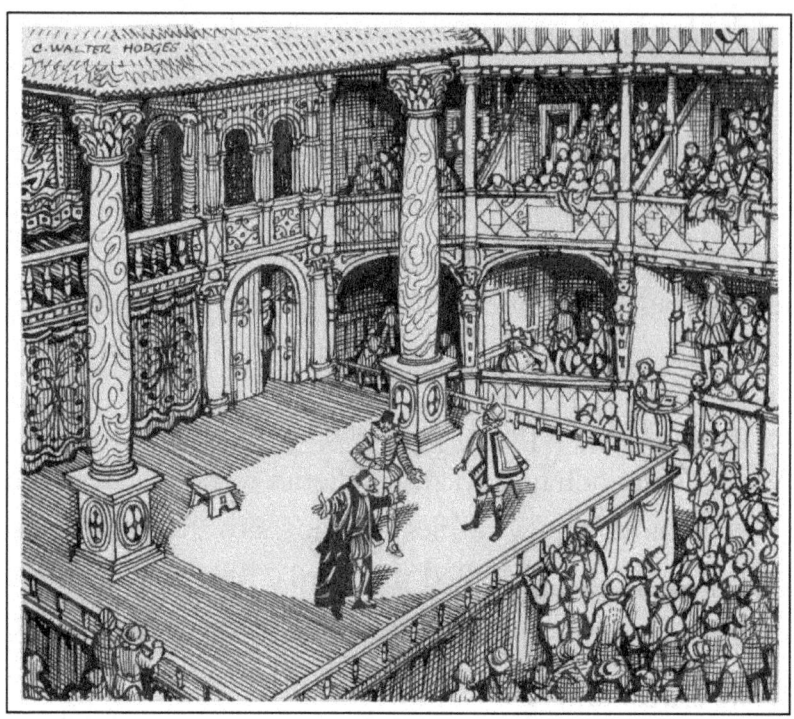

C. Walter Hodges' imagined reconstruction of *The Merchant of Venice,* Act I, scene 1

The Elizabethan Stage

The Globe's stage was rectangular and measured 43 feet wide by 27 feet deep. It stood at a height of five feet off the ground, leaving a space beneath the stage called the "cellarage," where a performer playing a ghost or demon could wait until he heard his cue to enter through a trap door in the stage floor, which is reminiscent of the hell mouth used in the old mystery plays.

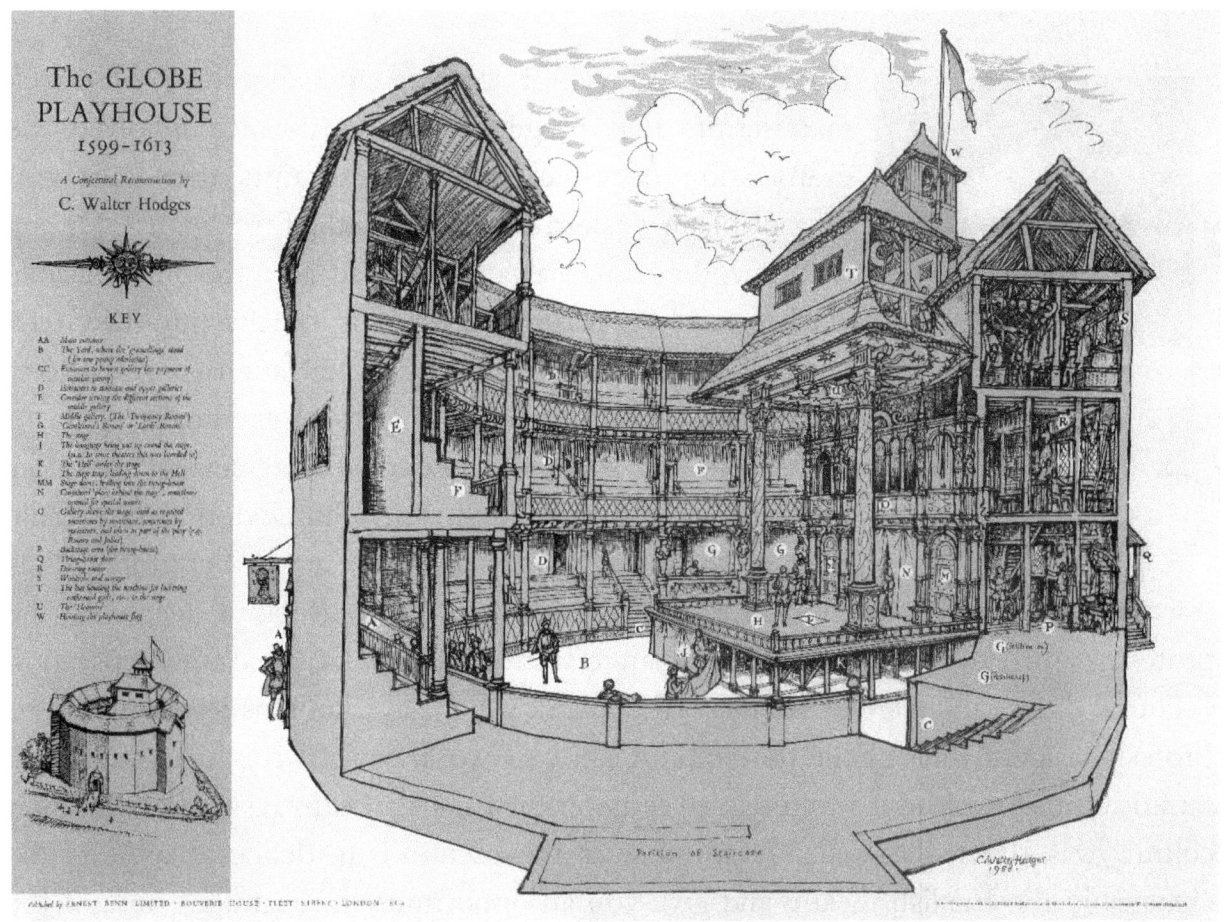

Conjectural Reconstruction of the Globe Theatre by C. Walter Hodges

Most of the action of the play occurred on the thrust stage, but C. Walter Hodge's drawing of the Globe reveals other spaces with special functions. On either side of the stage were large columns (see image) which supported a ceiling called "the heavens" that was typically painted with clouds or stars. The ceiling of the columned area also served as the floor of the "hut," which was built atop it. The hut, like the stage floor, had a trap door from which performers could ascend or descend by means of primitive stage machinery involving ropes, harnesses, and a winch, as in times past.

Against the back wall of the stage were two galleries, one upper and one lower. The lower gallery had a door on either side flanking a curtained area, which could be used for special scenes. The upper gallery had a twofold purpose: it could seat musicians or it could be used to perform scenes requiring elevated acting spaces, such as the famous balcony scene in *Romeo and Juliet*. The Lords' Rooms were on either side of the balcony.

How Did the Reformation Affect the Theatre?

Erasmus of Rotterdam published a Greek New Testament in 1516.

Part of the revival of learning and the study of Greek manuscripts that triggered the Renaissance involved the examination of Greek Bible manuscripts that had been unavailable in western Europe since the fifth century. During that time, the Latin Vulgate Bible had been the only available version, so it was natural for scholars to delve into the Greek texts, since Greek had been the original language of the New Testament. This translation effort eventually led to controversy as scholars discovered that several practices which had grown up in the Roman Church during the Middle Ages were not supported by the original Scriptures. This discovery launched an attempt to reform the Church, but as divisions deepened, the protestors (or Protestants) began to separate from Rome. In England, this separation occurred during the reign of Henry VIII, a break which gave impetus to the spread of Protestant ideas throughout the land. A shift in worldview of this magnitude has ramifications throughout a culture, and certainly the English theatre, as part of the larger culture, was affected as well. The purpose of this section is to delineate some of the changes in the English theatre and give you an opportunity to examine some of the changes yourself.

Henry VIII: The Demand for Religious Conformity

King Henry VIII of England
1491-1547

In this period, kings and queens determined what religion they would follow, and their subjects were obliged to follow suit. Following a different religion was, in their eyes, an act of treason, an offense for which execution was the customary punishment. During the reign of Henry VIII and that of his son Edward and daughters Mary and Elizabeth, England swung from Catholic to Protestant and back again every few years, and when the populace did not swing back and forth with the monarchs, dissenters were made into martyrs on both sides. In such tumultuous times, the monarchs tried to enforce their *dicta*, and Henry, the first king to break away from the authority of the pope, was not slow in laying out his official doctrine.

To prevent turbulence in England following his break with the Roman Church, for example, Henry VIII laid out his official Church doctrine in 1540, and then, in 1543, passed an Act for the Advancement of True Religion and for the Abolishment of the Contrary, charging that seditious people had tried to subvert official doctrine "not only by sermons but allso by prynted bokes prynted balades, *playes,* rymes, songes, and other fantasies." (Emphasis added.) This Act made it a crime for anyone to "express interpretations of Scripture contrary to the doctrine set forth or to be set forth by the king," and specifically singled out entertainers, saying, "No persons shall play in interlude, sing, or rhyme contrary to the said doctrine."[167] Of course, dialogue supporting Henry's point of view was still permitted on stage. This is evidenced by John Bale's play *King John*, which lionized an English king who, like Henry, had battled against the pope. This play was acceptable to Henry, but plays that supported the papacy were not permitted.

Protestant Reformers: Doctrine

Henry VIII's measures centered largely on his own headship of the Anglican Church and had not significantly affected doctrine or practices of the Church. However, there were Protestants in England who wished to carry the Reformation farther, and as they gained steam, Protestant-leaning members of the theatre community began editing the mystery plays to replace traditional Catholic teachings with Protestant ideas.

A good example of such editing can be seen in two versions of the Norwich Grocers' Play, which concerned the Creation and the Fall. The original version (Text A) was written in 1533 during the reign of Henry VIII. The Protestant revision (Text B) appeared in 1565 during the reign of Elizabeth I and was edited to reflect some of the ideas of the Reformed theologians. The exercise below is designed to shed light on the specific differences in the two texts.

EXERCISE 7.1: Comparing Traditional and Reformed Scripts

DIRECTIONS: Excerpts from both Text A and Text B of the Norwich Grocers' play appear in Appendix D. They cover the same sections of the play, but the editor of Text B has added some lines which highlight Protestant theology. Begin by reading the excerpts. Then, return to this exercise to analyze the differences in the two scripts.

1. View of marriage:

    a. How is the relationship between Adam and Eve portrayed differently in Texts A and B?

    b. Keeping in mind some of the Reformers' principles regarding the clergy, why do you suppose the nature of Adam and Eve's relationship was expanded in Text B?

2. Compatibility with Scripture:

    a. Review Genesis 2 and 3, and then respond: Does either text include anything non-Scriptural (that is, anything not found in Scripture)? If so, what?

    b. Does either text include anything that contradicts Scripture? Explain your answer.

3. Added characters:

    a. The editors of Text B added the Holy Spirit as a speaker in the last scene. In what way does this make a difference in the tone of the play's conclusion?

    b. What is your opinion about the fictional addition of words to be spoken by a member of the Holy Trinity?

Elizabeth I: The Threat of Political Turmoil

Not just religious doctrine, but also the accompanying political turmoil caused the Crown to rein in the playwrights. Knowing that a packed crowd at a theatre could be turned into a mob by ardent words, Queen Elizabeth appointed a Master of the Revels, Edmund Tilney, to whom all plays had to be submitted for approval before they could be performed. One play that did not pass muster was entitled *Sir Thomas More*. This play, which was probably written by Anthony Munday, concerns Henry VIII's execution of More, his Lord Chancellor, who had remained a steadfast Catholic during the English Reformation and would not recognize the king as the head of the Church. There was no way the queen was going to raise Catholic ire by allowing her father to be portrayed as a tyrant on the London stage, and Tilney made sure the play was never performed.

That Elizabeth did, indeed, have a legitimate fear of the link between stage and politics is proven by the rebellion of Robert Devereux [DĔ-və-rō], Earl of Essex, in 1601. Failing to accomplish the queen's objectives in Ireland and deemed as being too cozy with Irish hotheads, Essex had been deprived of office. But such an energetic noble was not about to go quietly. Essex and his allies, seeking to rebel against the queen, needed a way to stir up the populace to join them. To that end, they approached some actors in the Chamberlain's Men and asked them to perform a play about Richard II,[a] an English king who had been deposed and killed by his subjects. Fearing jail, the actors at first declined, but changed their minds when Essex offered them an extra forty shillings. Unfortunately for Essex, the performance did not bring about the desired result, and he was quickly arrested and sentenced to death. Although Augustine Phillips, an actor in the Chamberlain's Men, was required to give testimony about the incident, no actors ever were arrested, and the company was even invited to perform at court on the night before Essex was beheaded. It is doubtful, however, that they performed *Richard II*.

Robert Devereux, 2nd Earl of Essex (d. 1601)

---

[a] Recently some scholars have questioned whether it was indeed Shakespeare's version, as the actors had originally told Essex no one would attend such an "old" play, but since Phillips, a member of Shakespeare's troupe, testified they were approached by Essex's men, the weight of the evidence still seems to be on the side of Shakespeare's *Richard II*.

London City Council: Crime and Public Health

As long as the plays did not challenge the queen, Elizabeth encouraged the theatre community and is known to have truly enjoyed plays as a form of entertainment. But the monarch was not the only source of opposition to the theatre. The City Council also had concerns.

Spectators stood very close together to view a play, facilitating the spread of the plague.

First, the theatres were gathering places for pickpockets, prostitutes, and other unsavory sorts. The City had pushed the theatres outside the city limits for that reason, but crime was still rampant in Southwark, where The Swan, The Globe, and The Rose theatres were located. Secondly, during periods of contagion, the plague was easily spread from person to person as the groundlings stood close to each other around the stage. This was a serious threat to public health. And, third, employers complained about their apprentices sneaking away from work to see a play, which had to be performed during the day since the sun was their only source of light. These three factors—crime, plague, and interrupted commerce—kept the City Council busy with regulations it felt necessary for the good of the town.

Puritans: The Moral Dimension

Just as the pagan Greeks and Romans—as well as the early Christian leaders—had opposed the display of immoral behavior on the stage, so the Christian leaders of the sixteenth and seventeenth centuries spoke out against unseemly displays on the stage of their time. It would be hard to find a book about Elizabethan theatre that does not refer to "angry Puritans"[168] who made England a place where "no actor or spectator was safe."[169] These books focus primarily on the Puritan opposition to the theatre, but it is important to note that both Protestants and Catholics of the period opposed immorality on the stage. Christian opposition to the theatre in this period was not directed to the theatre itself as an evil institution, as evidenced by a plethora of "propaganda plays" in which both Catholics on the continent and Protestants in England used the stage to depict their group as heroes and the opposition as villains. Rather, the problem with the Elizabethan theatre was, once again, its immoral content, just as today's parents often criticize Hollywood for presenting inappropriate content for public consumption.

The comments of Puritan pamphleteer Philip Stubbs provide a good summary of the Puritan objections to the theatre. At the top of the list was the irreverence of the stage:

> All stage plays, interludes, and comedies are either of divine or profane matter. If they be of divine matter, then are they most intolerable, or rather sacrilegious for that [because] the blessed word of God is to be handled reverently, gravely and sagely, with veneration to the glorious majesty of God, which shineth therein, and not scoffingly, floutingly, and gibingly, as it is upon stages in plays and interludes. . . .[170]

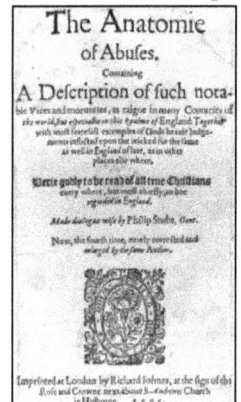

Frontispiece of *The Anatomy of Abuses*

Secondly, Stubbs objected to Sunday performances, which put the stage in competition with the pulpit:

> Do they not draw the people from hearing the word of God, from godly lectures and sermons? For you shall have them flock thither, thick and threefold, while the church of God shall be bare and empty.[171]

Third, he considered the content of the plays to be a threat to female chastity:

> For proof whereof, but mark the flocking and running to theatres and curtains, daily and hourly, night and day, time and tide, to see plays and interludes, where such wanton gestures, such bawdy speeches, such laughing and fleering, such kissing and business, such clipping and culling, such winking and glancing of wanton eyes, and the like is used, as is wonderful[a] to behold.[172]

Last, he called theatres "schools of mischief" and listed the subjects taught there: deceit, hypocrisy, lying, mocking, blasphemy, rebellion, treason, idleness, flattery, gluttony, substance abuse, impurity, arrogance, and defiance of God.

> If you learn . . . to commit all kinds of sin and mischief, you need to go to no other school, for all these good examples may you see painted before your eyes in interludes and plays.[173]

---

[a] unheard of

Certainly the Puritan voice was not the only one crying about the evil influences of plays. Matthew Parker, archbishop of Canterbury, denounced the stage, and, on the continent, Carlo Borromeo, Roman Catholic archbishop of Milan, opposed "theatrical performances, plays, things of this nature which take their origins from pagan practice and are contrary to Christian teaching."[174] Even Oxford University forbade plays in 1584. Thus, it is important to remember that as it always had—from Greece to Rome to Renaissance Europe—lewd behavior on the stage linked the theatre with immorality.

Statue of John Winthrop (National Statuary Hall Collection)

One last thing before we close: One often reads that Puritans were "killjoys" who objected to the theatre simply because they opposed anything fun. Perhaps Stubbs's comments above go some way toward showing that their objection was not to recreation *per se*, but to immoral recreation. What's more, part of their motivation was Christian charity. Puritan thoughts on this subject can be seen in "The Model of Christian Charity" written by John Winthrop shortly after the *Mayflower* set sail from England in 1630: "We must be willing to abridge ourselves of our superfluities, for the supply of others' necessities."[175] To this end, once the Puritans came to power in Parliament during the reign of Charles I, they passed a law that "all money taken as admission fees shall be forfeited to the churchwardens of the parish, and devoted to the use of the poor."[176]

Another re-purposing of the theatre district happened in 1644, when twelve buildings providing decent housing for the poor went up where the Globe had stood. Then in 1672 a Presbyterian[a] Meeting House was established in Globe Alley.[177] Thus, from the Puritan point of view, at least, before the end of the century, the once riotous neighborhood of the Southwark theatres was serving the charitable and spiritual goals of the faithful.

---

[a] Presbyterianism was that form of Calvinism which developed in Scotland. When King James VI of Scotland became King James I of England, Presbyterianism moved south into England. Puritan theology was also based on the teachings of John Calvin.

ELIZABETHAN PLAYWRIGHTS

Chapter 8

Introduction

Young American author Garth Risk Hallberg once said, "I associated excellence in writing with New York City." This nugget, modified by a few centuries, points to a truth about the English Renaissance: one can associate excellence in writing with London. Sixteenth-century London was a hub of activity. Publishers, explorers, philosophers, Reformers, and scientists—all were finding London the center of their universe. But, just as the Italian Renaissance was defined by art, the English Renaissance was defined by literature—and literature in that period meant plays. So who exactly were these giants of the English Renaissance? The purpose of this chapter is to introduce you to some of the playwrights and their major plays.

Playwrights

Christopher Marlowe

Christopher Marlowe (1564-93) is remembered not simply for being another member of the Elizabethan theatrical scene, but also for being an English spy with a mysterious death.

Christopher Marlowe

Born in Canterbury, Marlowe received his grammar school education at King's School, which was attached to Canterbury Cathedral and supported "fifty boys both destitute of the help of friends and endowed with minds for apt learning."[178] Sadly, he did not receive this scholarship until he was already fourteen years old, and the school only served students between the ages nine and fifteen. Proving himself able at King's, Marlowe received a scholarship to attend Corpus Christi College at Cambridge in 1580.

He took his Bachelor's degree in 1584 and soon began work on a Master's degree, at which time the narrative of his life becomes steeped in mystery. When the time came for Marlowe to receive his Masters of Arts, the college balked at giving him the degree on the grounds that he had exceeded the number of allowed absences. It was also rumored that Marlowe had converted to Catholicism while he was in the French city of Rheims [RĒMZ or, French, RĂNS], which most definitely would have been against the law in Elizabethan England. However, the college soon received a letter testifying on Marlowe's behalf that his time in Rheims had been spent "in matters touching the benefit of the country." Now, this letter was signed by four men, including the Archbishop of Canterbury and William Cecil, 1st Baron Burghley—the organizer of Queen Elizabeth's intelligence service, that is, her spies. Treason and assassination were always a possibility during the Reformation era, and it is believed that Marlowe associated with Catholics at Rheims in order to pick up any whisperings about a plot to overthrow Elizabeth and her Protestant government.

Who better to play the role of a spy than an actor who could "add colors to the chameleon" and "change shapes with Proteus for advantages"?[179] Back home in England, a traveling actor would also have a perfect cover for showing up in numerous spots about England without being suspected as a spy. It will be necessary to return to the spy business once again in the discussion of Marlowe's death, but at this point, we will move forward with his career as a dramatist.

Timur the Lame

In 1587, the same year Marlowe finished his education at Cambridge, he brought his play *Tamburlaine the Great* to the stage in London, a play which some consider the first play Shakespeare saw upon his arrival in London. The play concerns the Central Asian tyrant Timur the Lame, who died in 1405, and presented a wonderful role for tragedian Edward Alleyn. Marlowe's other plays are as follows:

- *Dido, Queen of Carthage*, which he wrote as a student at Cambridge.
- *The Jew of Malta*, 1589, a revenge tragedy based on religious conflict.
- *Dr. Faustus*, 1589 or 1593, a tragedy involving the fate of an alchemist who sells his soul to the devil in exchange for twenty-four years of unlimited magical power.
- *Edward II*, 1592, a history play about the assassination of the king.
- *The Massacre at Paris*, 1593, a play about the Massacre of St. Bartholomew's Day, when thousands of Huguenots [HYŪ-gə-nŏts] (French Protestants) were killed by Catholics in Paris, an event of recent memory, having occurred in 1572.

It is interesting to note that *The Massacre at Paris* was performed in January 1593, the year of Marlowe's mysterious death. Its subject matter was closely aligned with disturbances in London on May 5 of that year, when apprentices were attacking immigrant Huguenots, whom they charged with taking their jobs. One person deemed to be an instigator of the riots was the playwright Thomas Kyd, who was arrested and tortured. While searching Kyd's quarters, the authorities came across a composition about the Holy Trinity, which led to a charge of atheism against Kyd. However, under torture, Kyd claimed that the treatise belonged to Christopher Marlowe, his former roommate. Therefore, on May 20, 1593, Marlowe was arrested on a charge of atheism, but he was not tortured and was given what we would call probation. Ten days later he was dead.

It happened this way: On May 30, Marlowe spent the day with four persons at a boarding house (not a tavern, as many have suggested) run by the respectable Dame Eleanor Bull. There was much drinking, apparently, and late in the day an argument broke out between Marlowe and Ingram Frizer as to who would pay the bill. A knife was pulled and Marlowe was stabbed in the head, leaving a wound two inches deep and killing him instantly.

Now, that would be the end of the story were it not for the fact that Marlowe had been a spy who had recently been arrested on a charge of atheism. The matter is furthered muddied by the fact that the other two men present with Marlowe and Frizer were Robert Poley and Nicholas Skeres, both of whom had been involved with the Elizabethan spy ring. What's more, Frizer, who admitted to the stabbing with a claim of self-defense, was the personal servant of Thomas Walsingham, the founder of Queen Elizabeth's intelligence service. Conspiracy theories abound regarding who had a motive to murder Marlowe, and it has even been suggested that his death was faked so that he could escape the charge of atheism.

Plaque in Deptford, where Marlowe is buried. "Cut is the branch that might have grown full straight." *(Doctor Faustus)*

But was Marlowe an atheist? Determining Marlowe' religious views is problematic. At Cambridge, he had been accused of converting to Catholicism, and he did turn up at a Catholic school in France. However, as shown above, this could easily have been a cover if the queen had employed him as a spy. That he was not a Catholic is suggested by the fact that he was granted the Matthew Parker scholarship at Corpus Christi, which was intended for young men preparing to go into the Anglican ministry.

As we have seen, he was accused of atheism by Thomas Kyd (under torture) in 1593. Furthermore, Marlowe was a member of a group of "free thinkers" who had formed a secretive club called the School of Night, which included members of the nobility, scientists, astronomers, and mathematicians. It was, after all, the Renaissance, and various thinkers on the continent, such as Galileo, were beginning to re-examine long-held beliefs about the universe, a move which seemed to threaten powerful people in the Church and state. It cannot be known whether Marlowe was an atheist or just a person curious about new scientific discoveries and theories, but certainly the charge of atheism did bring him under suspicion and may have led to his death.

Whatever his religious views were, Marlowe's reputation as a dramatist is excellent. Some say that, had he lived, he would have excelled Shakespeare in the quality of his literature. His life and art were recalled in the anonymous play *Return from Parnassus*:

> JUDICIO
> Heological and diabolic
> Alas! Unhappy in his life and end;
> Pity it is that wit so ill should dwell.
> Wit lent from heaven, but vices sent from hell.[180] (1.2)

EXERCISE 8.1: Scriptural Connection *(Doctor Faustus)*

DIRECTIONS: Please begin by reading the introduction. Then read the excerpts from *Doctor Faustus* and answer the questions which follow.

INTRODUCTION: *One of Christopher Marlowe's most famous plays is* Doctor Faustus, *which concerns a learned German scientist who makes a deal with the devil. In exchange for twenty-four years of unlimited magical power, he promises to give his soul to Satan for eternity. This play is based on a German narrative called* Faust, *which was said to apply to two German scientists, both of whom died in 1540, "leaving a tangled legend of sorcery and alchemy, astrology, and soothsaying, studies theological and diabolical, necromancy, and, indeed, sodomy."*[181]

Excerpts from *Doctor Faustus*
By Christopher Marlowe

The first excerpt is a soliloquy rendered by Faustus at the beginning of the play, as he weighs the truth of Scripture against his own desires. The second is from the last soliloquy, which closes the play. The line numbers correspond to those of the full text. (NOTE: The Latin quotations from Jerome's Bible are almost immediately translated into English by the playwright. The one untranslated Latin statement will be treated in the questions below.)

Opening Soliloquy

FAUSTUS
Jerome's Bible, Faustus, view it well.
[Reads] Stipendium peccati mors est. Ha! Stipendium, &c.
"The reward of sin is death?" that's hard.
Si peccasse negamus, fallimur, & nulla est in nobis veritas:
"If we say that we have no sin,
We deceive ourselves, and there's no truth in us." 70
Why then belike we must sin,
And so consequently die.
Ay, we must die an everlasting death.
What doctrine call you this, *Che sera, sera:*
What will be, shall be? Divinity, *adieu.* 75
These Metaphysics of Magicians,
And Necromantic books are heavenly;
Lines, circles, scenes, letters and characters,
Ay, these are those that Faustus most desires.
O what a world of profit and delight, 80
Of power, of honor, of omnipotence
Is promised to the studious artisan?
All things that move between the quiet poles
Shall be at my command. Emperors and Kings,
Are but obeyed in their several provinces: 85
Nor can they raise the wind, or rend the clouds;
But his dominion that exceeds in this,
Stretcheth as far as doth the mind of man.

Postage stamp showing Faustus and Mephistopheles

> A sound magician is a mighty god:
> Here Faustus try thy brains to gain a deity.[182]

Questions:

1. In Lines #65-70, Faustus is reading from a Bible. What particular teaching from the New Testament is he reading about?

2. In Lines #71-75, does Faustus seem to understand the meaning of the scriptures he is reading?

3. In Lines #76-79, Faustus indicates a preference, not for Scripture, but for what?

4. In Lines #80-89, Faustus states his objective. Briefly summarize his statement.

Closing Soliloquy

> FAUSTUS
> *(To himself)* O, Faustus,
> Now hast thou but one bare hour to live,
> And then thou must be damned perpetually.
> Stand still, you ever-moving spheres of heaven,   2040
> That time may cease and midnight never come.
> Fair nature's eye, rise, rise again and make
> Perpetual day. Or let this hour be but a year,
> A month, a week, a natural day,
> That Faustus may repent and save his soul.   2045
> *O lente lente currite noctis equi.*
> The stars move still, time runs, the clock will strike.
> The devil will come and Faustus must be damned.
> O, I'll leap up to heaven; who pulls me down?
> One drop of blood will save me.   2050

Rend not my heart, for naming of my Christ.
Yet will I call on him. O spare me, Lucifer.
Where is it now? 'Tis gone.
And see a threatening arm, an angry brow.
Mountains and hills, come, come, and fall on me,   2055
And hide me from the heavy wrath of heaven.
No? Then will I headlong run into the earth.
Gape, earth! O no, it will not harbor me.
You stars that reigned at my nativity,
Whose influence hath allotted death and hell,   2060
Now draw up Faustus like a foggy mist
Into the entrails of yon laboring cloud,
That when you vomit forth into the air,
My limbs may issue from your smoky mouths,
But let my soul mount and ascend to heaven.   2065

[The watch strikes.]

O, half the hour is past! 'Twill all be past anon.
O, if my soul must suffer for my sin,
Impose some end to my incessant pain.
Let Faustus live in hell a thousand years,   2070
A hundred thousand, and at last be saved.
No end is limited to damnéd souls.
Why wert thou not a creature wanting soul?
Or why is this immortal that thou hast?
Oh πψτηαγορας[a] metempsychosis[b] were that true,   2075
This soul should fly from me, and I be changed
Into some brutish beast.
All beasts are happy, for when they die,
Their souls are soon dissolved in elements,
But mine must live still to be plagued in hell.   2080
Cursed be the parents that engendered me;

---

[a] Pythagoras, Greek mathematician, scientist, and philosopher (c. 570 – c. 495 BC)
[b] Pythagorean belief in the transmigration of the soul of a human or an animal into the body of another human or animal (reincarnation).

No, Faustus, curse thyself. Curse Lucifer
That hath deprived thee of the joys of heaven.

[The clock strikes twelve.]

It strikes, it strikes! Now body turn to air,   2085
Or Lucifer will bear thee quick to hell.
O soul be changed into small water drops,
And fall into the ocean ne'er be found.

[Thunder, and enter the devils.]

O mercy, heaven! Look not so fierce on me;   2090
Adders and serpents let me breathe awhile.
Ugly hell, gape not; come not Lucifer!
I'll burn my books! Oh, Mephistopheles!

Questions:

6. This is the closing of the play when Faustus realizes he must now hold up his end of the bargain and enter hell.

    a. What is the meaning of the Latin sentence, "*O lente lente currite noctis equi*"? (If unsure, type the words into the search bar on your Internet browser.)

    b. This Latin quote appears in Faustus' thoughts expressed in Lines #2037-2049. Briefly state the meaning of this passage in your own words.

7. What understanding of Scripture does Faustus show in Line #2050?

8. What does he wish to do in Lines #2051-2052a?

9. In Lines #2052b-2065:

   a. Faustus cries out not to Christ, but to whom and what?

   b. What is he asking all these things to do for him?

10. To what Roman Catholic doctrine (not retained by the Church of England) does Marlowe seem to reference in Lines #2066-2072?

11. Lines #2073-2074 present some linguistic problems.

   a. First, the word *thou (you)* in Line #2073 is a reference to himself. Second, in Marlowe's time, the word *wanting* meant *lacking*. In the space provided, summarize what Faustus seems to be wishing for here.

   b. In your own words, indicate what question Faustus asks himself in Line #2074.

12. In Lines #2074-78, Faustus wishes what? Why?

13. In Lines #2079-83, Faustus brings down three curses. What is each, and why does he call each down?

   First, he curses

   Second, he curses

   Third, he curses

14. In Lines #2085-93, what last ditch efforts to avoid hell does Faustus make?

MORE CHALLENGING:

15. Discuss Line #2090 with your classmates, using the three following questions:

    a. Is Faustus crying out for salvation or for something else? Explain your answer.

    b. Does Faustus believe what he expressed in Lines #2050-52? Explain your answer.

    c. If he did call out for Christ in these last seconds, could he still have been saved, according to Scripture? (You may wish to examine Luke 23:39-43 and Hebrews 3:14-19.)

16. Considering that Marlowe was accused of atheism more than once in his life, do you think the ideas in this play support or refute that charge? Explain your answer.

Thomas Kyd

Thomas Kyd was a major figure in the Elizabethan theatre and even an influence on Shakespeare. He was a Londoner through and through. Born there in 1558, he was educated at the Merchant Taylor's School, which was the largest school in England at the time, studying Latin, Greek, music, and classical theatre, and was imbued with the Greek idea of developing *mens sana in corpore sano,* "a healthy mind in a healthy body.

Like Shakespeare, Kyd did not attend university and, like Shakespeare, received the same snobbish reception from the Cambridge and Oxford poets.

A man of the Renaissance, Kyd flourished in the revival of the Greek and Roman plays. The plays of Seneca that Kyd read in school were, for him, not just dead documents of a dead culture, but vibrant works more than worthy of reintroduction into Europe. His play *The Spanish Tragedy* was, like Seneca's tragedies, centered on the theme of revenge and full of madness, violence, and blood (the lead character Hieronimo bites off his tongue moments before stabbing himself to death).

However, Kyd was not just an imitator. He experimented with plot structure and was the first to compose a work that had a play within a play, a technique later used by Shakespeare in *Hamlet*. One piece of dialogue in Act IV of *The Spanish Tragedy* even provides a hint that Kyd departed from the current notion that women should not perform in plays. Bellimperia, the woman whose sweetheart was murdered by her brother Lorenzo and his friend Balthazar, is to be avenged by the sweetheart's father, Hieronimo. In order to expose the truth, Hieronimo proposes that Lorenzo and Balthazar perform a play whose plot line rather obviously parallels their own evil deed, and while explaining the plot to them, he offers up this line about their players:

> Now, my good lord, could you entreat
> Your sister Bellimperia to make one?
> For what's a play without a woman in it?[183] (4.1)

Some might argue that Bellimperia was included as an actress in this ruse simply because she and Hieronimo were not planning to play-act the stabbing of the two, but *actually* to stab them. However, the line "For what's a play without a woman in it?" reveals perhaps Kyd's own opinion on the subject of women players.

Though Shakespeare is believed to have had better poetry in his plays, Kyd is nevertheless still praised for the liveliness and complexity of his plays. One scholar recently summed up Kyd's startling innovations this way:

> Bloody deeds were not now merely reported by a distraught nurse or breathless messenger [as in classical times] but staged in full view as living testimony to Fortune's fickleness or the instability of life in princely courts. . . . *The Spanish Tragedy* is generally endowed with frequent hints and clues as well as harsh evidence. One may consider, for example, the significance Kyd attaches to physical contact in the play built on images of violent death, illicit love, overt and

concealed cruelty. Characters therefore kiss, embrace, threaten, assault, execute one another; people fall to the ground, drop gloves, whisper confidences, give each other chains, letters, papers, gold; they enter bearing a book or a halter and poniard;[a] they fix up curtains, sit down at banquets, and run mad.[184]

In short, Thomas Kyd was a master at theatrics. As we have seen, he was accused of atheism in 1593 and, under torture, blurted out the name of Christopher Marlowe, who was, he claimed, an atheist. This claim may have led not only to Marlowe's death, but also to the reputation of Kyd, who afterwards isolated himself in his rooms, translating *Cornelia* from French until he died penniless the following year.

Ben Jonson

Ben Jonson
1532-1657

The playwright considered to be England's first poet laureate is Ben Jonson, who was born in London on June 11, 1572. His father, a clergyman, died shortly after his birth, and he was raised in the home of his step-father, a bricklayer. The spelling of Jonson's name has been the subject of some interest inasmuch as it has dropped the *h* which normally is used in the name and actually derives from a Scottish name, *Johnston*, suggesting his ancestors had made their way south from Scotland.

While he was growing up, he lived with his mother and stepfather in Westminster, the capital of the English government. He apparently was a clever boy and came to the attention of the renowned classical scholar William Camden, who paid for young Ben's education at the highly respected Westminster School. Leaving school in 1589 at the age of seventeen, he worked first as a bricklayer alongside his stepfather, then served with England's army in Flanders for a time before returning to London. It is at this point that his education and intellect took hold of his life, as he soon joined Philip Henslowe's theatre company.

In 1598, now twenty-six, Jonson wrote his first great play, *Every Man in His Humor*, in which William Shakespeare acted in 1616. Not long after the opening of his play, Jonson killed a fellow theatre figure named Gabriel Spencer in a duel for reasons still not known today. Certainly, it was not Spencer's first

---

[a] a sword

duel, as he had killed a man in a duel two months earlier. What happened next may interest all students of Latin. Though Jonson did spend a few weeks in prison, he was able to escape severe punishment by claiming "benefit of clergy," a privilege offered to people who could read Latin. Still, he was later arrested again for failing to pay one of his actors.

These insights suggest that "Jonson the man" may not have been as highly esteemed as "Jonson the poet." William Drummond of Hawthornden, who knew him, left us this description:

> He is a great lover and praiser of himself; a contemner[a] and scorner of others; given rather to lose a friend than a jest; . . . he is passionately kind and angry; careless either to gain or keep; vindictive, but, if he be well answered, at himself . . . ; oppressed with fantasy, which hath ever mastered his reason.[185]

As one might imagine, he was not always popular with his fellow poets, and in 1601 he wrote a satire, blasting his fellow poets for what he considered their shortcomings. Of course, they answered back, and the whole episode has come to be called the War of the Theatres. Were he alive today, he would probably be boisterous on *Twitter*.

Jonson wrote twenty plays and thirty-six masques. He was considered a better poet than Shakespeare in his time, and certainly they were friends—and rivals—in the theatre community of Elizabethan London. After Shakespeare died, Jonson wrote an elegy for him, which briefly mentions their shared endeavor, calling Shakespeare "the applause, delight, the wonder of our stage!"[186]

Despite the fact that Jonson had poked fun at the Scots in one of his plays, King James thought enough of his work to grant him a yearly stipend of 100 marks, which was later increased by Charles I to £100—and "a butt of Canary wine from the King's cellars," to boot.[187] However, for whatever reason, Jonson died a poor man, which meant that he could not afford a grave space in Poet's Corner in Westminster Abbey. Legend has it that in conversation with the dean of Westminster, he said, "I am too poor for that and no one will lay out funeral charges upon me. No, sir, six feet long by two feet wide is too much for me: two feet by two feet will do for all I want," so the dean gave him an eighteen-inch square space in the church floor, and, when the time came, Jonson

---

[a] One who shows contempt for another

was buried standing on his feet."[188] A respectful grave marker was placed over the spot, bearing his name (misspelled) among the words: "O Rare Ben Johnson,"

William Shakespeare

William Shakespeare
1546-1616

Though William Shakespeare is one of the most famous men of all time, very few records exist to document his life. Church baptismal records show that he was baptized at Stratford-on-Avon in Warwickshire on April 26, 1564. Since English custom was to baptize an infant three days after its birth, a birth date of April 23 has become the standard ascribed to young Will. He died in April 1616, some believe on his birthday.

A versatile playwright, Shakespeare wrote comedies, tragedies, and history plays—both Roman and English. In all, including those he composed in collaboration with others, he is attributed with 38 plays, 154 sonnets, and two narrative poems. The quality of his language and the universality of his themes have resulted in translations of Shakespeare into at least eighty languages, including Japanese, Chinese, and Bengali. One wonders, however, how much of the Shakespearean quality is lost without the *thee*'s, *thou*'s, *-eth*'s, and *-est*'s that are so characteristic of his work! The memorable line, "Romeo, Romeo, wherefore art thou Romeo?" becomes in French, for example, *"Romeo, romeo, donc c'est toi romeo"* and in Korean, *"romeo, romeo, geuleon kkadalg-e neoneun lom soida."*[a]

Shakespeare's father, a glover (maker of gloves), was a prosperous member of the rising middle class in England and owned a timbered house in the Tudor style on Henley Street, where it still stands today. As a lad between the ages of six and eight, the future poet was enrolled at the Stratford Grammar School, where he received a classical and Christian education. He did not attend university (more about this in Chapter 11).

Shakespeare's birthplace in Stratford-on-Avon, Warwickshire

After the death of Queen Elizabeth, Shakespeare continued his career as a member of the King's Men, sponsored by the new monarch, Elizabeth's Scottish cousin James I.

---

[a] Capitalization rules are different in other languages.

At the age of eighteen, he married Anne Hathaway and with her had three children: Susanna (b. 1583) and twins, Hamnet and Judith (b. 1585). From the birth of the twins until 1592, Will Shakespeare vanishes from the records for a period of time called the "lost years," as there is no accounting for his whereabouts. This has not stopped scholars from creating various theories, however, and the two most often mentioned are that (a) he had to escape the law for an act of poaching, and (b) he left town with a traveling theatre troupe that had made a stop in Stratford. Some believe that Shakespeare spent time in Italy during these years because many of his plays, notably *Romeo and Juliet*, have Italian settings and show familiarity with the area. Another theory is that he served for a while as a country schoolmaster, a claim with some support in that Alexander Houghton, schoolmaster in Lancashire at the time, mentioned one "William Shakeshaft" in his will. Sometime before 1592, Shakespeare made his way to London. There is a long tradition that he was employed by theatre managers to handle the horses of theatre patrons, though there is no documentation that he did so.

Woodcut of Robert Greene "suted in deaths livery," 1598

Theatre records tell us that he had been on the London stage several times by 1592, enough to raise the hackles of the more well-established theatre personalities who perhaps saw in him a serious threat of displacement. Robert Greene, for example, wrote:

> There is an upstart Crow, beautified with our feathers, that with his Tiger's heart wrapped in a Player's hide, supposes he is as well able to bombast out a blank verse as the best of you: and being an absolute *Johannes factotum*, is in his own conceit the only Shake-scene in a country.[189]

The reference to "a tiger's heart wrapped in a player's hide" echoes a similar line which Shakespeare wrote for the Duke of York in *Henry VI, Part 3,* where the duke barks to Queen Margaret: "O tiger's heart wrapped in a woman's hide" (1.4.140),[190] a line Greene seems to be mocking.

In addition to his literature, Shakespeare expanded into real estate. In about 1613, when he retired from the theatre and returned to Stratford, he invested his considerable wealth in real estate, purchasing the property still known as New House, which is a major tourist attraction today, as are his birthplace, the Stratford grammar school, and the Stratford church where he was buried in 1616. Visitors to the church often gaze at the full-color bust of the poet there and feel a certain disappointment that the face is somewhat fuller than is depicted in famous portraits they have seen in books throughout the years, but it has been said that when his wife Anne saw it for the first time, she said it was very like him. Even the great man put on a little weight as he aged.

The grave itself is inside the church, as was the custom of the time. Of course, there is a limit to the number of bodies that can be buried inside the walls of a small church, so the common practice was to disinter the remains from a previous grave and to replace them with another "occupant." Shakespeare reviled the practice and, to insure this would not happen to him, composed before his death a little piece of doggerel, which still rests on his grave in its original seventeenth-century orthography:

> Good frend for Iesvs sake forbeare,
> To digg the dvst encloased heare.
> Bleste be ỹ man ỹ spares thes stones,
> And cvrst be he ỹ moves my bones.

> [Good friend, for Jesus' sake forbear
> To dig the dust enclosèd here.
> Blessed be the man that spares these stones,
> And cursed be he that moves my bones.]

Social Status of Playwrights

Once in every generation, it seems, someone will sell some books by claiming to have proof that William Shakespeare did not write the plays of William Shakespeare. One of the reasons for such skepticism is snobbery, pure and simple, for William Shakespeare was not a Cambridge or Oxford man. He attended the Stratford grammar school and then ran off to join an acting troupe. Shakespeare's case is somewhat similar perhaps to that of Abraham Lincoln, a country lawyer whom many considered a hick, but who nonetheless stunned the world with his oratory.

Of the four authors profiled in this chapter, only Marlowe attended university, and even he did not attend on his own dime but received what we would call today a need-based scholarship. The Renaissance brought change not only in literature, art, and religion, but in economic circumstances as well. The medieval feudal system was not completely dead, but the sixteenth and seventeenth centuries saw the emergence of a rising middle class. Shopkeepers, artisans, clothiers, printers, tavern keepers, spinsters—all of these were flourishing and enhancing the wealth and stability of their families.

Just look at the four playwrights featured here: Christopher Marlowe's father was a shoemaker; William Shakespeare's, a glover; Thomas Kyd's, a scrivener; and Ben Jonson's, a bricklayer. What's more, the players and theatre owners were also from modest backgrounds. Richard Burbage's father was a joiner; Thomas Heywood's, a country parson; Edward Alleyn's, an innkeeper. Richard Tarleton's father was probably a pig farmer, and the player himself was a water-carrier and, along with his wife, ran a tavern. Yet all of these stars of the Elizabethan theatre were well educated, because they each received a classical education in an English grammar school.

ELIZABETHAN PLAYERS

Chapter 9

Introduction

In 1962, when President John F. Kennedy addressed a gathering to honor winners of the Nobel Prize, he proclaimed, "I think this is the most extraordinary collection of talent, of human knowledge, that has ever been gathered at the White House—with the possible exception of when Thomas Jefferson dined alone." It was a marvelous expression of the brilliance of an eighteenth-century American, but Kennedy's phrase about "the most extraordinary collection of talent" gathered in one place at one time also aptly defines the brightest constellation of players and playwrights simultaneously existing in sixteenth-century England. The plays of the period were masterpieces of world literature, but they would not have come to much without four "stars" of the Elizabethan heavens: Richard Tarlton, Will Kempe, Edward Alleyn, and Richard Burbage. The purpose of this chapter is to recount the amazing talents of these men.

Comic Actors

Richard Tarlton

Richard Tarlton (d. 1588) is considered to have been the greatest comic of Elizabethan times. Born in Shropshire, where some have reported his father was a pig farmer, Tarlton had modest origins, yet still managed to receive some schooling 300 years before education was compulsory in England. Though he could obviously read and write quite well, a contemporary commented that "he was only superficially seen in learning, having no more but a bare insight into the Latin language."[191] Deciding whether exposure to rudimentary Latin lessons makes him poorly educated is up to his fans to decide.

Richard Tarlton (d. 1588)

His birth year is unknown, but he must have been making a name for himself in the years before 1583, when he was admitted to the prestigious acting company called the Queen's Men. His "discovery" and transition from Shropshire to London is legendary.

While Tarlton was still living in Condover in Shropshire, it is said, "He was in the field keeping his father's swine, when a servant of Robert, Earl of Leicester, passing this way to his Lord's lands in his Barony of Denbighe, was so highly pleased with his happy unhappy answers, that he brought him to court, where he became the most famous jester to Queen Elizabeth."[192]

The description of Tarlton's "happy unhappy answers" is a reference to his quick wit and (and sometimes satirical) humor. A contemporary, who had seen him in action, once reported that he was a "wondrous, plentiful, extemporall wit, [and] hee was the wonder of his time."[193] Sometimes his biting observations got a little too close to the bone, as, for example, the time he made some biting remarks about Queen Elizabeth's two favorites—Walter Raleigh, Earl of Essex, and Robert Dudley, Earl of Leicester:

> At supper the queen would divert herself with her friends and attendants, and if they made her no answer, she would put them upon mirth and pleasant discourse with great civility. She would then admit Tarlton, a famous comedian and pleasant talker, and other such men to divert her with stories of the town and the common jests and accidents. . . . Tarlton, who was then the best comedian in England, had made a pleasant play, and, when it was acting[a] before the queen he pointed at Raleigh and said, "See! the knave commands the queen!" for which he was corrected by a frown from the queen; yet he had the confidence to add that he was of too much and too intolerable a power, and going on with the same liberty, he reflected on the too great power of the earl of Leicester, which was so universally applauded by all present that she thought fit to bear these reflections with a seeming unconcernedness. But yet she was so offended that she forbad Tarlton and all jesters from coming near her table.[194]

Tarlton died in September 1588, but his reputation certainly survived him. In fact, it is generally believed that the words spoken about Yorick, "the king's jester," in the famous graveyard scene in *Hamlet* refer to Tarlton. The melancholy Hamlet and his friend Horatio are wandering past a churchyard one day when two men, identified as First Clown and Second Clown, are digging a grave, jesting with each other as two grave diggers might in order to avoid thinking of their grim task. Hamlet strikes up a

---

[a] Note the use of the active form of present progressive tense. Where we would use *was being enacted*, the seventeenth-century writer used *was acting*. The passive form of present progressive tense did not become established in English until the eighteenth or nineteenth century.

conversation with the First Clown, asking him how long it takes a body to decay in the grave. This exchange then ensues:

FIRST CLOWN
Here's a skull now; this skull has lain in the earth
three and twenty years.

HAMLET
Whose was it?

FIRST CLOWN
A mad fellow's it was: whose do you think it was?

HAMLET
Nay, I know not.

FIRST CLOWN
A pestilence on him for a mad rogue! a' [he] poured a
flagon of Rhenish on my head once. This same skull,
sir, was Yorick's skull, the king's jester.

HAMLET
This?

FIRST CLOWN
E'en that.

HAMLET
Let me see.

[Takes the skull]

Alas, poor Yorick! I knew him, Horatio: a fellow
of infinite jest, of most excellent fancy: he hath
borne me on his back a thousand times; and now, how
abhorred in my imagination it is! my gorge rims at
it. Here hung those lips that I have kissed I know
not how oft. Where be your gibes now? your
gambols? your songs? your flashes of merriment,

that were wont to set the table on a roar? Not one
now, to mock your own grinning? quite chap-fallen?[195] (5.1.179-99)

As Shakespeare clearly knew, "*Mortuus est pro nobis*"

Will Kempe

The mantle of best comic actor of the Elizabethan stage next passed to Will Kempe (1550-1603). The first recorded mention of this great comedian was in 1585, when he was a member of Leicester's Company. Later he joined Strange's Men, moving on to a five-year stint with the Chamberlain's Men. In 1598, during his time with the Chamberlain's Men, he joined with William Shakespeare, Richard Burbage, and three others to be one of the six shareholders in the company. However, he quarreled with Shakespeare in 1599 and left the company for good.

Will Kempe (right) doing the morris dance

Kempe's brand of humor was the type that would produce great belly laughs. It is said the audience would break out in laughter if he just peeped from behind a curtain. The comic roles which Kempe played for Shakespeare include Dogberry in *Much Ado about Nothing*, Peter in *Romeo and Juliet*, and probably Lancelot Gobbo in *The Merchant of Venice*, Bottom in *A Midsummer Night's Dream*, and Falstaff in the history plays about Henry IV. Now, there is a curiosity about the play *Henry V*, the sequel to *Henry IV*: the beloved character Falstaff is mentioned in the play but never appears on stage. This has led one scholar to speculate that Kempe quit the company as Shakespeare was writing *Henry V*, and the playwright simply did not have time to find another comic actor. This theory is supported by the fact that Kempe had walked out on the Chamberlain's Men just as the company was finishing its last performance of *Henry IV, Part II*.[196]

Kempe's natural wit made him, like Tarlton, a great extemporaneous performer, so much so that some believe that his incessant ad libbing was at the bottom of his quarrel with Shakespeare. In fact, Shakespeare himself may have left us a description of his annoyance with Will Kempe in Act II of *Hamlet*, where the melancholy Prince Hamlet is getting up a sober play he hopes will prick the conscience of his stepfather, the king.

To bring off the desired effect, Hamlet tells one of the Danish actors how they should *not* perform:

> HAMLET
> O, reform it altogether. And let those that play
> your clowns speak no more than what is set down for them;
> for there be of them that will themselves laugh, to
> set on some quantity of barren spectators to laugh
> too; though, in the meantime, some necessary
> questions be then to be considered:
> that's villainous, and shows a most pitiful ambition
> in the fool that uses it.[197] (2.2.40-47)

However, Kempe was not finished with his shenanigans, as he now turned his attention to another feature of his merriment—the jig, or morris dance. The morris dance was a folk dance that had been around since the late fifteenth century. The dance was performed to the rhythmic beating of a tabor, the type of drum associated with marching soldiers. Such dancers were called *bel-shangles*, a reference to the strap of bells the dancers would wear on their shins to enhance the jovial effect of the dance.

After Kempe left the Chamberlain's Men, he undertook to jig all the way from London to Norwich, a distance of 100 miles, taking along his bells and his taborer. Afterwards, he wrote an account of his caper known as *Kemp's Nine Daies Wonder*, in which he described how various folks from the towns through which he passed would accompany him for a mile or two as he danced on to the next town—a butcher, a plumpish maiden "not passing fourteene yeares of age," two annoying lads, and a corpulent innkeeper. This last companion gave out after following Kempe only "two fields" and collapsed on the road.

Bel-shangles to Bojangles?

In the early twentieth century, an African-American tap dancer named Bill Robinson adopted the nickname Bojangles. Later, in 1968, Jerry Jeff Walker wrote a song, made famous by Bob Dylan, entitled "Mister Bojangles." The first stanza of the song goes this way:

I knew a man Bojangles and he'd dance for you
In worn out shoes,
Silver hair, ragged shirt and baggy pants,
That old soft shoe.
He'd jump so high, he'd jump so high,
Then he lightly touch down.
Mr. Bojangles, Mr. Bojangles, dance.

(Google Play Music)

"Dauncer," quoth hee, "if thou daunce a^a God's name, God speede thee: I cannot follow thee a foote farther, but adieu, good dauncer. God speed thee, if thou daunce a God's name."[198]

Will Kempe died in 1603, the same year that Queen Elizabeth passed. For years, he had lived and performed in Southwark, so perhaps it is not unreasonable to guess that it is indeed the actor's surname which is recorded in the burial register of St. Saviour's Church, Southwark, identifying the deceased simply as "Kempe, a man."

ACTIVITY 9.A: Freeze Tag Improvisation

DIRECTIONS: To practice the skill of ad libbing, for which Will Kempe was so renowned, a class can play the game Freeze Tag. It goes like this:

- Arrange the classroom chairs or desks in a circle.
- Send in two students, whom we will call Student A and Student B.
- Select another student to be the Timer.
- Student A begins the dialogue and action with a comment such as, "Oh, my gosh! We need to get you to a doctor!" or "I can't believe you just ate that!" Whatever is said should suggest a certain mood or attitude—concern, anger, curiosity, etc.
- Student B will improvise an answer, and the two will continue in conversation for a while, during which time they use gestures and movement appropriate to the dialogue.
- After a while, when the Timer notices Student A making an interesting gesture or movement, he or she calls out, "Freeze!" Both Student A and Student B freeze in place.
- While B is "frozen," A comes out and is replaced by another student, who must assume the exact same body language that the previous Student A had had when the action was frozen. The new Student A, assuming the same

---

^{a} in

position, starts a completely different dialogue with a completely different tone, and Student B again responds in kind.
- At a good point, the Timer freezes the action again, and Student B is replaced with a new student. Whenever there is a replacement, whoever is designated Student A starts a new dialogue. The action continues, rotating A and B every other time.
- The teacher will determine the length of time to devote to the game.

Tragic Actors

Edward Alleyn

Edward Alleyn
1566-1626

Edward Alleyn, called "Ned" by his contemporaries, was born in 1566 in the parish of St. Botolph's-without-Bishopsgate[a] in London. At the age of sixteen, he was already associated with the traveling troupe maintained by William Somerset, third earl of Worcester [WÜS-tər]), known as Worcester's Men. In 1585, he left this troupe and headed for London, where he hoped to play before the queen.

His introduction into the theatre community of London brought him into contact with theatre businessman Philip Henslowe, whose step-daughter he married. He became a theatre owner with Henslowe and later broadened out into real estate, as well as the other (more unsavory) attraction in Southwark—bear baiting—eventually becoming Bear Master under King James I.

Physically, Alleyn was an imposing man, standing nearly seven feet tall and speaking in stentorian tones, which made him perfect to play some of the Elizabethan theatre's most formidable characters, delivering immortal lines from some of the best plays of the period:

---

[a] In this name, the word *without* means *outside*.

1. As the cruel Tamburlaine in Christopher Marlowe's *Tamburlaine*:

   Holla ye pampered jades of Asia!
   What, can ye draw but twenty miles a day?[199] (4.3.1-2)

2. As Faustus, who sells his soul to the Devil, in Marlowe's *Doctor Faustus*:

   Was this the face that launch'd a thousand ships,
   And burnt the topless towers of Ilium. . . ?[200] (5.1.1874-75)

3. As the murdering Barabas of Marlowe's *The Jew of Malta*:

   The juice of Hebon and Cocytus' breath,
   And all the poisons of the Stygian pool,
   Break from the fiery kingdom, and in this
   Vomit your venom, and envenom her
   That, like a fiend, hath left her father thus![201] (3.4.101-103)

4. As the mad Orlando in Robert Greene's *Orlando Furioso:*

   Villain, provide me straight a lion's skin,
   Thou see'st I now am mighty Hercules;
   Look where's my massy club upon my neck.
   I must to hell,
   To seek for Medor and Angelica,
   Or else I die.[202]

5. As the Duke of York in Shakespeare's *Henry VI, Part 3*:

   O tiger's heart wrapt in a woman's hide!
   How couldst thou drain the life-blood of the child,
   To bid the father wipe his eyes withal,
   And yet be seen to bear a woman's face?[203] (1.4.140-44)

It is no wonder that, in 1598, Edward Guilpin included this reference to Alleyn's portrayal of such characters:

   What humors have possessed him so, I wonder,
   His eyes are lightning and his words are thunder: . . . .
   Stalking and roaring like Job's great devil.[204]

Because of his many business adventures, Alleyn was quite wealthy at the end of his career. In fact, he was so prosperous by 1613 that he was able to pay £35,000 for the manorial estate of Dulwich [DŬL-ĭch], where, in 1619, he founded a school, which he named the College of God's Gift at Dulwich. We get a glimpse into Alleyn's heart when we read that he populated the school with poor boys from his old neighborhood of St. Botolph's:

> Now, there is a legend about his founding of the school to the effect that Alleyn did so out of a sense of terror—and perhaps guilt—for a strange event that happened during a performance, of Christopher Marlowe's *Doctor Faustus*. Alleyn and six others were on stage costumed as devils when a mysterious eighth figure appeared, whom they believed to be an actual demon, if not Satan himself. Unnerved, Alleyn felt the need for atonement and, thus, began the process to set up the school.[205]

Edward Alleyn died on November 21, 1626, and was buried four days later in the chapel of the College of God's Gift at Dulwich, where his remains still lie beneath the floor. He is perhaps best remembered by the words of Thomas Heywood, written fourteen years earlier, that best express his contemporaries' regard for him: "Not Roscius nor Æsope,[a] those tragedians admyred before Christ was borne, could ever performe more in action than famous Ned Allen."[206]

> **The College of God's Gift at Dulwich**
>
> Edward Alleyn endowed the college of God's Gift at Dulwich with £800 per year for the support of one headmaster, one warden, four fellows (three clergymen, a warden, and an organist), four "poor Sisters," and twelve poor boys who were to be instructed till the age of fourteen or sixteen at which time they would be apprenticed for a trade or calling. The institution thrived and today is a boarding school with nearly 1,700 boys between the ages of seven and sixteen, dozens of whom are involved every year in plays performed in the Edward Alleyn Theatre at the school.

Richard Burbage

If Kempe was Shakespeare's go-to comic, his best tragedian was Richard Burbage, son of theatre owner James Burbage. Born in London in 1567, Burbage grew up amidst the bustling theatre business, learning firsthand from his father and, no doubt, spending hours in the playhouses watching rehearsals and listening to the interaction between players and playwrights. Since boys often played the female roles in this time period, it

---

[a] This is not a reference to Aesop, the Greek writer of fables, but to Clodius Aesopus, a Roman actor of the first century AD.

is even possible to imagine him first taking on the roles of children and, perhaps, females at about the age of eleven or twelve.

Little is known of Burbage's education, but, if it was like the standard grammar school education of the day, it focused on the classical languages (Latin and Greek) and the works of literature and theatre of the ancient world. But more central to the education of a future actor would have been the methods of the schoolmasters in the Tudor period: oral recitation, declamation, and memorization of long passages of literature. These methods would have trained young Richard's voice, assisted him in memorizing lines, and feeling comfortable in a performance environment

Strange's Men and the Admiral's Men both performed at James Burbage's theaters in the 1590s, around the time Richard was coming into manhood, and since it is known he was a popular actor by the age of twenty, it is safe to assume that early in his career he played with those companies. He was a member of the most prestigious company, the Lord Chamberlain's, by 1594, the year the troupe first formed a stock company, remaining with them for the rest of his life.

Richard Burbage
1568-1619

One of Burbage's earliest dramatic roles was that of Hieronimo in Thomas Kyd's *The Spanish Tragedy*, and during his career he played lead roles for all the major playwrights of the period. However, it was in the plays of William Shakespeare that Burbage made his name, the first actor ever to play such delicious roles as Romeo, Hamlet, Macbeth, Othello, Lear, and Richard III. In fact, his performance in Shakespeare's *Richard III* was so impressive that Reverend Richard Corbet (1582-1635) once recorded its effect on the imagination of an innkeeper in Leicester. With a keen interest in local history, the good fellow took Corbet and his traveling companions out to see the last battlefield of the Wars of the Roses, where King Richard had been killed by Henry Tudor. Corbet narrates the colloquial innkeeper's bombast this way:

> And on the morrow when he brought us nigh
> Where the two Roses joyn'd, you would suppose,
> Chaucer ne'er made the Romance of the Rose.
> Hear him: "See ye yon wood? There Richard lay
> With his whole army: Look the other way,

> And—lo!—where Richmond in a bed of gorss
> Encamped himself o'er night, and all his force:
> Upon this hill they met." Why, he could tell
> The inch where Richmond stood, where Richard fell:
> Besides what of his knowledge he could say,
> He had authentic notice from the play;
> Which I might guess, by's mustering up the ghosts,
> And policies, not incident to hosts;
> But chiefly by that one perspicuous thing,
> Where he mistook a player for a king.
> For when he would have said, "King Richard died"
> And called—"A horse! a horse!" — he, Burbage cried.[207]

People often ask if King Richard actually cried out for a horse at the Battle of Bosworth Field, but Corbet's anecdote goes some way toward showing that Shakespeare's account and Burbage's interpretation of it are the actual source for the famous line from Act V: "A horse! a horse! My kingdom for a horse!"[208] (5.4.7)

Burbage died on March 6, 1619, and the elegy composed concludes with lines that reveal the esteem in which his contemporaries held him:

> And now, dear Earth, that must enshrine that dust,
> By heaven now committed to thy trust,
> Keep it as precious as the richest mine
> That lies entomb'd in that rich womb of thine,
> That after times may know that much lov'd mould
> From other dust, and cherish it as gold:
> On it be laid some soft but lasting stone,
> With this short epitaph endors'd thereon,
> That every eye may read, and reading, weep:
> 'Tis England's Roscius, Burbage, that I Keep.[209]

Burbage was buried in Shoreditch, the original theatre district, near St. Leonard's Church, where five of his children already lay. Despite the elegy's suggested lofty epitaph, the stone on Burbage's grave suits the great actor well, reading simply, "Exit Burbage."

EXERCISE 9.1: Analyzing Acting Style

DIRECTIONS: Below is a description of the acting style of the great tragedian Richard Burbage written by Richard Flecknoe (c. 1600 – 1678). Please read the description and answer the questions that follow. (Spelling and punctuation have been modernized.)

Richard Burbage's Acting Style
By Richard Flecknoe

(1) Burbidge, of whom we may say that he was a delightful Proteus, so wholly transforming himself into his part, and putting off himself with his clothes, as he never (not so much as in the tiring house) assumed himself again until the play was done. (2) There was as much difference betwixt him and one of our common actors as between a ballad singer who only mouths it and an excellent singer who knows all his graces and can artfully vary and modulate his voice, even to know how much breath he is to give to every syllable. (3) He had all the parts of an excellent orator animating his words with speaking, and speech with action, his auditors being never more delighted than when he spoke, nor more sorry than when he held his peace; (4) yet, even then, he was an excellent actor still, never falling in his part when he had done speaking, but, with his looks and gesture, maintaining it still unto the height, he imagining *Age quod agis* only spoke to him: (5) so as those who call him a player do him wrong, no man being less idle than he whose whole life is nothing else but action, with only this difference from other men's—that as what is but a play to them is his business, so their business is but a play to him.[210]

1. In Sentence #1, there is a reference to Proteus, a figure from Greek mythology. In what way did Flecknoe believe Burbage was like Proteus?

2. In Sentence #2, there is a reference to the "tiring house," which was the dressing (or attiring) room. From that part of the sentence, what do we learn about Burbage's acting ability?

3. In Sentence #3, Flecknoe compares Burbage's style of acting to that of others by referring to ballad singers and excellent singers. In what way does he believe Burbage was like what he calls "excellent singers"?

4. Sentence #4:

   a. Was reciting his lines enough for Burbage? Explain your answer.

   b. What does *Age quod agis* mean? How does it help you understand Richard Burbage?

5. Sentence #5 contains a pun on the word *player*, which was the normal way of referring to an actor in the sixteenth century.

   a. What two meanings of *player* is he referencing here?

   b. What point is Flecknoe trying to make about Burbage by using this pun?

ELIZABETHAN AND JACOBEAN PLAYS

Chapter 10

Introduction

In his play *The Spanish Tragedy*, Thomas Kyd gives Hieronimo to say:

> Comedies are fit for common wits:
> But to present a kingly troop withal,
> Give me a stately-written tragedy;
> *Tragadia cothurnata*, fitting kings,
> Containing matter, and not common things.[211] (4.1)

But why give Comedy such short shrift? After all, American novelist Dawn Powell was on to something when she observed: "The basis of tragedy is man's helplessness against disease, war and death; the basis of comedy is man's helplessness against vanity (the vanity of love, greed, lust, power)."[212]

Tragedy

In his *Poetics*, Aristotle devoted more space to tragedy than to comedy, laying out principles that have long been followed by European (and later American) playwrights. To what degree a writer follows or deviates from Aristotle has often been a measure of the quality of a playwright, though certainly we see Shakespeare at times trying to wiggle out of his Greek strait-jacket, more of which below. Beginning with Aristotle, then, what exactly is tragedy, and what were its requirements?

Definition

In literature, the term *tragedy* has a specific meaning. It does not mean simply a catastrophe such as that wrought by war or typhoons. Rather, Aristotle taught that tragedy was to be "an imitation of an action that is serious, complete, and of a certain magnitude."[213] By *magnitude*, Aristotle meant that the more devastating the effects of the tragic experience, the more suitable it was for tragedy.

Plot in Tragedy

Probability: We often hear the saying, "Truth is stranger than fiction," which concisely states Aristotle's idea that the events in a play should grow out of each other and not depend on coincidence for resolution. Unlike the historian, who records what has already happened—no matter how improbable, the dramatist must construct the plot on what could actually happen according to "the law of probability or necessity."[214] For example, if a character is wandering in a desert and near death for lack of water, it would not be probable for him to "happen" across a well his ancestor had built many decades before. That would be just a bit too convenient and, therefore, not believable.

The only exception Aristotle allowed to the rule against coincidence was that any improbable element was to "lie outside the action of the play,"[215] as in the case of fate or the foreordination of God, or as an opening action in the play. For example, the prophecy that governed the action in Sophocles' *Oedipus Rex* occurred before the opening of the play, and in Shakespeare's *Macbeth*, the witches' prophecy that drove the action of the play was made in Act I.

Parts: As outlined in Chapter 4, Aristotle also stated that the plot of a tragedy would have three parts: Reversal (*peripeteia*), Discovery (*anagnorisis*), and a Scene of Suffering (*pathos*). In other words, the character's situation first changes from good to bad. Then at some point, the character discovers what is actually driving his misfortune. And at the end, the protagonist suffers for his or her errors.

Unities: Aristotle believed that plots should be worked out within certain limitations, which eventually came to be called the *unities* (the principle of oneness). To be specific, a play should have unity of place (one location), time (one day maximum), and action (nothing off topic).

Characters in Tragedy

Morality: Regarding characters, Aristotle stated that protagonists should be good persons with a moral purpose, someone like ourselves with whom the audience can identify. An audience is more likely to feel fear and pity for an essentially good person with a weakness than for a total villain.

Status: Aristotle believed that tragic figures must also be "above the common level,"[216] meaning they should be people of high status such as kings, queens, and nobles, so that the hero's downfall affects large numbers of people. For Aristotle, the life of a woman was less attractive as a topic, and that of a slave (or, as the Elizabethans might have said, a commoner) was "completely worthless."[217] Shakespeare followed this principle of high-status characters by writing plays about kings (*King Lear*), nobles (*Macbeth*), and military generals (*Othello*).

Tragic Hero: The *tragic hero* is the protagonist who brings disaster upon himself or herself due to a bad decision or weakness of character. One example is Shakespeare's Macbeth, who was not a thorough-going villain but was, in essence, a good man who succumbed to the very human trait of wanting better things for himself—or, in Macbeth's case, for his wife.

Tragic Flaw: In cases where one's greatest strength becomes, in the end, his or her greatest weakness, we refer to that characteristic as the character's *tragic flaw*. Shakespeare followed this principle in *Julius Caesar*, in which Brutus's greatest strength (his honor) ultimately brings him down because it subjected him to manipulation by Cassius. Goaded on by Cassius' flattery, Brutus commits a very dishonorable action, which results in remorse and ultimately suicide.

Catharsis

Aristotle required of drama that it affect the emotions of the audience, saying that "through pity and fear" a tragedy should bring about the "proper purgation" of emotion.[218] What exactly does purgation mean with respect to emotion? Anyone who has ever had a hearty laugh or a good cry knows that, afterward, he or she feels better. All the built-up tension has been relieved by these innate vehicles that carry emotional energy out of the body. This feeling of relief is exactly the effect that Aristotle was going for—a kind of calm after the emotional storm that the theatregoer has been observing and experiencing vicariously. This purging is generally referred to as *catharsis* (kə-THÄR-sĭs) [κάθαρσις].

Lars Jacob as Comedy and Tragedy

Comedy

Aristotle's Definition

In his *Poetics*, Aristotle had less to say about Comedy than Tragedy, but nevertheless laid the groundwork for Comedy in the western theatrical tradition, so once again our discussion should begin with him.

It is important to note that Comedy in the classic sense is not necessarily a play that produces laughter, as we might conceive of it today. In fact, sometimes the only difference between a comedy and a tragedy is the ending: a tragedy ends in a death, a comedy with a wedding. In short, the term *Comedy* includes any story that has a happy ending. Shakespeare's *Merchant of Venice*, for example, has some extremely tense scenes with overtones of impending torture, but it is classified as a Comedy because the torture is averted and the final scene involves happy husbands and wives. Still, the subdivision of Comedy into types allows for plays that produce plenty of laughter, as we shall see below. Aristotle's definition of Comedy includes a prescription for the type of characters whose lives are represented. He said, "Comedy is . . . an imitation of characters of a lower type—not, however, in the full sense of the word *bad*, the ludicrous being merely a subdivision of the ugly."[219] *Oxford Dictionaries* defines *ludicrous* as "so foolish, unreasonable, or out of place as to be amusing," and points out, interestingly, that the word is derived from the Latin word *ludrum*, meaning *stage play*. Below we will look at some of the types of play that fit this definition.

Comic Characters

Imperfections: The protagonist in a Comedy, though not a villain, is not necessarily moral, as the protagonist in a Tragedy is, though he or she will without question have certain foibles. The comic character might be conniving, puffed-up, bawdy, or selfish in ways that expose the human condition and evoke laughter. Aristotle drew this distinction: "Comedy aims at representing men as worse, Tragedy as better than in actual life."[220]

Social Status: Whereas Tragedy centered on high-status characters, Comedy could focus on "characters of a lower type."[221] Accordingly, Shakespeare's most famous comic character, Falstaff, is a petty thief and laggard who whiles away most of his time drinking ale and dozing in a tavern. He is, above all, a commoner of London, with whom Prince Henry enjoys frittering away his own time much to the dismay of his father, the king. Falstaff's shortcomings are depicted at the outset of *Henry IV, Part I*, when Prince Henry finds the old man lounging around in his (the prince's) apartments:

FALSTAFF
Now, Hal, what time of day is it, lad?

PRINCE HENRY
Thou art so fat-witted with drinking of old
sack, and unbuttoning thee after supper, and
sleeping upon benches after noon, that thou hast
forgotten to demand that truly which thou wouldst
truly know. What a devil hast thou to do with
the time of the day? Unless hours were cups of
sack. . . .[222] (1.2.6-8).

Types of Comedy

Comedy of Situation: Denton Jacques Snider once explained that, in a Comedy of Situation, "a person is placed in circumstances over which he has little or no control, and is made to pursue absurd and nugatory[a] objects without any direct fault of his own. His deception is brought about through the senses; his mistakes arise from false appearances which hover around him — in general, that which is phantom seems reality."[223] Shakespeare brilliantly displayed Comedy of Situation in *Midsummer Night's Dream*, in which Bottom the Weaver is placed under a spell by the mischievous faerie Puck, who changes Bottom's head to that of an ass and enchants Titania, the queen of the faeries, so that when she awakes, she will fall in love with the first thing she sees—the "ass." Bottom, naturally, is not quite sure what it is that the queen of faeries finds so fascinating in him.

Comedy of Character: Snider also explained that in a Comedy of Character, "[T]he individual is self-determined; his situation, in its essential points, is the consequence of his own action — of his own folly or weakness; he is not plunged into it from without, by fate or by accident." A classic example is Shakespeare's *The Merry Wives of Windsor*, in which Shakespeare's greatest comic character, the portly, aging Falstaff, gets his come-

---

[a] worthless

uppance when he connives to woo two wealthy married women in order to help himself to their wealth.

Tragicomedy

Tragicomedy, as the name suggests, is a play which mixes elements of tragedy and comedy. One kind of tragicomedy is truly dark in tone and content but has "a happy ending." *The Winter's Tale* by Shakespeare is one example, a play which portrays false charges of infidelity, madness, child abandonment, death, and grief but ends, nevertheless, happily when the abandoned child, now a young woman, returns home and her mother, dead for many years, returns to life. As is typical of Comedy, the play ends in a wedding.

Another kind of tragicomedy might have a serious subject which is relieved now and then by comic elements. When the darkness of a play is building tension and suspense in the audience, the author will write in a comic character, whose buffooning causes laughter, releasing the built-up tension. One of the most famous examples is in Act II of Shakespeare's *Macbeth*. In Scene 2, Macbeth commits two murders, comes to the verge of insanity when he starts hearing voices, is unable to wash the blood from his hands, and is called cowardly by Lady Macbeth, for whom he committed the murders in the first place. Dark indeed, so Shakespeare immediately follows in Scene 3 with a comic scene wherein the old gatekeeper at the castle renders some good lines in which he shows dismay at the knocking at the gate which requires him to fumble for the key and answer the door. This technique by which tension from a dark scene is reduced by a subsequent lighter scene is called *comic relief*.

Masques

Masques, which were popular in the seventeenth century, were elaborate plays centering on characters from classical mythology. They involved beautiful costumes, music, dancing, stage scenery (new to England), and stage machinery for special effects. Their cost, of course, was very high, and they were not performed in the public theatres but at court, where members of the nobility would often play a role. Because of the singing and dancing, which sometimes included members of the audience, the masque is thought of as the ancestor of twentieth-century musicals.

Ben Jonson is the English playwright whose name is most associated with masques. One of them, called *The Masque of Blackness*. Controversial in our time due to the use of "blackface" (body painting using soot and ash to depict an African character), the play appeared at a time when the English people were beginning to show great interest in the "red Indian" and the black African, who were considered exotic and, therefore, fascinating.[224] In fact, it was Anne of Denmark, the wife of King James I, who requested Jonson to write her a play in which she and her ladies-in-waiting could be costumed as "blackamoors." The play has little plot—after all, its purpose was mainly to allow lords and ladies to have a bit of fun at a party—but has all the marks of a masque: mythological characters (Oceanus, Niger, Aetheiop) and exotic costumes. Jonson himself described some of the costuming this way:

Queen Anne, consort of James I, in blackface for *The Masque of Blackness*, 1605

> The attire of the masquers was alike in all, without difference: the colors azure and silver; their hair thick and curled upright in tresses, like pyramids, but returned on the top with a scroll and antique dressing of feathers, and jewels interlaced with ropes of pearl. And for the front, ear, neck, and wrists, the ornament was of the most choice and orient pearl best setting off from the black.
>
> For the light-bearers, sea-green, waved about the skirts with gold and silver, their hair loose and flowing garlanded with sea grass, and that stuck with branches of coral.[225]

Witch Plays

When Queen Elizabeth I died without an heir in 1603, the Crown passed to her cousin James VI of Scotland. He was twenty years old. Since he was the first king of England to be named James, he was known there as James I, and is usually styled as James VI and I for this reason.

James was born into a Scotland that was already engaged in ridding the country of the practice of witchcraft. In 1563, during the reign of James's mother, Mary Queen of Scots, Parliament had passed a bill called the Scottish Witchcraft Act. This law required the death penalty for either practicing witchcraft or consulting with witches. English Parliaments under Henry VIII and Queen Elizabeth had also passed laws against witchcraft, but when James assumed the English throne, he expanded the law, requiring the death penalty to apply also to those who kept "familiars," evil spirits who took the form of household animals such as cats.

Unlike most people today, who consider witches to be mythological creatures or possibly a symbol of evil, people of James's day believed them to be absolutely real. We can debate whether there was any real power in witchcraft, but the important thing here is that the people of seventeenth-century England and Scotland definitely believed so, attributing the source of their power to Satan. There were actual practitioners of witchcraft, but, no doubt, some put on trial were innocent.

Though some might think that putting witches to death was too severe a penalty for the crime, it is important to remember the current notion that just as a murderer could kill one's body, a witch could kill one's soul. Therefore, they reasoned, if murderers were put to death, so witches should be. As a denizen of this culture and the head of the Church, to boot, James took his responsibility very seriously and even wrote a treatise on the subject entitled *Daemonologie* to educate the populace about the nature and types of witches. The preface to this work begins with these words:

> The fearful abounding at this time in this country, of these detestable slaves of the Devil, the witches or enchanters, hath moved me (beloved reader) to dispatch in post, this following treatise of mine, not in any way . . . to serve for a show of my learning and ingine,[a] but only (moved of conscience) to press thereby, so far as I can, to resolve the doubting hearts of many; both that such assaults of Satan are most certainly practiced, and that the instruments thereof merit most severely to be punished.[226]

Playwrights had long known that they would be able to maintain their freedom by presenting kings and queens with versions of life and history that reflected the royal worldview. Therefore, English playwrights soon began to compose plays about witchcraft to please the new king, the most well-known being Shakespeare's *Macbeth*. The first thing to say about plays with a theme of witchcraft is that the playwrights rarely made witches the objects of humor. They clearly presented them as evil and sometimes focused on whether they could find eternal salvation in Christ, even if repentant.

---

[a] Ingenuity, mental ability

One such play was *The Late Lancashire Witches* by Thomas Heywood and Richard Brome, which opened at the Globe in 1634 during the reign of Charles I. This play was based on the transcript of a series of actual witchcraft trials that took place in Pendle, Lancashire, in February of that year and resulted in the hangings of nine people. Many of the trappings of witchcraft that are stereotypical today were depicted in this play, especially teleportation by broom (more of which anon).

The play could be classified as a tragicomedy since it does not actually end in a death. Instead, the witches are led off to be put on trial (when the play was written, verdicts had not yet been reached). For the most part, the play has an uncanny tone, but one scene in which invisible witches descend and break up a wedding cake has been termed a "farce."[227]

The Sound of Elizabethan Plays

Present-Day British English

Students who are called upon to play a part in which the characters are English (either in Shakespeare or otherwise, as in *My Fair Lady*) sometimes like to make a stab at the intonation and pronunciation of words as spoken in Standard British English today. One can find videos online that will explain how to hold the tongue to make certain sounds, and so on, but there is one trick that will bring about a number of results with one simple move: jut your jaw out so that your lower teeth are just slightly in front of your upper teeth. By doing so, your mouth is in such a position that it is almost impossible to make a post-vocalic *r* (that is, an *r* that follows a vowel).

Benedict Cumberbatch as Sherlock Holmes, 2010

To actually see this jaw position, view the following interview with English actress Emma Thompson, which appears on *YouTube* at this URL:

<https://www.youtube.com/watch?v=7MgM3jL6XUE>.

Try reading the following lines from Hamlet first with your jaw in normal position for American English, then with the jaw thrust forward for a more British sound. Listen closely to what happens to the *r* in some of these words. Speaking to the ghost of Hamlet's father, Horatio says:

> What art thou that usurp'st this time of night,
> Together with that fair and warlike form
> In which the majesty of buried Denmark
> Did sometimes march? by heaven I charge thee, speak![228] (1.1.54-58)

A bit of practice every day should soon have you sounding as if you just got off a flight from London.

ACTIVITY 10.A: Practicing an English Accent

DIRECTIONS: This exercise will give you the opportunity to practice reading Shakespeare's Sonnet XVIII with your jaw thrust forward to produce a more British-sounding accent. To hear it first read by an English actor, pull up the video of English actor Michael York. Listen to the sound of the words and watch what the actor is doing with his jaw. URL:

<https://www.youtube.com/watch?v=1AfeHREVp4I>.

Sonnet XVIII

Shall I compare thee to a summer's day?
Thou art more lovely and more temperate:
Rough winds do shake the darling buds of May,
And summer's lease hath all too short a date:
Sometime too hot the eye of heaven shines,
And often is his gold complexion dimmed,
And every fair from fair sometime declines,
By chance, or nature's changing course untrimmed:
But thy eternal summer shall not fade,
Nor lose possession of that fair thou ow'st,
Nor shall death brag thou wander'st in his shade,
When in eternal lines to time thou grow'st,
So long as men can breathe, or eyes can see,
So long lives this, and this gives life to thee.

The Early Modern Accent

All of us have heard various English-language accents in movies and on television: American, English, Scottish, and Australian, for example. Besides the position of the jaw, there are vowel sounds that also distinguish the accents. One example is the contraction *can't*, which is pronounced in the United States as /kănt/, but in England, as /känt/. Even within the United States, the word *aunt* might be pronounced either as /ănt/, rhyming with the name of the insect, or as /änt/, which sounds more British.

From examples such as this, we can conclude that words (mainly the vowels in the words) may differ as one moves geographically, that is, through space, but what about moving through time? For example, a student might look at this famous passage from *Hamlet* and wonder why the second and fourth words are spelled alike but are pronounced (in American English) quite differently:

> Doubt thou the stars are fire;
> Doubt that the sun doth move;
> Doubt truth to be a liar;
> But never doubt I love.[229] (2.2.124-27)

This is the point at which the student may start to wonder, "Hey, what's up with Shakespeare? He couldn't even rhyme his words!" Well, the answer is that in Shakespeare's time, they did rhyme. The word *love* would have been pronounced with the same vowel sound as in *move*.

If we transfer these principles to Early Modern English, which was Shakespeare's language, we see that, as with Chaucer's poetic lines, Shakespeare's would have been received differently by his audience than by ours. Returning to the original quotation from Hamlet, we now can understand why *love* would have been pronounced as /lūv/. Give it a try by reading these lines aloud so that the two italicized words rhyme:

> Doubt thou the stars are fire;
> Doubt that the sun doth *move*;
> Doubt truth to be a liar;
> But never doubt I *love*.

By Shakespeare's time, enough had changed that the final *-e* was no longer articulated in English words so that both *move* and *love* would have been articulated as one-syllable words, just as they are today. However, the articulation of the suffix *-ed* was in a state of flux in Shakespeare's time, which gave him great flexibility in making his lines scan in iambic pentameter. One often finds *-ed* pronounced /əd/, as in the line from *Julius Caesar*, "The good is oft interrèd with their bones." Most editors assist the reader by using a stress mark above the *e*, as you see in *interrèd*, signaling to the reader to pronounce the word as /ĭn-TĀR-əd/, but in cases where Shakespeare's words would have sounded the same as ours, they employ an apostrophe, to indicate that the *e* has been collapsed, as we see in Horatio's line about the ghost in *Hamlet*:

What, has this thing appear'd again tonight?[230] (1.1.30)

In both cases, the past tense suffix *-ed* follows an *r*. In one word it is articulated; in the other, it is not. In present-day English, the vowel in the past tense suffix is only spoken if it follows *t* or *d* (*wanted, wounded*), but all others have been clipped just to the consonant (*puffed, waned*). Amazingly, there are a few adjectives which have retained the full pronunciation of the *-ed* suffix: *wicked, learned, beloved, blessed*, and (when reading from the King James Bible) *hallowed*.

One last word to actors: Lately there has been a publishing trend whereby the accent mark and/or the apostrophe are no longer printed in Shakespearean text. For example, online sources often render *interrèd* as *interred*, and the Folger Shakespeare Library renders *appear'd* as *appeared*. Still, the actor needs to know when to and when not to articulate the vowel.

ACTIVITY 10.B: The Sound of Shakespeare's English

David Crystal, Honorary Professor of Linguistics at the University of Wales, has done considerable research on the pronunciation of Early Modern English, which he calls Original Pronunciation (OP). He has made available on *YouTube* a video in which he and his son Ben read the same Shakespearean lines, Ben with the present-day pronunciation, and David with the original. The examples they have chosen to read reveal some puns that Shakespeare's audience would have caught, but which are entirely lost in modern renderings. The ten-minute video can be viewed at this URL:

< https://www.youtube.com/watch?v=gPlpphT7n9s >.

In some ways, David Crystal's presentation sounds much like the way a Scot would read the lines. One Scottish actor whose pronunciation can be used for comparison is David Tennant, who plays the BBC's tenth Dr. Who. Now, Tennant is perfectly capable of imitating almost any accent, but you can hear him read Shakespeare's Sonnet XVIII with his native Scottish flair at this URL:

<https://www.youtube.com/watch?v=nD6Of-pwKP4&list=PLUbjVS8GVE8-0fiG7uNOORIdpegLI-aAY#t=1.5234042>.

After listening, try to pinpoint with your class exactly what features of the Scottish dialect match that of Crystal's OP.

WHY SHAKESPEARE?

Chapter 11

Introduction

If old English teachers were like old disc jockeys, they would probably have read enough William Shakespeare in their time to have a hunch why he has been at Number One on the charts, so to speak, for the past 500 years and shows no sign of slipping anytime soon. But what about the young people just launching out on the sea of English-language literature who often ask, "What's the big deal about Shakespeare?"

Thus, in a book about theatre written for young people, it behooves "ye olde English teacher" to set down on paper just what it is that sets the Bard of Avon apart from any other word-weaver in the English-speaking world. Below is a list (probably incomplete) of the many reasons why Shakespeare remains unsurpassed.

Let's begin with Aristotle's *Poetics* and see if Mr. Shakespeare measures up to the standard that was established in the Classical Age.

Action (or Plot)

Aristotle believed that, before anything else, a quality play required a good tale. Otherwise, who would stay through the fifth act? On this score, Shakespeare truly measures up. He had a way of packing theatres just on the strength of his plots alone. He used not only plots, but sub-plots, and in *Hamlet* actually had three plots going at once—and a play-within-a-play, to boot. Another example of a plot with pleasant twists and turns is *A Comedy of Errors*, in which an audience member's brain gets quite a workout tracking all the confusion resulting from the appearance in Ephesus of two persons (a master and servant) who are identical twins—unknown to each other—of well-known persons in town (also a master and servant). And we can't forget *Othello,* in which the audience watches the machinations of the villain, Iago, as he sets up a complicated plot that will lead to the ruin of his rival. By exercising not only the imagination, but the intellect, the audience becomes enthralled with the play.

Character

Shakespeare's characters are always individuals, not types. They have such staying power that they are remembered as if they had been real people. Even people who have never read *Romeo and Juliet*, for instance, nevertheless know the names of the two "star-crossed lovers" whom Shakespeare created five centuries ago. His characterization of Richard III, moreover, was so robust that, single-handedly, he turned the last Plantagenet king into such a villainous monster that even today reputable historians must begin their work with Shakespeare's depiction seared in their minds. Even the characters Shakespeare borrowed from the ancients were vastly re-worked (one could even say improved) by his wizardry. His re-drawing of the lovers Pyramus and Thisbe into hilarious comic figures in *A Midsummer Night's Dream* has meant that many people are only aware of Shakespeare's duo, not the classic pair. The breathlessness of Juliet, the wickedness of Iago, the witchery of Prospero, the madness of Lear, the mirth of Falstaff—all these (and more) provide evidence of Shakespeare's unmatched proficiency at characterization.

Idea

A work that achieves the status of a classic is one that addresses a universal idea, or theme. As with action and character, Shakespeare excels in this realm as well, providing perspectives on such human interests as justice in *The Merchant of Venice*, honor in *Julius Caesar*, and war in *Henry V*. He shows us the consequences of rash behavior in *Romeo and Juliet*, the evils of acting without knowing all the facts in *Othello*, and the horrors induced by a guilty conscience in *Macbeth*. He presents to his audience the onerous "lot of woman," by inserting a serious conversation into his *Comedy of Errors*. He addresses the supernatural in *Macbeth* and *The Tempest*, as well as the depravity of the human heart in *Titus Andronicus*, yet never loses sight of the Christian worldview:

> Let never day nor night unhallowed pass,
> But still remember what the Lord hath done.[231]
>
> (*Henry VI, Part II*, 2.1.94-94)

Diction

The term *diction* refers to the way an author uses language. Since the English of Shakespeare was what we now call the Early Modern form of the language, his works present a challenge to audiences today. Two complaints normally crop up with beginning Shakespeare students. The first concerns the use of the second-person pronouns *thou, thee, thy,* and *thine,* an issue addressed in the next chapter. The second concerns Shakespeare's word choice. "Why can't Shakespeare just say things straight out instead of couching everything in 'fancy words'?" students often ask.

American actor Kevin Conway answered the question this way:

> In a contemporary play, somebody would say, "Hey, you, go over there, get that thing and bring it back to me." That would be the line. Shakespeare says it: "Be Mercury, set feathers to thy heels, / And fly like thought from them to me again"[232] (*King John* 4.2.182-83).

Much more creative, isn't it? It leaves the average writer saying, "I wish I had written that!" A closer look at that quotation reveals not only the creative word choice Shakespeare used, but also his inclusion of a metaphor, a simile, and a classical allusion—and all in perfect iambic pentameter. And he went on like that for line after line, poem after poem, play after play—for twenty-five years!

Shakespeare's diction allowed for tone (serious, sarcastic, affectionate, etc.), rhetorical form (such as the elements of the progymnasmata), and the compression of lofty thoughts into tight epigrams. Moreover, he created 1,700 new words that have become basic vocabulary in today's language (e.g., *blanket, dawn,* and *skim milk*), and he invented expressions so apt that their use over time has almost turned them into trite clichés. Such phrases as *bated breath, break the ice,* and *for goodness' sake* were all Shakespeare's inventions.

What is more, figures of speech were almost exhaled by Shakespeare with his every breath. One wonders if he learned all those tropes at the Stratford grammar school or if they just came naturally to him. Whatever the case, if Shakespeare and any other writer (including Aristotle himself) were to run a "trope race," so to speak, it would not be at all surprising if Shakespeare took the gold in the Literary Olympics every year. He is that good. Since a claim such as this requires some support, a hefty list is available for your amazement and amusement in Appendix E, but here let us content ourselves with a trope that Shakespeare could use like no other: *antanaclasis,* a type of pun in which a word is often repeated as different parts of speech and/or with different meanings.

One example comes from *Romeo and Juliet,* when the nurse arrives with the news of Romeo's fight with Tybalt. The nurse is so upset at Tybalt's death that she simply cries out, "He is dead!" leading Juliet to believe (mistakenly) that Romeo is dead. To show Juliet's inner turmoil, Shakespeare continues for seven lines, jumbling together the words *eye, I,* and *aye* (a synonym for *yes*). The lines suggest confusion at first, but, when analyzed, show Shakespeare's masterful wordplay. Note that he plays with spelling here as well, though the audience would just have heard the oral presentation:

> JULIET
> Hath Romeo slain himself? say thou but "I,"
> And that bare vowel "I" shall poison more
> Than the death-darting eye of cockatrice:
> I am not I, if there be such an I;
> Or those eyes shut, that make thee answer "I."
> If he be slain, say "I"; or if not, no:
> Brief sounds determine of my weal or woe.[233] (3.2.43-51)

Not only the language of the sixteenth century, but also the religious and political environment affected Shakespeare's style. Because Shakespeare was born while Elizabeth I was queen, he was raised in the Protestant Church of England, and the queen took it seriously: church attendance was mandatory. Therefore, in the Stratford church, the future poet became well versed in Scripture, which he memorized from the Geneva Bible (King James had not come along yet). Quotations and echoes of these Bible verses would be sprinkled throughout his plays in future years. In *Hamlet*, for example, when the young prince is goaded into participating in a contest of swordsmanship, his friend Horatio, fearing he is overmatched, offers him a way out:

> HORATIO
> If your mind dislike anything, obey it. I will
> forestall their repair hither and say you are not fit.
>
> HAMLET
> Not a whit. We defy augury. There is [a]
> special providence in the fall of a sparrow. (5.2.231-34)

Hamlet's words here are a clear echo of Jesus' words from Matthew 10:29, which reads in the Geneva version, "Are not two sparrows sold for a farthing, and one of them shall not fall on the ground without your Father?"

Now, in 1604, shortly after coming to the throne, King James I decided to authorize the translation of the Bible from Greek into English. At the time, Shakespeare was well known to the king as a member of his acting troupe and, arguably, the ablest handler of the English language, which leads some people to wonder if he was invited to help polish the translations done by scholars of theology. In this regard, one theorist, with perhaps too much time on his hands, once discovered what some think is Shakespeare's signature in the Bible. The whirlwind of attention focuses on Psalm 46. Counting down 46 words in the KJV version of that psalm leads us to the word *shake*, while counting up 46 words leads us to the word *spear*. This fact in and of itself is not remarkable. However, the polishing of the text would have been done in 1611, which just happens to be the year Will Shakespeare turned 46, so the question arises: Did

King James Bible 1611

Shakespeare, in fact, sneak his signature into this psalm? Some smile with glee at the thought and others frown with disapproval, and, of course, we will never know for sure, but you can examine the "evidence" by reading the psalm yourself:

Psalm 46
King James Version

God is our refuge and strength, a very present help in trouble.

Therefore will not we fear, though the earth be removed, and though the mountains be carried into the midst of the sea;

Though the waters thereof roar and be troubled, though the mountains *shake* with the swelling thereof. Selah.

There is a river, the streams whereof shall make glad the city of God, the holy place of the tabernacles of the most High.

God is in the midst of her; she shall not be moved: God shall help her, and that right early.

The heathen raged, the kingdoms were moved: he uttered his voice, the earth melted.

The Lord of hosts is with us; the God of Jacob is our refuge. Selah.

Come, behold the works of the Lord, what desolations he hath made in the earth.

He maketh wars to cease unto the end of the earth; he breaketh the bow, and cutteth the *spear* in sunder; he burneth the chariot in the fire.

Be still, and know that I am God: I will be exalted among the heathen, I will be exalted in the earth.

The Lord of hosts is with us; the God of Jacob is our refuge. Selah.

Song

Song refers to the musical interludes of the Chorus. In Shakespeare's plays, the Chorus appears usually as a prologue (introduction) or epilogue (conclusion). Instead of the group of singers or chanters common to Greek plays, Shakespeare's Chorus was an individual who spoke directly to the audience. Shakespeare also wrote songs to help set the mood of a scene and included singers and musicians in his plays.

Spectacle

The term spectacle refers to the visual interest of the play. By Shakespeare's time, stage machinery had advanced considerably, and, as we have seen, the Elizabethans were able to manage smoke, fire, and cannon bursts onstage; to build stage machinery which would allow characters to "fly"; and to use elaborate and colorful costumes as "eye candy" for the audience. And, if Elizabethan special effects fell short of the real thing, Shakespeare would employ language to enhance the visual image in the listener's mind, as when he implied the existence of dark clouds, as in *The Tempest* when Miranda says, "The sky, it seems, would pour down stinking pitch."[234] (1.2.3)

Psychology

But beyond satisfying Aristotle, what sets Shakespeare apart from the many other European authors who also followed Aristotle's lead? To answer that question, let us turn to the field of psychology.

Emotions

Shakespeare understood human beings so well that his plots and characters burst with rich insights into the human condition. He shows, for example, the effects of jealousy (Othello in the play *Othello*), envy (Cassius in *Julius Caesar*), betrayal (Cressida in *Troilus and Cressida*), lust for power (Lady Macbeth in *Macbeth*), peer pressure (Cassio in *Othello*), guilt (Macbeth and Lady Macbeth in *Macbeth*), remorse (Brutus in *Julius Caesar*), and manipulation (Iago in *Othello*).

What is more, Shakespeare was far ahead of his time in his understanding of specific mental disorders, which even in the twenty-first century are still being researched and named. Below are some of the mental conditions he explored with various characters centuries before they were scientifically studied.

Borderline Personality Disorder (BPD)

In *Antony and Cleopatra*, Shakespeare delineated the classic features of borderline personality disorder. Psychiatrist Dr. Jonathan D. Lewis put it this way:

> What took a committee of distinguished psychiatrists decades to define, a single genius accomplished in the space of perhaps a month. . . . Shakespeare creates a Cleopatra who demonstrates affective [emotional] instability, identity disturbances, a hunger for proclamations of love, feelings of emptiness at the prospect of being abandoned, an intense and unstable relationship with Antony, an extensive history of suicidal behavior, and uncontrolled anger in a frantic attempt to avoid being abandoned by the latest of her many lovers. Shakespeare's Cleopatra is the quintessential borderline personality.[235]

Depression

The Mayo Clinic defines depression as "a mood disorder that causes a persistent feeling of sadness and loss of interest." Depression is all-consuming. It affects how a person feels, thinks, and believes and "can lead to a variety of emotional and physical problems."[236] The Shakespearean character that best expresses the symptoms of depression (called *melancholy* at that time) is Jaques in *As You Like It*, who, feigning madness, is described in Act II by a person who observed him lying under an oak near a brook:

> FIRST LORD
> The wretched animal heaved forth such groans
> That their discharge did stretch his leathern coat
> Almost to bursting, and the big round tears
> Coursed one another down his innocent nose
> In piteous chase (1.2.37-41)

Then in Act 4, Jaques' own line acknowledges the condition:

> JAQUES
> [I]t is a melancholy
> of mine own, compounded of many simples, extracted
> from many objects, and indeed the sundry
> contemplation of my travels, in which my often
> rumination wraps me in a most humorous[a] sadness.[237] (4.1.18-22)

Schizophrenia

Schizophrenia is a serious mental disease characterized, in part, by hearing voices, losing touch with reality, and speaking in a nonsensical way. Several of Shakespeare's characters exhibit these symptoms, most notably Lady Macbeth, who sees floating daggers and permanent bloodstains on her hands. In response to his wife's hallucinations and disordered speech, Macbeth beseeches the physician, "Canst thou not minister to a mind diseased?"

But *Macbeth* is not the only play that depicts schizophrenia. Psychiatrist N. M. Bark has argued that Shakespeare's understanding of schizophrenia even penetrated to the characteristic of "clothing redundancy," the wearing of multiple layers of clothes.[238] This fixation is displayed by Edgar, in his disguise as Tom, in *King Lear*:

> GLOUCESTER
> What are you there? Your names?

> EDGAR
> Poor Tom, that eats the swimming frog, the
> toad, the tadpole, the wallnewt, and the water; that

---

[a] moody

in the fury of his heart, when the foul fiend
rages, eats cow dung for sallets, swallows the old
rat and the ditch-dog; drinks the green mantle of
the standing pool; who is whipped from tithing to
tithing, and stock-punished, and imprisoned;
*who hath had three suits to his back and six shirts to
his body* . . . . [239](Emphasis added.) (3.4.36-47)

Such attention to detail proves Shakespeare to have been an astute observer of human behavior.

Ophelia Syndrome

Professor Thomas G. Plummer used Shakespeare's character Ophelia from the play *Hamlet* to coin the term *Ophelia Syndrome*. Plummer refers to the conversation between Ophelia and her bossy father, Polonius, who asks her what she thinks of "the Lord Hamlet" in this passage from Act 1:

> POLONIUS
> What is between you? give me up the truth.
>
> OPHELIA
> He hath, my lord, of late made many tenders
> Of his affection to me.
>
> POLONIUS
> Affection! puh! you speak like a green girl,
> Unsifted in such perilous circumstance.
> Do you believe his tenders, as you call them?
>
> OPHELIA
> I do not know, my lord, what I should think.
>
> POLONIUS
> Marry,[a] I'll teach you.[240] (1.3.107-12)

---

[a] When *marry* appears at the beginning of a sentence, it is an interjection used for transition.

The term *Ophelia Syndrome*, then, describes one person's dependence (in this case Ophelia's) on another's perceptions (in this case Polonius's). It is not a healthy practice, and it ends badly for Ophelia. She commits suicide in Act 4.

Obsessive-Compulsive Disorders

Dr. Bruce Hubbard has stated that obsessive worriers "are plagued by thoughts and images of disastrous outcomes that in reality may never come to be."[241] As a result, they simply do nothing. The passage below from *Measure for Measure* shows that Shakespeare understood this incapacitating fear:

> ISABELLA
> Alas! what poor ability's in me
> To do him good?
>
> LUCIO
> Assay the power you have.
>
> ISABELLA
> My power? Alas, I doubt—
>
> LUCIO
>   Our doubts are traitors
> And make us lose the good we oft might win
> By fearing to attempt.[242] (1.4.81-87)

Paranoia

Psychologists Daniel Freeman and Jason Freeman have defined *paranoia* as "the unrealistic belief that other people want to harm us" and point to Shakespeare's Leontes for an example:[243]

> LEONTES
> There is a plot against my life, my crown;
> All's true that is mistrusted: that false villain
> Whom I employed was pre-employed by him:
> He has discovered my design, and I
> Remain a pinched thing; yea, a very trick
> For them to play at will.[244] (*The Winter's Tale* 2.1.58-63)

Sociology

In addition to understanding the mind of the individual, Shakespeare showed he had a grasp of social relationships at all levels. In fact, some of his most memorable lines are those which express the joys and woes of various relationships, as in the following quotations:

The Soldiers' Bond

In *Henry V*, Shakespeare characterized the bond between soldiers:

> HENRY V
> This story shall the good man teach his son;
> And Crispin Crispian shall ne'er go by,
> From this day to the ending of the world,
> But we in it shall be remembered—
> We few, we happy few, we band of brothers;
> For he today that sheds his blood with me
> Shall be my brother . . . [245] (4.3.58-64).

Civil Factions

In *Romeo and Juliet*, Shakespeare exposed the devastating results of civil feuds:

> PRINCE ESCALUS
> Where be these enemies? Capulet! Montague!
> See, what a scourge is laid upon your hate,
> That heaven finds means to kill your joys with love . . . [246] (5.4.301-303).

Influence

In *Twelfth Night*, he showed the limits of an individual's influence:

> SIR TOBY BELCH
> Dost thou think, because thou art virtuous,
> there shall be no more cakes and ale?[247] (2.3.114-15)

Leaders and Followers

In *Henry IV, Part 2*, he commented on the responsibilities of leadership:

HENRY IV
Uneasy lies the head that wears a crown.[248] (3.1.31)

In *Henry V*, he examined the sometimes conflicting claims of duty and moral responsibility:

HENRY V
Every subject's duty is
The king's; but every subject's soul is his own.[249] (4.1.182)

The Accused and the Courts

In *The Merchant of Venice*, he addressed the issues of mercy and justice:

PORTIA
The quality of mercy is not strained.
It droppeth as the gentle rain from heaven
Upon the place beneath. It is twice blessed:
It blesseth him that gives and him that takes.[250] (4.1.190-93)

Racial and Ethnic Groups

In *The Merchant of Venice*, he drew attention to the common humanity of all people:

SHYLOCK
        I am a Jew. Hath not
a Jew eyes? Hath not a Jew hands, organs,
dimensions, senses, affections, passions? Fed with
the same food, hurt with the same weapons, subject to
the same diseases, healed by the same means,
warmed and cooled by the same winter and summer
as a Christian is? If you prick us, do we not
bleed? If you tickle us, do we not laugh? If you
poison us, do we not die? And if you wrong us, shall
we not revenge?[251] (3.1.57-66)

In *The Comedy of Errors*, he drew attention to the hostile relationship between persons of different nationalities:

> DUKE SOLINUS OF EPHESUS
> Merchant of Syracuse, plead no more;
> . . . .
> [I]f any born at Ephesus
> Be seen at Syracusian marts and fairs;
> Again, if any Syracusian born
> Come to the bay of Ephesus, he dies,
> His goods confiscate to the Duke's dispose . . .[252] (1.1.3, 16-20).

Parents and Children

In *A Midsummer Night's Dream*, he raised questions about the fairness of a father's selecting a husband for his daughter:

> HERMIA
> I do entreat your grace to pardon me
> . . . .
> But I beseech your grace that I may know
> The worst that may befall me in this case,
> If I refuse to wed Demetrius.
>
> THESEUS
> Either to die the death or to abjure
> Forever the society of men.[253] (1.1. 60, 64-68)

In *King Lear*, he also addressed the ways in which children can disappoint their parents:

> LEAR
> How sharper than a serpent's tooth it is
> To have a thankless child![254] (1.4.302-303)

Health

Health and physical well-being are, of course, just as important as mental well-being, so it is not surprising to discover that Shakespeare was keenly aware of body issues, too. Still, his goal was not simply to comment on physical conditions that any person can easily perceive, but to illustrate how physical weaknesses affect one's life and relationships.

Perceptions of Body Types

In *Julius Caesar*, Shakespeare shows us the influence of stereotypes based on body type:

> CAESAR
> Let me have men about me that are fat;
> Sleek-headed men and such as sleep o' nights:
> Yond Cassius has a lean and hungry look;
> He thinks too much: such men are dangerous.[255] (1.2.202-205)

Aging

Like all of humankind, Shakespeare had to grow old. However, even in his first play, when he was only twenty-seven, he already showed an understanding of our common fate:

> TALBOT
> O young John Talbot! I did send for thee
> To tutor thee in stratagems of war,
> That Talbot's name might be in thee revived
> When sapless age and weak unable limbs
> Should bring thy father to his drooping chair.[256] (*Henry VI, Part 1*, 4.5.1-5)

Substance Abuse

In *Othello*, the manipulative Iago capitalizes on Cassio's sensitivity to alcohol by pressuring him to drink against his will. He then exploits the resulting drunkenness by seeing to it that Cassio loses his position of trust with Othello. Cassio's comment:

> OTHELLO
>   O God,
> that men should put an enemy in their
> mouths to steal away their brains![257] (2.2.308-310)

Reactions to Deformity

Even in an "enlightened" time such as ours, when we strive to treat the disabled as we would anyone else, people often feel uncomfortable around a person who is "different" in some visible way. In previous centuries, it was even worse. Physical deformity was seen as the mark of Cain, an outward sign of inward evil, a perception Shakespeare used to effect in his depiction of King Richard III. Knowing that one of Richard's shoulders was slightly higher than the other (we now know that he had scoliosis), Shakespeare led King Henry VI to hurl these insults at Richard:

> HENRY
> The owl shrieked at thy birth—an evil sign;
> The night-crow cried, aboding luckless time;
> Dogs howled, and hideous tempest shook down trees;
> The raven rooked her on the chimney's top,
> And chattering pies in dismal discords sung.
> Thy mother felt more than a mother's pain,
> And, yet brought forth less than a mother's hope,
> To wit, an indigested and deformèd lump,
> Not like the fruit of such a goodly tree.
> Teeth hadst thou in thy head when thou wast born,
> To signify thou camest to bite the world.[258] (*Henry VI, Part III* 5.6.45-55)

Infirmity

It is hard to imagine, in all history, a person more powerful than the Roman general Julius Caesar, yet Shakespeare did not shy away from pointing to Caesar's infirmities. In *Julius Caesar*, he commented on three such deficiencies in Act I alone. He refers to Caesar's loss of hearing ("Come on my right hand, for this ear is deaf"); lack of endurance ("Caesar cried 'Help me, Cassius, or I sink!'"); and epileptic seizures:

> CASSIUS
> He had a fever when he was in Spain,
> And when the fit was on him, I did mark
> How he did shake: 'tis true, this god did shake;
> His coward lips did from their color fly,
> And that same eye whose bend doth awe the world
> Did lose his luster: I did hear him groan:
> Ay, and that tongue of his that bade the Romans
> Mark him and write his speeches in their books,
> Alas, it cried "Give me some drink, Titinius,"
> As a sick girl.[259] (1.2.223, 118,131-35)

Laughter and Health

Most of the excerpts above show Shakespeare's awareness that physical features can negatively influence the way one person feels about another, but let us end on a happier note. We learn from the Bible that "a joyful heart is good medicine" (Prov. 17:22a), a truth which Shakespeare put to use in *The Comedy of Errors*, when Antipholus of Syracuse describes his servant as:

> A trusty villain, sir, that very oft,
> When I am dull with care and melancholy,
> Lightens my humor with his merry jests.[260] (1.2.19-21)

Summing Up

We began with the question, "Why Shakespeare?" Thus, we should close by reiterating the key points from the lists above. Shakespeare had a masterful—and arguably unmatched—command of the English language in terms of word choice and figures of speech, and on top of that, had keen insights into the sometimes disordered ways humans think, interact with others, and allow physical impairments to become barriers. And that spectacular combination is only magnified by the fact that he did it all within the framework of iambic pentameter! In short, it is fair to say that crossword puzzles, Sudoku, Rubik's Cubes, Gordian knots, and Shakespearean plays can all exercise your mind—but, of these, only Shakespeare can also move your heart. The only word to describe the man is *genius*.

SUBTEXT

Chapter 12

Introduction

The subtext of a play can be defined as the story-behind-the-story, the driving force that causes characters to speak or behave in a certain way, to hide their feelings, to fake their feelings, to hint at their feelings, or to show their feelings. Subtext can be compared to an iceberg. We normally see only what is above the water line, but below there is something much more massive than we can even imagine (see Fig. 1). Similarly, what a person wishes to show of himself to others is like the tip of the iceberg that everyone can see, while the part the character hides from others is like the monstrous berg beneath the water. That component represents the hidden emotion that is driving the action of the play and is referred to as the play's *subtext*. To present subtext, the playwright manipulates the language of the play, and the actor employs gesture, body language, intonation, movement, and facial expression to present the subtext on stage. The purpose of this chapter is to identify some techniques that are used and to provide you the opportunity to practice using subtext to convey meaning.

Fig. 1

Subtext via Body Language and Facial Expression

How did Jesus comport himself after his arrest? Was he belligerent? Holier-than-thou? Angry? We learn something about the way Jesus behaved before the authorities in Luke 23. First, Luke narrates Jesus' interaction with Pilate:

> And Pilate asked him, "Are you the King of the Jews?" And he answered him, "You have said so." Then Pilate said to the chief priests and the crowds, "I find no guilt in this man."

From this exchange, we can conclude that Jesus was humble and respectful before the Roman authority. Pilate, seeing humility, immediately moved to dismiss him. Next, Luke describes what happened when Jesus appeared before Herod, the Jewish authority: "He [Herod] was hoping to see some sign done by him. So he questioned him at some length, but he made no answer" (8-9). Jesus chose to remain silent. He did not boast. He did not show off. He did not chastise the authorities. He was simply silent, and yet the silence itself reveals much about the character of the man who was surrendering to the will of God and taking on the sins of the whole world. Even without a stage play, Luke's readers can sense the body language and attitude of Jesus. Actors, of course, are charged with conveying the personality of their character by comporting themselves in ways that suggest the "inner man," so to speak.

ACTIVITY 12.A: Perceiving Subtext

DIRECTIONS: Communication involves body language and facial expression. This activity will allow you to perceive a person's mood or emotion by examining those two aspects of communication. The activity has two components: one as classwork with everyone working together; and one as homework, working alone.

A. Classroom Exercise

Using the picture of the girl at the right, evaluate her body language and facial expression to determine her emotion and create a subtext to explain what caused her to feel the way she does in the picture. If you work with a partner, explain your ideas to the whole class when ready.

B. Homework Exercise

Search old magazines or the Internet to find pictures of people whose facial expressions communicate a certain mood. Imagine the subtext for the expression. In other words, what caused the person to feel this way? Is the person's expression sincere or feigned? For example, a person can look happy but feel anger internally. Bring the picture to class, allow everyone to see it, and then explain to your classmates what subtext you created for the "character" in the image.

Subtext and Intonation

Linguists differentiate between *segmentals* (the sounds used to pronounce words) and *suprasegmentals* (the tone of voice in which the words are spoken). By the intonation with which a person says a word, the listener will know something about his or her attitude.

Take the simple word *right*, for example. This word could be enunciated with completely different tones, depending on the situation:

- A person confirming that he or she understands.
- A person with an encouraging manner, who means, "Yes, now you get it!"
- A person who is questioning whether something is ethical.
- A person speaking ironically, who actually means, "Not right."

In 1951, comedian Stan Freberg did a radio monologue which remains today a classic in intonation and subtext.

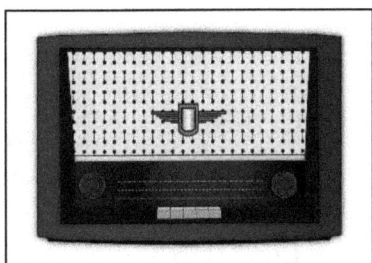

The skit was intended to make fun of the melodramatic dialogue so characteristic of daytime soap operas. Entitled "John and Marsha," it consisted of only two words: *John* and *Marsha*. By saying the same two words in different ways, Freberg conveyed quite different moods, and he performed so well that the piece still serves as an excellent example of subtext and intonation.

ACTIVITY 12.B: Subtext and Intonation

DIRECTIONS: Call up Stan Freberg's performance of "John and Marsha" on *YouTube* at this URL:

<https://www.youtube.com/watch?v=KkfwmB8jeSU>

After listening, discuss the skit with your classmates. Are the lines isolated examples of subtext, or, taken together, do they tell a story? Afterward, practice saying the following lines with different intonations, gestures, movements, and facial expressions:

1. "Who's that?"
2. "Why?"
3. "Oh, no."
4. "Forget it."
5. "Okay."
6. "I can't do it."

Subtext in Shakespeare

One can see an example of subtext at work in a Shakespearean play in Act 2, Scene 2, of *Julius Caesar*. By this point, the audience is well aware that there is a conspiracy to assassinate Caesar at the Senate House on a certain day. One of the conspirators is Decius Brutus. Now, just before Decius Brutus enters, Calpurnia, Caesar's wife, has implored Caesar not to go to the capitol that day because the augurers have warned of blood in the streets, the clamorous whinnying of horses, and the groaning of men. She feels he may be killed. Caesar, of course, cannot allow people to think that he, such a great man, is afraid, but out of his love for Calpurnia, he agrees not to go. At that moment, the conspirator Decius Brutus arrives to escort him to the Senate House. As you read the dialogue, note the hidden feelings of both Caesar (who wants to appear neither a coward nor a bad husband) and Decius Brutus (who has to find a way to get Caesar to the Senate House, no matter what). It reads as follows:

Enter DECIUS.

CAESAR
Here's Decius Brutus, he shall tell them so.

DECIUS
Caesar, all hail! good morrow, worthy Caesar:
I come to fetch you to the senate-house.

CAESAR
And you are come in very happy time,
To bear my greeting to the senators   65
And tell them that I will not come to-day:
Cannot, is false, and that I dare not, falser:
I will not come to-day: tell them so, Decius.

CALPURNIA
Say he is sick.

CAESAR
          Shall Caesar send a lie?   70
Have I in conquest stretched mine arm so far,
To be afraid to tell graybeards the truth?
Decius, go tell them Caesar will not come.

DECIUS
Most mighty Caesar, let me know some cause,
Lest I be laughed at when I tell them so.   75

CAESAR
The cause is in my will: I will not come;
That is enough to satisfy the senate.
But for your private satisfaction,
Because I love you, I will let you know:
Calpurnia here, my wife, stays me at home: 80
She dreamt to-night she saw my statue,
Which, like a fountain with an hundred spouts,
Did run pure blood: and many lusty Romans
Came smiling, and did bathe their hands in it:
And these does she apply for warnings, and portents, 85
And evils imminent; and on her knee
Hath begged that I will stay at home to-day.

DECIUS
This dream is all amiss interpreted;
It was a vision fair and fortunate:
Your statue spouting blood in many pipes, 90
In which so many smiling Romans bathed,
Signifies that from you great Rome shall suck
Reviving blood, and that great men shall press
For tinctures, stains, relics and cognizance.
This by Calpurnia's dream is signified. 95

CAESAR
And this way have you well expounded it.

DECIUS
I have, when you have heard what I can say:
And know it now: the senate have concluded
To give this day a crown to mighty Caesar.
If you shall send them word you will not come, 100
Their minds may change. Besides, it were a mock
Apt to be rendered, for someone to say
"Break up the senate till another time,
When Caesar's wife shall meet with better dreams."
If Caesar hide himself, shall they not whisper 105
"Lo, Caesar is afraid?"

Pardon me, Caesar; for my dear dear love
To our proceeding bids me tell you this;
And reason to my love is liable.

CAESAR
How foolish do your fears seem now, Calpurnia!   110
I am ashamèd I did yield to them.
Give me my robe, for I will go.²⁶¹ (2.2.1036-1038)

ACTIVITY 12.C: Detecting Subtext in *Julius Caesar*

DIRECTIONS: Discuss with your classmates how the actors might employ gesture, facial expression, and so on, when taking the subtext of the above scene into account. Act out your ideas to see what might work best.

Subtext and Early Modern Pronouns *(Thou vs. You)*

Shakespeare and his contemporaries were writing at a time when the English language was in its Early Modern form. Some students opine that Shakespeare is "too difficult" because of problems presented by the second-person pronouns *thou* and *you*; nevertheless, understanding the pronoun system of earlier times is important to the dramatist since the earlier pronouns added a subtext that would have been readily apparent to earlier audiences because social and emotional ramifications were associated with their use. These pronouns can convey a wide range of emotions: snobbery, arrogance, hatred, humility, subservience, fondness, friendliness, flirtation, and love. The material below is designed to raise your awareness of this connection between pronouns and subtext.

Pronoun Chart for Early Modern English

The chart below lays out the English pronouns as they existed from the late fifteenth-century to the mid- to late seventeenth century. These dates are coterminous with the Tudors and Stewarts—the two dynasties who ruled England during the lives of Shakespeare and his contemporaries.

Singular vs. Plural

At first glance, one sees that almost all the pronouns remain unchanged in the twenty-first century, with second person singular being the only odd-man-out.

Person	Singular	Plural
1st Person	I	We
2nd Person	thou	you
3rd Person	he, she, it	they

Variation in the singular and plural forms of second-person pronouns was (and is) characteristic of most European languages, as shown in this chart:

Language	2nd-Person Singular	2nd-Person Plural
Latin	tū	vōs
French	tu	vous
Spanish	tú	vosotros/-as
German	du	ihr/sie
English	thou	you

The use of *thou* for singular and *you* for plural is apparent in the King James Version of the Bible, as the following illustrations indicate:

SINGULAR (left): "And I say also unto *thee*, that *thou* art Peter, and upon this rock I will build my church." Mt. 16:18 (KJV)

PLURAL (right): "Let *your* light so shine before men, that they may see *your* good works, and glorify *your* Father which is in heaven. Mt. 5:16 (KJV)

An extra twist is that Early Modern English had, in addition to *thou*, one other second-person pronoun: *ye*. Though *ye* had been a plural pronoun in Middle English, by Shakespeare's time it was used for both singular and plural, thus:

Person	Singular	Plural
2nd Person	thou/ye	you/ye

Examine these examples of second person pronouns from *Henry VIII* by William Shakespeare:

Singular	Plural
Thou KING HENRY (to Wolsey) Thou art a cure fit for a king.	**You** WOLSEY Ladies, you are not merry.
Ye KATHARINE (to Wolsey) Ye tell me what ye wish for both—my ruin.	**Ye** KATHARINE Ye speak like honest men; pray God, ye prove so!

Case in Second-person Pronouns

In Modern English first-person and third-person pronouns still adjust for case (e.g., *I/me/my; he/him/his*). Similarly, the second-person pronoun was inflected in Early Modern English, as shown in the chart below:

Case	Singular	Plural
Nominative	thou	you
Objective	thee	you
Possessive	thy/thine	your/yours
Reflexive	thyself	yourselves

The following chart displays the case forms of second-person as used by William Shakespeare in *Macbeth*.

Case	Singular
Nominative	DUNCAN Where camest thou, worthy thane?
Objective	DUNCAN *[to Banquo]* let me enfold thee And hold thee to my heart.
Possessive	**Thy** ROSS *[to Macbeth]* The king hath happily received, Macbeth, The news of thy success.
	Thine MACBETH *[to Macduff]* My soul is too much charged With blood of thine already.

The reflexive pronouns *thyself, yourself,* and *yourselves* operated somewhat differently from what grammar books teach today. In our time, the reflexive is not to be used in the subject position. For example, we would not say, "Yourself is welcome." However, in Early Modern English, one finds the word as both a subject and an object:

Reflexive Pronoun *(-self)*	Singular
Object Position	BANQUO *[to Macduff]* Dear Duff, I prithee, contradict thyself, And say it is not so.
Reflexive Pronoun *(-self)*	Singular
Subject Position	ROSS He finds thee in the stout Norwegian ranks, Nothing afeard of what thyself didst make.

If the two parts *thy* and *self* were separated by the word *own*, which begins with a vowel, the form *thy* changed to *thine*, following the rule which still pertains today regarding the articles *a* and *an*:

Reflexive Pronoun *(-self)*	Singular
Thine is used here for because the word following it begins with a vowel (cf. *a/an*).	POLONIUS This above all – to thine own self be true.

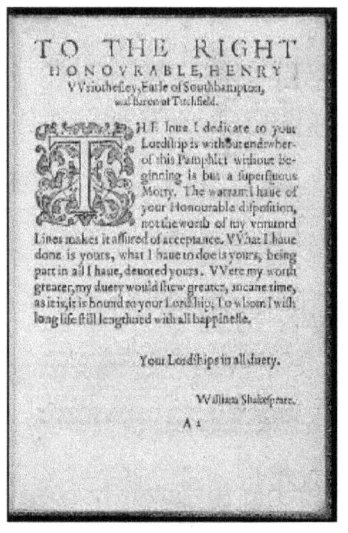

Shakespeare's letter to his patron, using the respectful form *you*

Cultural Use of Second-person Pronouns

Important to the Shakespearean actor is an understanding of how and in what situations *thou* and *you* forms are used. To express anger, characters will not use the same second-person pronoun as they would in expressing fondness, for example. In addition, there is a social component. That is, pronoun selection would vary to reflect social class. Knowing these subtleties can assist actors in knowing what tone of voice the they should use to present the lines. The information below will help you sort out the differences and give you an opportunity to examine and present scenes from some of Shakespeare's plays.

Formal/Informal: In Modern English, we use *you* in both formal and informal situations. However, that was not always the case. In Elizabethan times, the singular forms *(thou/ thee/ thy)* were used in informal, personal conversations such as those between family members and close friends. This was not a mandatory selection, however. In *Romeo and Juliet*, Benvolio is not only Romeo's cousin, but also his best friend. As the character switches forms, the actor's task would be to figure out the underlying tone of voice that would accompany the switch. Following is an example from Act I, Scene 1, in which Romeo enters with a downcast face, lamenting the fact that he has been jilted by Rosaline:

Situation	Pronoun Usage
Benvolio addresses his friend Romeo in the standard, respectful way.	BENVOLIO Tell me in sadness, who is that you love.
When Romeo continues to mope, Benvolio shifts to the affectionate form, revealing the closeness that underlies his advice to his cousin.	BENVOLIO Take thou some new infection to thy eye, And the rank poison of the old will die.

In short, the informal pronoun *thou* is delivered in a fond tone of voice, while the formal *you* is delivered in a more reserved manner.

Social "Superiors" and "Inferiors": It has been argued that one reason the singular form *thou* disappeared from the English language in the eighteenth century is that the democratizing influence of the American Revolution drove it out. Before that time, there were certain linguistic norms that revealed a distinction in social class, just as the sumptuary laws had made clothing a distinguisher of class. The general practice in English discourse in Early Modern English was as follows:

Prince Hal (a royal) hanging out with Falstaff (a commoner) in *Henry IV, Parts 1 and 2.*

Commoners used *you* when addressing nobles and royals.

Nobles and royals used *thou* when addressing commoners.

An example of this usage can be found in the opening scene of *As You Like It* in which the faithful servant Adam is speaking to Orlando, the son of the noble whom Adam serves.

Situation	Pronoun Usage
The servant addresses the noble.	ADAM Yonder comes my master, *your* brother.
The noble responds to the servant.	ORLANDO Go apart, Adam, and *thou* shalt hear how he will shake me up.

In this case, the social "inferior" (Adam) speaks to the noble with the polite form *your*, while the social "superior" (Orlando) speaks to the servant with the informal form *thou*.

Moreover, one finds passages in Shakespeare where an understanding of the pronoun system adds dimension to characterization. Below, for example, is an excerpt from Act I, Scene 2 of *Richard III*. Richard, still the Duke of Gloucester but already plotting to usurp the throne, happens across the Lady Anne, who is accompanying the corpse ("corse") of her father-in-law, Henry VI, whom Richard has murdered. With her are some gentlemen and guards, who are carrying the funeral bier. Notice how Richard's pronouns change when his attitude toward these men changes:

Situation	Pronoun Usage
As Gloucester (Richard) begins the dialogue, he uses the respectful form when addressing the guards.	GLOUCESTER *[to the guards]* Stay, you that bear the corse, and set it down. LADY ANNE What black magician conjures up this fiend, To stop devoted charitable deeds? GLOUCESTER Villains, set down the corse; or, by Saint Paul, I'll make a corse of him that disobeys.
When the guards (his "inferiors") do not comply with his request, he abruptly shifts to the pronoun *thou* in order to pull rank.	GENTLEMAN My lord, stand back, and let the coffin pass. GLOUCESTER Unmanner'd dog! stand thou, when I command: Advance thy halbert higher than my breast, Or, by Saint Paul, I'll strike thee to my foot, And spurn upon thee, beggar, for thy boldness.

Gentleness and Anger: The exchange between Duke Richard and the guards illustrates not only the social distance between them, but also the anger Richard feels when his order is disobeyed. Given the times, this might not seem unusual, but the remainder of the dialogue in this scene illustrates that pronoun usage can also represent an emotional distance between characters of the same social rank. Notice the Lady Anne's use of pronouns as she addresses, first, the guards (her "inferiors") and then Richard (her social equal).

Richard Mansfield as Richard III and Beatrice Cameron as Lady Anne, 1890
Folger Shakespeare Library

Situation	Pronoun Usage
Here Lady Anne addresses her "inferiors" respectfully.	LADY ANNE *(to the guards)* What, do you tremble? are you all afraid? Alas, I blame you not; for you are mortal, And mortal eyes cannot endure the devil.
Here she addresses her "equal" disrespectfully.	*(to Gloucester)* Avaunt, thou dreadful minister of hell! Thou hadst but power over his mortal body, His soul thou canst not have; therefore, be gone.

This scene is one of Shakespeare's most famous scenes and shows his mastery of language and characterization as Lady Anne, who begins with utter contempt for Richard, ends by accepting his ring and hinting at romance to follow. The scene shows not only Richard's mastery of manipulation, but Shakespeare's mastery of his art. The scene is too long to excerpt in whole, but the chart below will display the relevant lines:

Situation	Pronoun Usage
Anne uses *thou* as she calls Gloucester the devil.	LADY ANNE Foul devil, for God's sake, hence, and trouble us not; For thou hast made the happy earth thy hell, Fill'd it with cursing cries and deep exclaims.
Gloucester uses *you*, not returning the animus.	GLOUCESTER Lady, you know no rules of charity, Which renders good for bad, blessings for curses.
The tone begins to change, as Gloucester changes from *you* to *thou*. His use of *thou* is different from hers: he is showing (or feigning) affection.	LADY ANNE I would I were, to be revenged on thee. GLOUCESTER It is a quarrel most unnatural, To be revenged on him that loveth you. LADY ANNE It is a quarrel just and reasonable, To be revenged on him that slew my husband. GLOUCESTER He that bereft thee, lady, of thy husband, Did it to help thee to a better husband.
Gloucester uses the singular form to continue his feigned affection, while Anne uses it to continue her contempt.	*(She spitteth at him.)* GLOUCESTER Why dost thou spit at me? LADY ANNE Would it were mortal poison, for thy sake!
In this dramatic exchange, Richard asks Anne to kill him, since she hates him so. His pronouns show a continued affectionate tone.	GLOUCESTER *(He lays his breast open: she offers at it with his sword.)* Nay, do not pause; for I did kill King Henry, But 'twas thy beauty that provoked me. Nay, now dispatch; 'twas I that stabb'd young Edward, But 'twas thy heavenly face that set me on. *(Here she lets fall the sword.)* Take up the sword again, or take up me.
Anne is moved by Richard's demonstration of love and addresses him with *thy*, perhaps in a softer, more affectionate manner.	LADY ANNE Arise, dissembler: though I wish thy death, I will not be thy executioner.

Situation	Pronoun Usage
Gloucester promises to see to a respectful burial for Henry, then come to her. Notice the switch from *thee* to *you*, as he brings the wooing scene to an end.	GLOUCESTER That it would please thee leave these sad designs To him that hath more cause to be a mourner, And presently repair to Crosby Place; Where, after I have solemnly interr'd At Chertsey monastery this noble king, And wet his grave with my repentant tears, I will with all expedient duty see you: For divers unknown reasons. I beseech you, Grant me this boon.
At the close of the scene, Anne switches to the respectful *you*, signaling her change of heart.	LADY ANNE With all my heart; and much it joys me too, To see you are become so penitent.

ACTIVITY 12.D: Delivering Lines with Second-person Pronouns

DIRECTIONS: Below is an excerpt from *Romeo and Juliet*. Please begin by reading the introduction. Then read the excerpt and discuss the questions which follow. Before the class, act out some of the parts, using the body language and tone of voice indicated by the pronoun usage.

INTRODUCTION: *The back-story to the opening scene of* Romeo and Juliet *is that two houses of Verona, the Montagues (Romeo's family) and the Capulets (Juliet's family), have been engaged in hostilities for some time. Frays have often broken out in the streets of Verona, as the young men— teenagers, really—taunt each other in the streets. In this scene, the Capulets encounter some Montagues in the marketplace and, as usual, engage in verbal one-upmanship. Notice how the conversation begins somewhat civilly with the polite form* (you), *but as tension builds, the pronouns shift to the more rude form* (thou). *Note: The line numbers are for the purposes of the exercise only.*

Excerpt from *Romeo and Juliet*
By William Shakespeare

[Enter two friends, Gregory and Sampson, of the House of Capulet, strolling in the marketplace of Verona.]

GREGORY
Draw thy tool! here comes
two of the house of the Montagues.
. . . .
I will frown as I pass by, and let them take it as
they list.

SAMPSON
Nay, as they dare. I will bite my thumb at them; 5
which is a disgrace to them, if they bear it.

[Enter ABRAHAM and BALTHASAR of the House of Montague]

ABRAHAM
Do you bite your thumb at us, sir?

SAMPSON
I do bite my thumb, sir.

ABRAHAM
Do you bite your thumb at us, sir?

SAMPSON
(Aside to GREGORY) Is the law of our side, if I say 10
ay?

GREGORY
No.

SAMPSON
No, sir, I do not bite my thumb at you, sir, but I
bite my thumb, sir.

GREGORY
Do you quarrel, sir? 15

ABRAHAM
Quarrel sir! no, sir.

SAMPSON
If you do, sir, I am for you: I serve as good a man as you.

ABRAHAM
No better.

SAMPSON
Well, sir.

GREGORY
Say "better:" here comes one of my master's kinsmen. 20

SAMPSON
Yes, better, sir.

ABRAHAM
You lie.

SAMPSON
Draw, if you be men. Gregory, remember thy swashing blow.

[*They fight.*]

[*Enter BENVOLIO, a friend of Romeo and the peacemaker of the Montagues. Notice that his name, Benvolio, suggests the Latin for good will.*]

BENVOLIO
Part, fools!
Put up your swords; you know not what you do. 25

[*He beats down their swords.*]

[*Enter TYBALT, hothead of the House of Capulet, drawing his sword.*]

TYBALT
What, art thou drawn among these heartless hinds?
Turn thee, Benvolio, look upon thy death.

BENVOLIO
I do but keep the peace: put up thy sword,
Or manage it to part these men with me.

TYBALT
What, drawn, and talk of peace! I hate the word,   30
As I hate hell, all Montagues, and thee:
Have at thee, coward!

[They fight.][262]

Questions:

1. Line 1:

    a. When Gregory addresses Sampson, what pronoun does he use?

    b. What seems to be the underlying purpose (emotion) behind that usage?

2. Lines 7-32:

    a. The two groups dislike each other, but what pronoun do they use throughout from Line 7 to Line 25?

    b. How does this change from Line 26 to 32?

    c. What does the switch in pronouns signify here?

d. Does this switch parallel the stage action? Explain your answer.

3. Act out the scene, showing changes in body language and tone of voice as the scene progresses. If your teacher permits, use dowels or yardsticks as swords to show how the character might wield his weapon as he speaks.

EXERCISE 12.1: Subtext in a Seventeenth-century Witch's Play

DIRECTIONS: Turn to APPENDIX F, where you will find an excerpt from Act IV, Scene 2 of *The Late Lancashire Witches* by Thomas Heywood and Richard Brome. After reading the introduction and the excerpt, return to this page for the exercise below. On a separate piece of paper, jot down each instance in the scene where a character is saying something but masking inner thoughts or worries. (You can use line numbers to save time.) Be sure to indicate what the subtext (the inner feeling) is. Discuss your answers with your class.

Example:

Lines: 51-55

Characters: Generous and Robert

Subtext: Robert is well aware the horse has been ridden, and to a witches' meeting, at that. He is pretending it has not been ridden and hopes Generous will not become aware of what has happened.

SPECTACLE ON THE ELIZABETHAN STAGE

Chapter 13

Introduction

The massive Greek and Roman amphitheatres of the classical period had fallen into ruins in the medieval period, and when theatre started up again in northern Europe, it began with portable stages that could be stored in the winter months and brought out in the spring for roving street performances. However, the sixteenth century saw the next major development in theatrical stages in the West—the privately owned playhouse. The purpose of this chapter is to explore this new stage and the opportunities it created for special effects.

Stagecraft

One way to look at Shakespeare's stage is to perceive it as having as many as four different playing areas—upstage (unroofed), downstage (set off by columns and roofed), the inner room behind the curtain, and the balcony. In an area when scenery was not employed, such a configuration afforded the playwrights (and actors) some flexibility for the staging of various scenes. For example, Albert Harris Tolman once suggested the following staging for the tent scene in Act IV of *Julius Caesar*:

> In IV, ii, the front stage represents the space before Brutus's tent; at the end of this scene, Brutus and Cassius pass to the back stage, the interior of the tent, for scene iii.[263]

The German scholar Alois Brandl went even further. He believed that at times action would be simultaneous in more than one of the playing areas. Since we know that there were, in fact, three playing areas on medieval pageant wagons (which the Renaissance generation would have seen as children), it is not a great leap to think that just because Shakespeare is not performed that way in our times, it never was.

Brandl offered this example from Act IV, Scenes 4 and 5, of *Romeo and Juliet*:

(1) Downstage

In the reception hall that is upon the back stage, Capulet and the nurse are busily engaged in preparing the meal for the wedding guests; servants with food, firewood and baskets are hurrying to and from the kitchen.

Movement from (1) to (2)

The nurse is sent up into Juliet's chamber in order to waken the prospective bride.

(2) Balcony

Above in the balcony, we see her draw back the window curtain, but she cannot arouse the sleeper. Below the clatter of preparation continues. The nurse becomes anxious and calls for help.

Movement from (1) to (2)

Lady Capulet climbs the stair and beholds the sad spectacle. Capulet appears; both lament over the body of their daughter.

(3) Upstage

In the meantime, musicians have drawn near upon the front stage [inasmuch as] Paris will [be expected to] carry away his bride with cheery piping.

Sounds from both (1) and (2)

Thus, the festive tumult ever increases on the floor of the stage, as does the noise of lamentation above in the chamber, and both of them are both seen and heard by the spectator, until, at last, the words of Capulet spoken to Paris from the window put an end to this shocking contrast.[264]

This concept led Brendl to conclude, "In the modern theater with all its elaborate apparatus and decorations, half of the effect of such scenes is lost."[265] Indeed.

Spectacle and Special Effects

Though Spectacle was the feature Aristotle cared about the least, he still acknowledged that in tragedy, "spectacular equipment" for the production of special effects would be necessary, as long as its purpose was to enhance the emotional response.[266] Just as in real life people experience fear when the skies flash lightning and roar thunder, so will they in a theatrical storm created by special effects with state-of-the-art technology, whatever that is at any given moment in history.

In our own time, special effects are given much more importance than they were in times past. In an era of computer-generated "virtual reality," moviemakers have had a heyday creating fantastic special effects that dazzle the eye, and companies like Aquavision have developed amazing special effects involving laser beams and water curtains for live shows both indoors and outdoors. Though such techniques create a feast for the eyes, sometimes media critics lament the fact that we are losing the ability to imagine things in our "mind's eye," which would have been one of the primary sources of enjoyment for the playgoers of bygone times. Let us begin this chapter, therefore, with an analysis of the issue, as it was presented by the all-time great, William Shakespeare.

EXERCISE 13.1: Special Effects Analysis

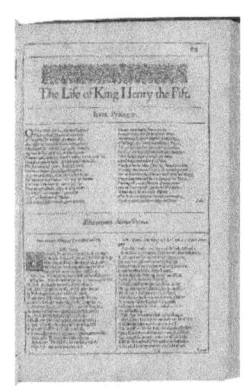

DIRECTIONS: Please begin by reading the introduction and completing the pre-reading activity. Then, read the excerpt and respond to the questions that follow.

INTRODUCTION: *William Shakespeare is well known for a series of history plays that involved the intrigues of the Plantagenets, but none presented the staging problems brought about by* Henry V, *which required the depiction of the battles of Harfleur and Agincourt. Fortunately for the student of Shakespeare, the author laid out some of the problems he had in effecting realism on the modest stage of the Globe theatre. Below you will have the opportunity to consider his problem and his options.*

1. Before reading the prologue, brainstorm with your classmates the kinds of things you would expect to see in a twenty-first century movie about England's fifteenth-century invasion of France. Jot down a list in the space provided.

Now read the prologue, keeping in mind the playwright's need for verisimilitude (realism).

CHORUS
O for a Muse of fire, that would ascend
The brightest heaven of invention,
A kingdom for a stage, princes to act
And monarchs to behold the swelling scene!
Then should the warlike Harry, like himself, 5
Assume the port of Mars; and at his heels,
Leash'd in like hounds, should famine, sword and fire
Crouch for employment. But pardon, and gentles all,
The flat unraised spirits that have dared
On this unworthy scaffold to bring forth 10
So great an object: can this cockpit hold
The vasty fields of France? or may we cram
Within this wooden O the very casques[a]
That did affright the air at Agincourt?
O, pardon! since a crooked figure may 15
Attest in little place a million;
And let us, ciphers to this great accompt,[b]
On your imaginary forces work.
Suppose within the girdle of these walls
Are now confined two mighty monarchies, 20
Whose high upreared and abutting fronts
The perilous narrow ocean parts asunder:
Piece out our imperfections with your thoughts;
Into a thousand parts divide one man,
And make imaginary puissance;[c] 25
Think when we talk of horses, that you see them
Printing their proud hoofs i' the receiving earth;
For 'tis your thoughts that now must deck our kings,
Carry them here and there; jumping o'er times,
Turning the accomplishment of many years 30
Into an hour-glass: for the which supply,
Admit me Chorus to this history;

---

[a] helmets
[b] account
[c] power

> Who prologue-like your humble patience pray,
> Gently to hear, kindly to judge, our play.[267]

2. In this passage, Shakespeare used a series of metaphors to explain his predicament.

   a. (Lines 1-4) First of all, knowing what he sorely lacks, what does Shakespeare wish for?

   b. In his ideal theatre, what would his actors be? What would his audience be?

   Actors:

   Audience:

   c. If we could transport Shakespeare into our own time, what "bright inventions of heaven" might he find available in our entertainment technology?

   d. (Lines 5-6) Shakespeare notes that, if he had what we call "special effects," he would be able to present King Henry (Harry), one of England's most popular kings as:

   e. (Lines 7-8) What horrors of war does he list, and how would he portray them if he had the means?

   f. In Line 3, what did he say he would need for a stage? But then in Line 10 he laments he has only what?

Line 3:

Line 10:

   g. In Lines 11-12, he compared a theatre to what?

Considering there were no airplanes in Shakespeare's time, we can assume he was probably referring to the "theatres" where the cock fights were held. Yet he has only this small space to depict what?

   h. In Line 13, he calls his theatre a "wooden O" in which he must present helmets. This may seem odd unless we consider Shakespeare's diction. In the space below, jot down the meaning of the term *synecdoche* (consult a dictionary if you are not sure). Then explain what Shakespeare really meant by *presenting casques in a "wooden O."*

   i. Lines 20-22: What does he say he must present within that space?

   j. Lines 30-31: In addition to the limits of space, what other limitation does he have?

3. (Lines 33-34) With all his limitations acknowledged, how does the speaker conclude?

Weapons

17th-century Fencing School

Tragedies involving murder and history plays involving battle scenes both required weapons as props. Typically, companies would have daggers and swords of various types (poniards, rapiers, military swords) amongst their properties. In order to learn how to use them, London's actors took lessons from an Italian fencing master named Rocco Benetti, who set up a school at London's only indoor theatre, Blackfriars. William Shakespeare, who took some of Benetti's classes, showed his familiarity with fencing terminology in *Romeo and Juliet* when Mercutio describes the skill of his rival, Tybalt:

> MERCUTIO
> More than prince of cats. Oh, he's the courageous
> captain of compliments. He fights as you sing
> prick-song, keeps time, distance, and proportion.
> He rests his minim rests[a] one, two, and the third in
> your bosom—the very butcher of a silk button, a duelist, a
> duelist, a gentleman of the very first house
> of the first and second cause.[b] Ah, the immortal
> *passado,* the *punto reverso,*[c] the *hay*![d][268] (2.4.20-27)

---

[a] Rests in music, applied here to pauses in action
[b] The first and second causes for which a man should fight
[c] A backhanded stroke
[d] Sometimes spelled *hai*, meaning, "You have it," used when the thrust reaches the antagonist. Modern fencers holler, "Ha!"

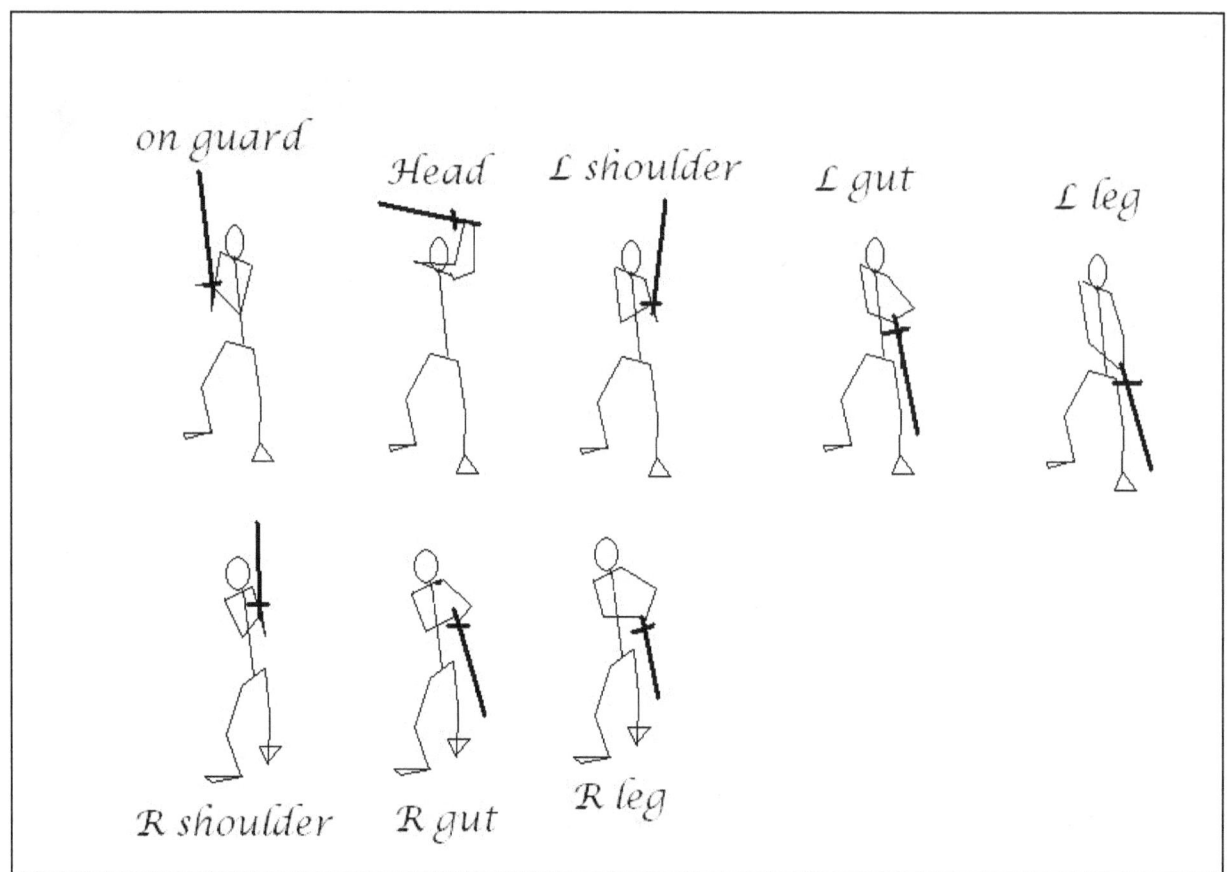

Fig. 1 Fencing positions from *Wikiwood*

It is commonly believed that "the very butcher of a silk button" was a reference to Benetti himself. Certainly George Silver, a writer on fencing during the period, described Benetti similarly saying: "There was an Italian teacher of defence [sic] in my time who was so excellent in his fight that he would have hit any Englishman with a thrust just upon any button in his doublet, and this was much spoken of."[269] Was there a trick to the trade? Silver certainly believed so, pointing out that when teaching noblemen to fight, Benetti "caused some of them to wear leaden soles in their shoes, the better to bring them to nimbleness of feet in their fight."[270] No doubt, Benetti used similar methods with the actors who sought him out.

In addition to swords, cannons—complete with gunpowder and wadding—would be set up in the attic area above the "Heavens." This created disaster in 1613 when the wadding caught fire and set the thatched roof ablaze during a performance of Shakespeare's *Henry VIII*. The entire theatre burnt to the ground.

Another military weapon used onstage was the pike. A pike is shaped like a long pole, running from 10 to 25 feet long and weighing approximately 5 to 13 pounds. In the exercise below you will be able to imagine (and possibly enact) a scene involving two actors, each with a pike and a rapier (a thin-bladed, 41-inch long sword).

ACTIVITY 13.A: Special Effects with Stage Weapons

DIRECTIONS: Please begin by reading the introduction. Then proceed to the excerpts and the questions which follow them. As you read the dialogue, try to imagine what actions each character would be performing with his pike. How easy or difficult would this be in a space the size of an Elizabethan stage with groundlings standing about? If space permits, use a baton or dowel to try out some possible maneuvers. (For safety, a dowel shorter than an actual pike is recommended.)

INTRODUCTION: In Thomas Heywood's play, The Four Prentices of London, *four brothers have been separated by the fortunes of war and each believes the others to be dead. When two of them, Guy and Eustace, stumble across each other in the course of the play, neither recognizes the other. Each deems the other to be an enemy, and a fight ensues. When they enter, each is carrying a rapier and a pike. As the two prepare to fight, they conduct a war of words, each boasting of his physical prowess, especially his skill with a pike. Two other characters, Robert and the Palatine, are onstage and step in at the end.*

Excerpt from *The Four Prentices of London*
By Thomas Heywood

GUY
Give me thy pike. I'll toss it like a reed,
And with this bulrush make mine enemy bleed:
Rapier and pike, is that thy honored play?
Look down, ye gods, this combat to survey.

EUSTACE
Rapier and pike, this combat shall decide: 5
gods, angels, men, shall see me tame thy pride.

GUY
Thou dost thy self wrong to o'er charge thine arm
With such a weapon as thou canst not wield:

I'll teach thee; thou shalt like my zany[a] be:
And feign to do my cunning after me. 10

EUSTACE
Thou wouldst instruct thy master at this play:
Think'st thou this rye-strew can o'er-rule my arm?
Thus[b] do I bear him when I use to mark.
Thus can I fling him up and catch him thus:
Then thus, to try the sinews of my arm. 15

[They toss their pikes]

GUY
But thou should'st charge him thus, advance him thus.
Thus should'st thou take him, when thou seest from far
The violent horses run to break our ranks.

EUSTACE
All that is nothing, I can toss him thus.

GUY
I thus: 'tis easier sport than the balowne.[c] 20

EUSTACE
We trifle time, this shall thy rage withstand.

GUY
With this, our host shall pierce thy sovereign's land.

[They fight. Robert and the Palatine cast their warders between them and part them.][271]

ACTIVITY 13.B: View and Do: Stage Combat from *Robin Hood*

Shortly after the movie *Robin Hood*, starring Russell Crowe, was produced in 2010, a documentary entitled *The Real Robin Hood* was made by the movie's producer Ridley Scott and actors Russell Crowe and Cate Blanchett. Among other things, the video

---

[a] A clown (This word was introduced to the English language by Shakespeare.)
[b] Here *thus* means *in this manner* and should take the stress with each use.
[c] A game played with a leather "balloon" (bag or handball)

provides demonstrations of fighting with various swords. If possible, secure a copy of the video and watch those segments with your class.

Then, to practice stage combat, create a harmless "sword" by cutting pool noodles in half and practice the fencing positions in Fig. 1. Employ some of the tips provided in the video as well.

ACTIVITY 13.C: View and Do: Stage Combat in *Romeo and Juliet*

The fight scene in William Shakespeare's *Romeo and Juliet* was masterfully directed and filmed in Franco Zeffirelli's 1968 movie version of the play. The two sword fights in Act III were acted by Leonard Whiting (Romeo), Michael York (Tybalt), and John McEnery (Mercutio). The fracas begins before Romeo, who is now kin to Tybalt because of his secret marriage to Juliet, appears fresh from the chapel. He is happy and desires no trouble with the Capulets, but Tybalt and Mercutio are hotheads and have no interest in Romeo's peacemaking. The scripted dialogue is brief, and the stage directions are terse, as seen in this sequence:

- *Mercutio draws.*
- *Mercutio challenges Tybalt.*
- *Tybalt draws.*
- *They fight.*
- *Tybalt stabs Mercutio under Romeo's arm.*

On paper, it is a rapid sequence. What makes it credible—and cathartic—is the staging of the fight. Zeffirelli, working in the medium of film, set the fight in an actual town square in a European city, and with the greater expanse, could do much more than could be done on the stage. If possible, view the fight between Mercutio and Tybalt, as well as the subsequent fight between Romeo and Tybalt. After viewing, discuss Zeffirelli's concept of the fight with your classmates. What subtext underlies the scene?

INSTRUCTIONS: Assign roles to at least five students. Three, playing Mercutio, Tybalt, and Romeo can memorize and present the fight scene in 3.1.74-90, and the other two, that of Romeo and Tybalt in 3.1.124-43. For swords, use the pool noodles created for the previous activity. Perform the scenes for the class.

Decapitation

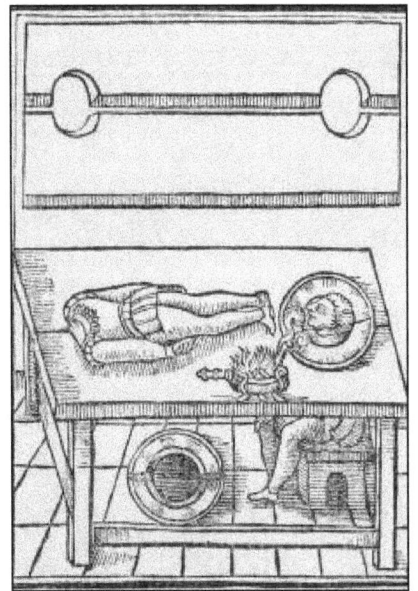

Fig. 2. "The Decollation of John Baptist" from *The Discoverie of Witchcraft*

Reginald Scot, a Member of Parliament in the reign of Elizabeth I, was convinced that the "magic" attributed to witches was nothing more than trickery, and he set out to prove it. The result was his book *The Discoverie of Witchcraft*, published in 1584. On the frontispiece of his text, Scot specified his goal of "proving that the compacts and contracts of witches with devils and all infernal spirits or familiars, are but erroneous novelties and imaginary conceptions. . . ." His ultimate purpose was to end the "unchristian practices" involving torture and execution.[272]

Scot's text is important for the history of the Elizabethan theatre in that he details how fakesters brought off their tricks. For example, he explained that with two boys, dressed in identical costumes, one could bring off the apparent beheading of John the Baptist. To be specific, a hole the size of a boy's neck would be cut into a platter. Then two holes the same size as that of the platter would be drilled in a table top, one at each end, and the platter would be placed over one of them. The boy playing John would sit under the table with his head poking through the hole to simulate a detached head lying on the platter. The other boy would lie on the table with his head poking downward through the second drilled hole "so as his bodie shall seeme to lie on the one end of the boord, and his head shall lie in a platter at the other end" (see Fig. 2). To increase the goriness of the scene, the "conjurors" would touch up the head on the platter by putting about the boy's neck "a little dough kneded with bullocks blood, which being cold will appear like dead flesh; & being pricked with a sharp round hollow quill, will bleed, and seeme very strange."[273]

Smoke and Fire

Several plays from the period required flashes or bolts of lightning. Flashes could be created by throwing resin powder into the flame of a candle, causing a mini-explosion, a "flash in the pan," as the old idiom has it; and bolts of lightning could be created by using a device called a *swevel*. This technique involved affixing a firecracker at the top of a wire running from the roof of the theatre to the floor of the stage. On cue, a stagehand, probably working from the tiring house above the stage, would light the firecracker, causing it to shoot downward from the top of the wire to the stage floor, creating sparks all along its path. Firecrackers were also used in the portrayal of devils. In Thomas Middleton's *Women Beware Women,* we find this exchange:

John Dee
1527- c. 1609

> GUARD
> Here take this caltrop, then convey it secretly
> Into the place I show'd you: look you, sir,
> This is the trap-door to't.
>
> WARD
> I know't of old, uncle, since the last
> Triumph. Here rose up a devil with one eye,
> I remember, with a company of fireworks at's[a] tail.[274] (5.1)

In Christopher Marlowe's *Doctor Faustus*, actors portraying devils even placed firecrackers in their mouths to suggest the fires of hell. Even without fire, smoke could be created by using chemicals, alcohol, and salts, and depending on the combination used, the smoke might be black, white, yellow or red. The stagehand producing the smoke would probably have been positioned in the cellarage with smoke emerging via the trap door.[275]

Optical Illusions

Stage directions in *Macbeth* call for daggers to float and witches to vanish. How could the people of the late sixteenth and early seventeenth centuries have brought off these effects? In search of an answer, Iain Wright, professor of English at Australian National

---

[a] at his

University, turned to the writings of Renaissance scientists, who were then making an effort to manipulate the physical world, or what they called "natural magic." Wright was drawn to the works of John Dee, an Elizabethan-era philosopher and alchemist, who was particularly interested "in how specially modified mirrors could create tricks of the light, making things appear as if by magic." In Dee's preface to *Euclid's Geometry*, written in 1570, Professor Wright found the link he needed. He explained it this way:

> In the preface, Dee takes a survey of the state of modern science. There is a whole section called the art of perspective, which is what they called *optics*. In that, I suddenly ran up against this description of a man starting back with amazement at a floating dagger, and of the "marvellous glass" that produced it. Finding it was pure chance really, a lucky break.[276]

Thus, we see that illusions from "smoke and mirrors," as the saying goes, were already dazzling audiences in Elizabethan England.

Music and Sound Effects

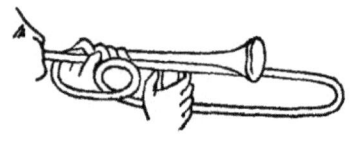

An alto sackbut

Music was widely employed in plays of this period. We have already seen that the musicians even had a special section above the stage, and in some scenes, such as Capulet's party in *Romeo and Juliet*, musicians would even have been onstage as part of the action. For softer music, they used lutes, recorders, and viols, but louder sounds, like those employed in a battle scene, were created by trumpets, drums, and fifes, probably from the cellarage. In his diary, Philip Henslowe mentioned a number of instruments in the inventory of the Rose Theatre: three trumpets, a drum, a treble viol, a bass viol, a sackbut (similar to a trombone), some timbrels (similar to tambourines), chiming bells, a cithern (similar to today's guitar), and a bandore[a] (similar to a bass guitar).[277] A deeply resonant bell seems also to be called for at the close of *Midsummer Night's Dream*, when Duke Theseus says, "The iron tongue of midnight hath told twelve."

To create thunder, stagehands could roll a cannonball across the floor of the tiring house or bend a metal sheet back and forth. Probably standing below the trap door, actors could offer up battlefield groans and ghostly wailings. To suggest birds, an actor could imitate the crowing of the rooster, as in the opening scene of *Hamlet*, or a

---

[a] The word *bandore* was gradually clipped to become the word *banjo*.

screaming owl and crying crickets, as in the second act of *Macbeth*. These lines from the last scene of *Midsummer* also suggest animal cries as "noises-off":

ROBIN GOODFELLOW
Now the hungry lion roars,
And the wolf behowls the moon.[278] (5.1.388-87)

Flying

Nowadays we tend to view witches flying on broomsticks as a child's tale acted out on Halloween and, thus, give little credence to the phenomenon. Yet in the Elizabethan and Jacobean periods, teleportation via long-handled brooms awakened by magic was considered quite real. Therefore, in the witch plays of the Jacobean period, a "flying machine" was necessary. As shown in earlier chapters, the ascent and descent of gods, goddesses, or angels were performed by means of a winch. However, in London's roofed theatre, Blackfriars, it was possible to devise machines which would allow motion from left to right and back again to create the illusion of free flying. In addition, an Italian architect named Nicola Sabbatini designed a *deus ex machina* sturdier than the old Greek machine. Called a *cloud machine*, it involved a platform about the width of a sidewalk and long enough to hold up to four actors, who could be raised or lowered as needed. The platform was covered up with a horizontal "cloud" attached to the front of the platform so that the "car" of bygone days was not visible to the audience.

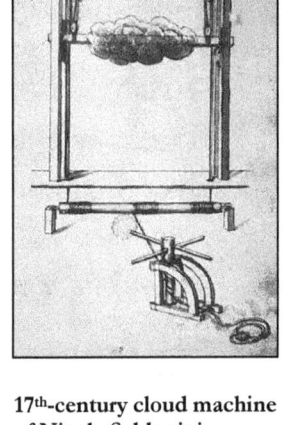

17th-century cloud machine of Nicola Sabbatini

17th-century wire flying system of Giacomo Torelli. Note cloud effect at top.

In his play, *The Witches of Lancashire*, Thomas Heywood included a somewhat comical scene (excerpted below) involving an unseen spirit that descends from above and interferes maliciously with a group gathered for a wedding feast.

DOUGHTY
On, in the name of wedlock, fiddlers, on!

LAWRENCE
On with your melody!

[The fiddlers pass through, and play the battle as they exit.]

BANTAM
Enter the gates with joy,
And as you enter, play "The Sack of Troy."

[[Enter a] spirit [above]]

JOAN
Welcome, bride Parnell.
Bridegroom Lawrence eke.[a]

SEELY
[To Lawrence] In you before,[b] for we this cake must break
Over the bride. *[Exit Lawrence]*

[As they lift up the cake, the spirit snatches it and pours down bran.]

Forgi' me! What's become O' th' cake, wife?

JOAN
It slipped out of my hand and is fallen into crumbs, I think. *[Aside]* "Crumbs?"
The devil of crumb is here—but bran, nothing but bran? What prodigy is this?

PARNELL
Is my best bride's cake come to this? Oh, woe worth it!

[Exit Parnell, Seely, Joan, and maids.]

WHETSTONE
How daintily the bride's hair is powder'd with it!

ARTHUR
My hair stands on end to see it!

BANTAM
And mine!

---

[a] also
[b] Enter ahead of me

SHAKESTONE
I was never so amaz'd!²⁷⁹ (3.1.43-58)

EXERCISE 13.2: Special Effects Platt Sheet

DIRECTIONS: The purpose of this exercise is to undertake a special effects survey of Shakespeare's *Macbeth*. Divide the members of the class into five groups, one for each act in Shakespeare's *Macbeth*. You may use any edition of the play that is available to you in a library or on the Internet. (A particularly useful web site is <http://shakespeare.mit.edu/macbeth/full.html>.) Your task is to create a platt sheet for the act your group has been assigned. Note the cues the stagehand would be listening for as well as the special effect that would immediately follow the cue. An example is provided below with text from the first act of Shakespeare's *Julius Caesar*. Write by hand, as would have been done in Elizabethan times. To make the platt sheet readable at a glance, find a way to set the cues apart from the effect (sample on next page).

Script

BRUTUS
Follow me, then.

Exeunt

Scene II. CAESAR's house.

Thunder and lightning. Enter CAESAR, in his night-gown.

CAESAR
Nor heaven nor earth have been at peace tonight:
Thrice hath Calpurnia in her sleep cried out,
"Help, ho! they murder Caesar!" Who's within?

> ### Platt Sheet
>
> Speaker: BRUTUS
>
> Line: Follow me, then.
>
> Effect: Roll cannon ball to create sound of thunder

RHETORIC IN RENAISSANCE PLAYS

Chapter 14

Introduction

Imagining the boy Will Shakespeare with a satchel and hornbook in tow may not be the first mental image we have of him, but indeed the great man did once "creep like snail unwillingly to school," (*As You Like It*, 2.7.153-54) as he once put it. How, then, did his education in the grammar school at Stratford-on-Avon shape his art? For an answer, one can turn to historian George A. Kennedy, who explained sixteenth-century developments in English education, thus:

> In the mid-sixteenth century, practical handbooks of rhetoric began to appear in English. That such works were written is an indication that some English schoolmasters for the first time recognized a need to train students in the composition and appreciation of English. This feeling was contemporary with assertions of nationalism under the Tudor kings, including the independence of the Anglican Church from Rome and its substitution of an English liturgy for the Latin mass. The new English rhetorics[a] . . . show *how rhetoric was taught when the great writers of the Elizabethan Age, including Shakespeare, were young students.*[280] (Emphasis added.)

The heart and soul of rhetoric in grammar and logic schools was, and still is, the progymnasmata, the preliminary exercises that a student was expected to master before advancing to full-blown rhetoric. What the great playwrights cut their teeth on as young students became radiantly displayed later in the plays they wrote.

The chart that follows provides a list of the elements of the progymnasmata as well as passages where each is exemplified in the plays of Shakespeare and his contemporaries:

---

[a] Textbooks of rhetoric

PROGYMNASMATA ELEMENT	AUTHOR	PLAY	DETAILS
Fable	William Shakespeare	*Coriolanus* Act I, sc. 1	Menenius tells the fable of the Belly and the Limbs as a metaphor for the state and the people.
Narrative	Thomas Kyd	*The Spanish Tragedy* Act I, sc. 1	The ghost of Andrea narrates the actions that have preceded the action of the play.
Description	Christopher Marlowe	*Dr. Faustus* Act V, sc. 2	Evil Angel describes a Place (Hell). Faustus describes Time and Motion.
Proverb	John Pickering	*Horestes* ll. 276-85	Employs a variation of "Time and tide wait for no man" ("let slyp no time ne tyd")
Chreia	Thomas Kyd	*The Spanish Tragedy* Act III, sc. 13	Three quotations in Latin—two from Seneca, one from Romans 12:19
Refutation	Christopher Marlowe	*Doctor Faustus* (passim)	Throughout the play, there is an ongoing debate as to whether Faustus is beyond redemption or not.
Confirmation			
Commonplace	William Shakespeare	*The Merchant of Venice* Act IV, sc. 1	"The quality of mercy" speech exemplifies a judicial use of Commonplace.
Encomium	William Shakespeare	*Julius Caesar* Act III, sc. 2	Antony's speech ("I come to bury Caesar, not to praise him") is an artful Encomium of Caesar.
Invective	Ben Jonson	*Bartholomew Fair* Act I, sc. 3	Quarlous speaks an Invective against Zeal-of-the-Land Busy, a Puritan.
Comparison	William Shakespeare	*A Comedy of Errors* Act II, sc. 1	Luciana laments the differences between the lives of men and women.
Speech in Character	Christopher Marlowe	*Tamburlaine* Act IV, sc. 2	Tamburlaine's raving reveals his maniacal mind.
Thesis	William Shakespeare	*Henry V* Act IV, sc. 1	Henry argues that every man's conscience is his own.
Legislation	William Shakespeare	*Henry V* Act I, Scene 1	The English lords are trying to determine if their king can lawfully claim the throne of France.

EXERCISE 14.1: Examining a Shakespearean Encomium

DIRECTIONS: Please begin by reading the introduction and the excerpt. Then answer the questions which follow.

INTRODUCTION: *The following passage is an Encomium from the closing scene of William Shakespeare's play* Henry VIII. *It depicts that moment when Henry first sees his newborn daughter, Elizabeth (the future Queen Elizabeth I), who is brought to him in the arms of Thomas Cranmer, Archbishop of Canterbury. It is Cranmer who delivers the Encomium.*

Excerpt from Henry VIII
By William Shakespeare

ARCHBISHOP CRANMER
Let me speak, sir,
For heaven now bids me; and the words I utter
Let none think flattery, for they'll find 'em truth.
This royal infant—heaven still move about her!—
Though in her cradle, yet now promises   25
Upon this land a thousand blessings,
Which time shall bring to ripeness: she shall be—
But few now living can behold that goodness—
A pattern to all princes living with her,
And all that shall succeed: Saba[a] was never   30
More covetous of wisdom and fair virtue
Than this pure soul shall be: all princely graces,
That mold up such a mighty piece as this is,
With all the virtues that attend the good,
Shall still be doubled on her: truth shall nurse her,   35
Holy and heavenly thoughts still counsel her:
She shall be loved and fear'd: her own shall bless her;
Her foes shake like a field of beaten corn,
And hang their heads with sorrow: good grows with her:
In her days every man shall eat in safety,   40
Under his own vine, what he plants; and sing

---

[a] Queen of Sheba (Saba), the Biblical queen who visited King Solomon, as recorded in I Kings 10.

    The merry songs of peace to all his neighbors:
    God shall be truly known; and those about her
    From her shall read the perfect ways of honor,
    And by those claim their greatness, not by blood.   45
    Nor shall this peace sleep with her: but as when
    The bird of wonder dies, the maiden phoenix,
    Her ashes new create another heir,
    As great in admiration as herself;
    So shall she leave her blessedness to one,   50
    When heaven shall call her from this cloud of darkness,
    Who from the sacred ashes of her honor
    Shall star-like rise, as great in fame as she was,
    And so stand fixed: peace, plenty, love, truth, terror,
    That were the servants to this chosen infant,   55
    Shall then be his, and like a vine grow to him:
    Wherever the bright sun of heaven shall shine,
    His honor and the greatness of his name
    Shall be, and make new nations: he shall flourish,
    And, like a mountain cedar, reach his branches   60
    To all the plains about him: our children's children
    Shall see this, and bless heaven.

    KING HENRY
    Thou speakest wonders.[281] (5.4)

Questions:

1. BACKGROUND: This Encomium is adapted to the dramatic context.

    a. To whom was Cranmer speaking? (Check Line 63 if unsure.)

    b. How does that explain the absence of the Background portion of the encomium?

2. EDUCATION / INFLUENCES: Cranmer does not name specific people as Elizabeth's teachers and influences, but instead identifies her tutors as:

   a. Line 35:

   b. Line 36:

3. VIRTUES: What virtues are specified in the following lines?

   a. Line 28:

   b. Line 43:

   c. Line 44:

4. ACHIEVEMENTS: In Line 54, Cranmer lists five achievements that Elizabeth will make by the end of her reign.

   a. What are they?

   b. Which two of these five are detailed in Lines 40-42?

   c. The fifth item may seem strange to list as an "achievement." Re-read Lines 37-39 and, in your own words, summarize what Cranmer means here?

5. Instead of ending the Encomium at Line 45, why do you suppose Cranmer shifts the focus to Elizabeth's successor in Lines 46-62? (HINT: The play was written in about 1613.)

Modes of Persuasion

Without question, among all the monologues of the Elizabethan era, the best representation of the modes of persuasion is the speech of Mark Antony in Act III of Shakespeare's *Julius Caesar*. Caesar has just been assassinated, Brutus has explained to the mob why the death of Caesar was justified, and the mob at this point is jeering the dead Caesar. Antony's job is to meet his hearers in their anger toward Caesar and turn that anger toward  the conspirators. Shakespeare well understood that he could not write a brief speech for such a situation. It consumes 195 lines and provides a marvelous example of the three modes of persuasion:

Ethos—which is an appeal to ethics. Its purpose is to establish the character or credibility of the speaker. After all, who would believe a rogue?

Logos—which is an appeal to logic. Its purpose is to persuade by laying evidence before the hearers.

Pathos—which is an appeal to the emotions. Its purpose is to persuade an audience by arousing in them such feelings as righteous indignation, patriotism, or respect.

An examination of Antony's monologue will reveal how these three approaches work together.

Excerpts from *Julius Caesar*
By William Shakespeare

Antony approaches his task humbly, assuring the mob that his purpose is not in opposition to that of the honorable Brutus, who, having just explained his reasons for the murder of Caesar, has yielded to Antony:

ANTONY

          [Ethos]
Friends, Romans, countrymen, lend me your ears.
I come to bury Caesar, not to praise him.
The evil that men do lives after them;
The good is oft interrèd with their bones.

> So let it be with Caesar. The noble Brutus
> Hath told you Caesar was ambitious.
> If it were so, it was a grievous fault,
> And grievously hath Caesar answered it.
> Here, under leave of Brutus and the rest
> (For Brutus is an honorable man;
> So are they all, all honorable men),
> Come I to speak in Caesar's funeral.[282] (3.2.42-53)

This statement of an honorable purpose is supplemented some lines later with the following:

> O masters, if I were disposed to stir
> Your hearts and minds to mutiny and rage,
> I should do Brutus wrong and Cassius wrong,
> Who, you all know, are honorable men.
> I will not do them wrong. I rather choose
> To wrong the dead, to wrong myself and you,
> Than I will wrong such honorable men. (90-96)

Having shown his love of honor (his character), Antony moves from Ethos to Logos. He begins to remind the Romans of all that Caesar has done for them, and he continues to remind them of Brutus's honorable intent. However, notice that as he moves ahead, one senses the actor would begin to use the word *honorable* in a gradually more sarcastic tone:

ANTONY

[Logos]
> He was my friend, faithful and just to me,
> But Brutus says he was ambitious,
> And Brutus is an honorable man.
> He hath brought many captives home to Rome,
> Whose ransoms did the general coffers fill.
> Did this in Caesar seem ambitious?
> When that the poor have cried, Caesar hath wept;
> Ambition should be made of sterner stuff.
> Yet Brutus says he was ambitious,

And Brutus is an honorable man.
You all did see that on the Lupercal
I thrice presented him a kingly crown,
Which he did thrice refuse. Was this ambition?
Yet Brutus says he was ambitious,
And sure he is an honorable man.
I speak not to disprove what Brutus spoke,
But here I am to speak what I do know.

You all did love him once, not without cause.
What cause withholds you, then, to mourn for him?—
O judgment, thou art fled to brutish beasts,
And men have lost their reason!—Bear with me;
My heart is in the coffin there with Caesar,
And I must pause till it come back to me. (54-76)

That Antony has succeeded in his logical appeal is borne out by the immediate responses of the plebians:

FIRST PLEBEIAN
Methinks there is much reason in his sayings.

SECOND PLEBEIAN
If thou consider rightly of the matter,
Caesar has had great wrong. (77-79)

Now Antony launches more fully into his emotional appeal, using the old "forbidden fruit" trick, telling the crowd that he dare not read Caesar's will because of the effect it might have on them. Of course, this makes them clamor all the more, so Antony continues:

ANTONY

[Pathos]

Have patience, gentle friends. I must not read it.
It is not meet you know how Caesar loved you.
You are not wood, you are not stones, but men.
And, being men, hearing the will of Caesar,
It will inflame you; it will make you mad.

'Tis good you know not that you are his heirs,
For if you should, O, what would come of it? (109-15)

As the scene proceeds, the plebians persist in their demand to hear Caesar's will, so Antony gathers them around the corpse of Caesar, reminisces about Caesar's valor, and throws back Caesar's cloak to expose his bloody wounds to the men of Rome, a move calculated to further inflame the crowd. But he is not done yet. An analysis of the rhetorical appeals in the remainder of the speech awaits below, giving you the opportunity to ferret out the stages for yourself.

ACTIVITY 14.A: Listening to Marc Antony's Oration

Over the years, several excellent actors have delivered Antony's speech in film or video, some of which have been placed on *YouTube*. If time permits, view one or two of the following and note how various actors employ voice, facial expression, and gesture as their character moves back and forth between Ethos, Logos, and Pathos (you may need to forgive an old-fashioned costume or two):

- Marlon Brando, 1953 (partial, 3 min.)
- Robert Stephens, 1969 (13:31 min., 31 sec.)
- Charlton Hesston, 1970 (9 min., 47 sec.)
- Richard Pasco, 1979 (partial, 6 min. 25 sec.)
- Damien Lewis, 2016 (partial, 2 min. 33 sec.)

EXERCISE 14.2: Identifying Rhetorical Appeals

After the crowd has become inflamed by the sight of the gory corpse, Antony continues to speak and, once again, draws on all three persuasive appeals—ethos, logos, and pathos.

> ANTONY
> I come not, friends, to steal away your hearts.
> I am no orator, as Brutus is,
> But, as you know me all, a plain blunt man
> That love my friend, and that they know full well   185
> That gave me public leave to speak of him.
> For I have neither wit, nor words, nor worth,
> Action, nor utterance, nor the power of speech

> To stir men's blood. I only speak right on.
> I tell you that which you yourselves do know, 190
> Show you sweet Caesar's wounds, poor poor dumb mouths,
> And bid them speak for me. But were I Brutus,
> And Brutus Antony, there were an Antony
> Would ruffle up your spirits and put a tongue
> In every wound of Caesar that should move 195
> The stones of Rome to rise and mutiny. (3.2)

1. Which lines represent Ethos (the ethical appeal)?

2. Which line represents Logos (the logical appeal)?

3. Which lines represent Pathos (the emotional appeal)

After Antony reaches a fever pitch in these lines, the plebians cry out, "We'll mutiny!" But Antony calls them back to hear the will:

> ALL PLEBEIANS.
> Most true. The will! Let's stay and hear the will. 205
>
> ANTONY
> Here is the will, and under Caesar's will
> To every Roman citizen he gives,
> To every several men, seventy-five drachmas.

In lines 208-12 (omitted here), the plebians shout for revenge, but Antony continues:

> Moreover, he hath left you all his walks,
> His private arbors, and new-planted orchards,
> On this side Tiber. He hath left them you, 215
> And to your heirs forever—common pleasures
> To walk abroad and recreate yourselves.
> Here was a Caesar! When comes such another?

4. Do Antony's lines (206-17) have ethical, emotional, or logical appeal? Explain your answer.

5. With what appeal does Antony close in Line 218? Why do you suppose he finishes with this type of appeal?

Finally, worked to a frenzy, the people run into the streets to avenge Caesar's death

> FIRST PLEBEIAN
> Never, never!—Come, away, away!
> We'll burn his body in the holy place
> And with the brands fire the traitors' houses. (219-21)

Once the mayhem has begun, Antony mutters to himself:

> ANTONY
> Now let it work. Mischief, thou art afoot;
> Take thou what course thou wilt. (226-27)

6. Why do you suppose Shakespeare wrote this additional remark for Antony, instead of finishing with the crowd roaring off for revenge?

RENAISSANCE THEATRE TIDBITS FROM PRIMARY SOURCES

Chapter 15

Introduction

Sports fans are aware that numerous superstitions have grown up around the sport of baseball. Wade Boggs of the Detroit Tigers, for example, would eat only chicken before a game. Scott Erikson would dress only in black and utter nary a word to anyone before a game in which he was pitching. More obvious to the fans was pitcher Jose Valverde's ritual. He would come out of the bullpen with his mouth full of water, then spit an equal amount to his right and to his left, and conclude with a slap of his glove against his thigh. Then, carrying his hat and glove—one in each hand—he would run to the mound, being certain never to step on any line on the field.[283] Baseball is full of such stories. But who knew that actors display such superstition? Originating in the early seventeenth century, the superstition still affects the theatrical community today. It even has a name: the *Macbeth* curse.

The *Macbeth* Curse

Why would an otherwise perfectly normal actor or director suddenly exit the theatre, spin around three times, spit, quote an insult from Shakespeare, and wait to be invited back inside? Because that little ritual is considered the antidote to the *Macbeth* curse. It seems that whenever *Macbeth* is performed, calamity results, and, according to the legend, it all began at the first performance of the play when a boy playing the role of Lady Macbeth died backstage while awaiting his cue. Bad luck has followed this play since that night. Why? Well, some believe that when Shakespeare was writing the play, he inserted into the script an actual witch's incantation, unintentionally bewitching the play forever after. Results of the hex include the following, arranged by century:

1672: An actor in Amsterdam substituted a real knife for the stage knife and actually killed the actor playing Duncan.

1703: On the day the play opened, a violent storm beset England.

1721: On a whim, a nobleman in the audience hopped onto the stage during a performance of the play. (It seems he needed to get to the other side to chat with a friend.) Angry, the actors ushered him off the stage. He returned a few minutes later and set fire to the theatre.

1775: When the great actress Sarah Siddons was playing Lady Macbeth one night, her spectators were somehow so overwhelmed with disapproval that she was "nearly ravaged" by the mob.

1882: All was well until the swordfight in Act V, Scene 8, when J. H. Barnes actually thrust his sword through the chest of William Rignold. (Fortunately, Rignold survived.)

1926: While Sybil Thorndike was performing the role of Lady Macbeth, a fellow actor suddenly lunged at her throat and tried to strangle her—for real!

1937: Lilian Baylis died of a heart attack during a rehearsal of *Macbeth*. In the same show where Lilian Baylis died, Laurence Olivier was nearly killed by a falling weight.

1942: When John Gielgud was playing the title role, three actors died—those playing King Duncan and the two witches. Later, the costume and set director committed suicide surrounded by his creations for the performance of *Macbeth*.

1947: In the final scene of the play, the actor Harold Norman was to perform the death scene of Macbeth. He did fall to the ground, as planned, but crawled backstage and cried out he had been stabbed. He later died at a hospital.

1953: Charlton Hesston, in the role of Macbeth, was riding his horse in an action scene when he suddenly dismounted and started screaming, "Get them off me!" It appears the laundress had soaked his tights in kerosene, and he suffered burns when it reacted with the sweat of the horse. In the same play, a planned fire at Macbeth's castle turned disastrous when a gust of wind blew flames into the audience.

1960: While props were being unloaded from a ship for a performance in South Africa, a stagehand shouted the title, *"Macbeth!"* Suddenly a spear fell from the box and ran him through.

1988: In Spain, Bantcho Bantchevsky, an 82-year-old singing coach, fell to his death from a balcony during the intermission at a performance of *Macbeth*.

Because of all these mishaps associated with the play, an unwritten rule has arisen: actors are never to say the name of the play while in the theatre. Instead, they call it "the Scottish play." So concerned were producers in 2013 that when Alan Cumming played Macbeth at the Ethel Barrymore Theatre in New York, they went to the expense to have a sign made and posted it at the entrance: "The producers ask that you refrain from speaking the name of the play you are about to see while within these walls." Reportedly, all went well.

Now, all of these incidents are perhaps a little unnerving, but the worst disaster to befall a performance of Macbeth happened in New York on May 10, 1849. In the years preceding the disaster, two actors—the British William Macready and the American Edwin Forrest—had become bitter rivals. Their hatred of each other was exacerbated by the English press, who would insult Forrest as an oafish bumpkin of an American, "fighting words" to an American public who still felt the sting of what they considered British snobbery. When Macready came to New York to perform the role of Macbeth, Forrest's fans decided they would pack the theatre and make things very nasty for Mr. Macready, but they probably never anticipated the actual result. Shortly after the ultimate disaster, a pamphlet was published reporting the details to the curious public. Excerpts appear below.

Excerpts from "Account of the Terrific and Fatal Riot at the New-York Astor Place Opera House"

> On the night of the 10th of May 1849, the Empire City, the great metropolis of the Union, was the scene of one of those horrors of civilization, which for a time make the great heart of humanity stop in its beatings. In the darkness of night, thousands of citizens were gathered in a central square of the most aristocratic quarter of New York—gathered around one of its most conspicuous and magnificent edifices, the Astor Place Opera House. . . .
>
> Around this edifice, we say, a vast crowd was gathered. On the stage the English actor Macready was trying to play the part of Macbeth, in which he was interrupted by hisses and hootings, and encouraged by the cheers of a large audience, who had crowded the house to sustain him. On the outside a mob was gathering, trying to force an entrance into the house, and throwing volleys of stones at the barricaded windows. In the house, the police were arresting those who made the disturbance—outside they were driven back by volleys of paving stones.

In the midst of this scene of clamor and outrage, was heard the clatter of a troop of horse approaching the scene. "The military—the military are coming!" was the exclamation of the crowd. Further on was heard the quick tramp of companies of infantry, and there was seen the gleam of bayonets. A cry of rage burst from the

Astor Place Riot, New York, 1849

mob. The appearance of an armed force seemed to inspire them with a sudden fury. They ceased storming the Opera House, and turned their volleys against the horsemen. Amid piercing yells and execrations, men were knocked from their horses, the untrained animals were frightened, and the force was speedily routed, and could not afterwards be rallied to perform any efficient service.

Now came the turn of the infantry. They marched down the sidewalk in a solid column; but had no sooner taken up a position for the protection of the house, than they were assailed with volleys of missals. Soldiers were knocked down and carried off wounded. Officers were disabled. An attempt to charge with the bayonet was frustrated by the dense crowd, seizing the muskets, and attempting to wrest them from the hands of the soldiers. At last the awful word was given to fire—there was a gleam of sulphurous light, a sharp quick rattle, and here and there in the crowd a man sank upon the pavement with a deep groan or a death rattle. Then came a more furious attack, and a wild yell of vengeance! Then the rattle of another death-dealing volley, far more fatal than the first. The ground was covered with killed and wounded—the pavement was stained with blood. A panic seized the multitude, which broke and scattered in every direction. In the darkness of the night yells of rage, screams of agony, and dying groans were mingled together. Groups of men took up the wounded and the dead, and conveyed them to the neighboring apothecary shops, station-houses, and the hospital.

The horrors of that night can never be described. We looked over the scene that misty midnight. The military, resting from their work of death, in stern silence were grimly guarding the Opera House. Its interior was a rendezvous and a hospital for the wounded military and police. Here and there around the building, and at the corners of the streets were crowds of men talking in deep and earnest tones of the indignation. There were little processions moving off with the dead or mutilated bodies of their friends and relations. A husband, uttering frenzied curses, followed his mortally wounded wife to the hospital. An aged mother found her only son, the sole support of her declining years, in the agonies of death. Many a wife sat watching at home, in terror and alarm for her absent husband. It was an evening of dread—and it became a night of horror, which on the morrow, when the awful tragedy became more widely known, settled down upon the city like a funeral pall. The result of that night's work was the death of twenty-two victims, either shot dead upon the spot or mortally wounded, so that they died within a few days; and the wounding of some thirty more, many of whom will be maimed for life.[284]

APPENDIX A: Robin Hood Fragment in Modern English

Sir Sheriff, for thy sake, / Robin Hood will I take.
I will thee give gold and fee. / This behest[a] thou hold me
Robin Hood, fair and free, / under this lind[b] shoot we.
With the shot I will / All thy lusts to fulfill
Have at the prick,[c] / And I cleave[d] the stick.   5
Let us cast the stone. / I grant well, by Saint John.
Let us cast the axletree.[e] / Have a foot before thee
Sir knight, you have a fall / And I the Robin quite shall
Out on thee I blow mine horn. / It were better to be unborn.
Let us fight at once. / He that fleeth, God give him mischance.   10
Now I have the mastery here. / Off I smite this sorry swire.[f]
This knight's clothes will I wear, / And in my hood his head will bear.
Wellmet,[g] fellow mine![h] / What hearest thou of good Robin,
Robin Hood and his meinie?[i] / With the sheriff taken be.
Set on foot with good will, / And the sheriff will we kill.   15
Behold well Friar Tuck, how he doth his bow pluck.
Yield you, sirs, to the sheriff, / Or else shall your bows cleave.
Now we be bounden all in same. / Friar Tuck, this is no game.
Come thou forth, thou false outlaw! / Thou shall [be] hanged and drawn
Now, alas, what shall we do? / We must to the prison go.   20
Open the gates fast anon / And let these thieves in go!

---

[a] promise
[b] linden tree
[c] point
[d] split
[e] unclear word in original (exaltre); could be axletree (a bar of wood connecting wheels on a carriage)
[f] neck
[g] hello
[h] my fellow
[i] band

APPENDIX B: *Translation of St. Nicholas Excerpt*

GETRON:
Tomorrow will be the feast
Of Nicholas, whom all Christianity
Ought to honor faithfully,
To revere and to bless.
Therefore, hear my plans:
Let us go to his sacred festivals;
Let us praise his wonderful works;
Let us pray for his intercession. . . .

Meanwhile, let someone come dressed like Nicholas;
Let him grab the boy, who is holding a goblet and a sack of new wine,
Let him place the captured [boy] in front of the doors,
And let him go away, as if he were not certain.
Then in truth let one of the citizens speak to the boy.

CITIZEN:
Boy, who are you, and where do you wish to travel?

BOY:
I come to this place; I will not go further.
I am the only son of Getron.
To Nicholas be praise and glory,
Whose favor has led me back here.

APPENDIX C: Excerpt from The Conversion of St. Paul

The *Conversion of St. Paul*, which is a Digby play, was written in the dialect of East Anglia, probably in the late fifteenth century, though additions were made in a distinctly different handwriting in the sixteenth century, probably during the Protestant Reformation. Because it is a conversion narrative, it is classified as a miracle play and was not part of a Corpus Christi cycle. In terms of the progymnasmata, it can be viewed as an Expanded Narrative of Acts 9, which records the conversion of Paul on the Damascus road.

Some have viewed certain lines of dialogue in this play as examples of medieval Christendom's anti-Semitism. However, Professor Heather Hill-Vasquez has made a good case for the idea that the accusations hurled at Caiaphas and Anna in the play are actually those of Protestant reformers to the Catholic clergy.[285] Moreover, one must also keep in mind that Paul's criticisms of the Sanhedrin in the first days of the Christian era should be viewed in their historical context of one son of Abraham arguing with other sons of Abraham with whom he has recently come to disagree.

The text that follows is an abridged version of the play rendered, for the most part, in Modern English to enhance readability. The Middle English version with annotations is available online.[286]

Since these plays were not part of the Corpus Christi plays, they were not presented on pageants. As you read, therefore, try to imagine how the two (or three) stages would have been arranged and what features they would have required. The special effects, stage properties, and costuming of this play also provide insights into medieval theatre.

Excerpt from *THE CONVERSION OF ST. PAUL*
From the Digby Manuscript

CHARACTERS

Saul / Paul of Tarsus
Caiaphas
Ananias (the priest)
First knight
Second knight
God
Ananias (the disciple)
Belial
Mercury
Servant of the priests
Angel

SETTING

Ancient Israel and Syria

TIME

AD 50

Station 1: Jerusalem

> NARRATOR
> Rex gloriae, all-powerful king
> And Mary, the most excellent queen,
> Who bore the blessed Jesus,
> Who suffered pain for us.
>
> Good friends, we come before you all
> To show you here our tale--
> The conversion of St. Paul--
> Which the Book of Acts does tell.

Right soon we will begin
To the best that we can do
Your attention we will win
And this tale unfold to you.

[An interlude of dance]

[Here Saul enters with the first knight, appareled in their best like adventurous knights, saying:]

SAUL
I am the most dreaded man on earth
I am, of all, most noble
No man can pass my worth
East or west or global.

All fear me. My name is Saul.
The disciples of Christ, they tremble
I threaten each and all.
They destroy our laws and temple.
On Jesus, they do call.

[Caiaphas and Ananias the priest enter with papers in hand.]

CAIAPHAS
Our task for you is simple.
The rebels—put down all!

ANANIAS THE PRIEST
We grant you here permission
To fill them all with woe
And stop their lawless mission.
Spare no one—friend or foe!

[Hands Saul the papers.]

SAUL
Instructions, I will fulfill
I give you here my oath

I spare neither man nor woman.
To you I will bring both.

Now, knights, we seek the road
To Damascus as fast as we can
Our horses here we load
All weight they can withstand.

[Here Saul goes a little aside to prepare to ride. The second knight comes to Saul with a horse.]

SECOND KNIGHT
Look, Paul, your palfrey's ready
All decked out for your journey.

SAUL
Please, friend, hold him steady.
To Damascus now, I turn ye.

[Here Saul rides forward with the two knights about the place and out of the place.]

NARRATOR
[Pointing to the next station] We show you here our version
Of Paul on Damascus Road
Where you will see his conversion
And also his sin unload.

Station 2: The Road to Damascus

SAUL
To Damascus I will go. I here devote my life
To pursuing the disciples and closing up their churches.
No joy for any of them—not man, nor child, nor wife.
If they return to our laws, their freedom they can purchase.

[Here comes a light with great tempest, and Saul falls off his horse. The second knight runs away, but the first knight remains. Then God speaks from heaven:]

GOD

[Speaking from above] Saul! Saul! Why do you persecute me?
It's hard to kick against the goads.
I, the maker of heaven and earth
Will lift your sinful load.

SAUL

O, Lord, I am afraid! I'm trembling with fear!
What shall I do? Please tell me now.

GOD

Arise and go to a city near
And I'll save you and lift your frown.

[God withdraws.]

SAUL

O merciful God! What's wrong with me?
My legs are weak, and I am lame.
My eyes are blind, I cannot see,
For help I call on Jesus' name.

FIRST KNIGHT

You don't need Christ. You just need me.
I'm true to you, and here's my hand. *[Reaches down to help Saul]*

SAUL

Thank you, friend knight, thank you indeed.
Lead on to Damascus' land.

GOD

Ananias, Ananias! Where are you, Anani?

DISCIPLE ANANIAS

I'm here, my Lord, I'm with you, really. What do you ask of me?

GOD

Go into the street called Straight. It's nigh.
I'll lead you to a certain house where Saul we will set free.
Though once a wolf, he now is meek, so mild and so tame.

DISCIPLE ANANIAS

I'm trembling, Lord. Saul frightens me.
He kills each one who says your name.

GOD

No, Ananias, no. To see you, he'll be glad.
Be not afraid. I've chosen him to take my name to kings,
And to the folk of Israel and on Mount Gilead.
A learned man is Saul, you'll see. I promise you these things.

DISCIPLE ANANIAS

I will fulfill this, your command. I'll make my way to Saul.

GOD

Good Ananias, fare thee well. Find Saul and tell him all.

[Ananias goes toward Saul, who is now alone, in a posture of prayer.]

DISCIPLE ANANIAS

New man, friend Saul, God sent me here.
He asks you pray and be steadfast
Remember him—the light, the fear!
And on the ground, you fell aghast.
Lo! He stands a man upright
Or throws him to the ground
This is his power. You need it sore,
His power celestial, all around.

SAUL

I welcome now this gratification.
I'm right glad it is thus.

[Here the Holy Spirit appears above them.]

DISCIPLE ANANIAS

Be of good cheer and jubilation
The Holy Spirit comes on us.
Put out your hand and go with me
I now restore your sight.

SAUL
Blessed Lord, I thankful be
You've lifted here my plight.
Where I was blind, I now can see.
And ask you please to baptize me.

DISCIPLE ANANIAS
Saul, to this well of virtue come.

[They move to the baptismal font.]

Kneel on the ground and here receive
This christening from the font.

[Saul kneels.]

Of you, your sins, he will relieve.
The devil comes to naught.

[Ananias baptizes Saul.]

SAUL
Glad as a bird in flight am I. I'm happy to receive
This blessed sacrament, so dear. No more the devil can deceive.

DISCIPLE ANANIAS
Come on your way. Do not delay. Disciples wait for you.
In Damasc town you'll live with them and they will tutor you.

[They leave in procession, Ananias leading.]

[There is an interlude of dance.]

NARRATOR
Thus Saul now converted be and serves the Lord quite true.
We commit you all to the Trinity, and end this Station Two.

Station 3: Back to Jerusalem

NARRATOR
The might of the Father, in this rotation,
Grant to you all—of high or low degree—
An understanding of this little station
Which is good and profitable for ye.

[The narrator steps aside. The two knights, back from the road to Damascus, report to Caiaphas and Ananias the priest at their platform or acting area.]

FIRST KNIGHT
Caiaphas and Ananias, hear our report profound.
A fearsome light glided from the sky
And smote noble Saul to the ground
As he unto Damascus went, disciples to espy.

SECOND KNIGHT
It ravished him. His spirits turned numb.
A sweet, melodious voice did speak
And chided him for all he'd done.
Disciple Ananias it told him he should seek.
And be baptized and live among the meek.
Against our law he is completely won.

CAIAPHAS
I'm sure this is not true! What?
Saul converted from our law?
But in Damascus he's been taught
And at tradition he does claw.

ANANIAS THE PRIEST
Caiaphas, hear my true word. I know with every breath
He'll not turn back no matter what.
We him must take and put to death
And all the rebels he once sought.

[They retire.]

[A devil enters with thunder and fire to boast about himself. He takes a seat in a chair.]

BELIAL
Ho! Ho! Behold me! I am the prince of parts infernal
Next unto Lucifer, I am in majesty.
By name, I am called the god Belial.
No one matches me in might or excellency.
My power is principal and of most sovereignty.
In the temples and synagogues, whoever denies me to honor
My bishops, through my motion, will him soon devour.

I have moved my prelates, Caiaphas and Anna,
To pursue and put down, by power royal,
Through the cities of Damascus and Lydda
All who worship the high God supernal.
Their death is conspired, without any favor at all.
My bishops have chosen one most rigorous
For them to pursue. His name is Saul.

[Mercury enters, with an explosion, coming in haste, crying and roaring.]

MERCURY
Ho, out! Out! Alas, this sudden chance!
Well we may bewail this cursed adventure!

BELIAL
Mercury, what ails you? Your tale enhance!
Who hereabouts has caused you this displeasure?

MERCURY
Displeasure enough! Of that you may be sure!
Our law will soon be clean down laid.
For it's decaying now. And more will fail, I am afraid.

BELIAL
How can that be? It simply can't be true!
Consider, fool, how long our law has reigned.
How people love to sin – their crimes to do –
Their hearts with folly and with pride are stained.

Even if they stray from off our path,
By their sins they've never earned or gained
We have the power to bring them back again.
So then what fury have you seen that troubles you?

MERCURY
Ho, out! Out! Saul—the one I trusted in—
Has turned away and is our cruel foe.
He serves almighty God and is baptized
And forth into the world he does go!

BELIAL
Out! This grieves me worse than all hell's pains!
More painful this, than the infernal dungeon!

MERCURY
Complaining does no good. Save breath.
We must find someone who will put Saul to death!

BELIAL
Well said, Mercury! Of council, you are able!
Ho, Saul, you will repent that you've been unstable.

[Belial and Mercury leave with fire and tempest.
Saul enters dressed as a disciple. He addresses the audience directly.]

SAUL
The Lord whose word has shaped the sand and sea
Can save you all—standing and sitting here—
From all the power of hell's dread misery.
Let us not spill his mercy, meek and dear.
Beloved friends, know ye the mortal sins,
Seven princes of poison that lead astray?
"Pride is the beginning of all sins,"
Says Holy Scripture. Pride is the great root.
Then Wrath and Envy and Sloth do enter in!
Put Gluttony, Lechery, and Greed out of your sight.
These branches of wickedness snare all men!
And women, too, are not immune.

These Sins lead us all down to doom.
To slay your body Sin doesn't need a knife.
Keep clean your body from Sin uncouth,

Let meekness and mercy guard your life.
With my own mouth, I tell this truth.
Steady your sights and guard your eye:
The messenger of folly can only lie.

[Two servants of the chief priests enter to arrest Saul.]

SERVANT OF THE PRIESTS
What? Is this not Saul? The one
Who journeyed to Jerusalem
To set disciples on the run?

SAUL
Yes, for sure. Saul is my name.
I had power in full dominion—
To hide that from you would be a sin
And on my head it would bring shame—
Under Caesar and priests of the religion
And temples of Jews, that are very hateful
Against almighty Christ.

SERVANT OF THE PRIESTS
To Ananias, I must take you in.
And Caiaphas will pour on you the blame.
Come! On your way! And no delay!

SAUL
I will follow you, for better or worse.

[The servant of the priests leads Saul to the chief priests.]

SAUL
(To the priests) I serve Christ Jesus, he almighty
Creator and maker of sand and sea,
Who is Omnipotent King of heaven's glory,

Who comforts all—both slave and free.
Against his power nothing may stand.
Emperor he is of both heaven and hell.
His goodness and grace all things excel!

[Recedit paulisper; that is, he withdraws for a little while.]

CAIAPHAS
This hurts my heart, Saul's situation.
He is so marvelously changed!
I think he's bewitched by conjuration
Or else the devil has him in chains.
Friend Ananias, what say you?

ANANIAS THE PRIEST
Unto my heart it does great ill.
But, for his falseness, we shall him spill;
By my assent, to death we will him bring.
So more mischief he cannot spring.

CAIAPHAS
We will command the gates all round
And walls, also, in every place,
That from this city he shan't go out,
For he must now his death embrace.

ANANIAS THE PRIEST
This traitor rebel—may he never prosper,
Who brings deceit unto us all!
(To the guards) Now, every guard keep well his wall!

SERVANT OF THE PRIESTS
He can't escape. The gates are shut.
All places are secure and well.
Except for some device, he can't go out
By any way that I can tell.

[An angel appears to Saul.]

ANGEL
Holy Saul, I give you admonition.
The priests are searching. They take great pains
To put you to death. But by God's provision
You will live longer and obtain.
And after your death you will reign
Above in heaven, with our Lord's grace.
Convey yourself now to another place.

SAUL
The Lord's pleasure ever must be done.
With the disciples' help I can escape
In a basket with a rope anon.

God's ways will make them gape.
I trust in him who is the true Lord
To resist their malice and cruel furor.

Epilogue

NARRATOR
Thus leave we Saul within the city
In care of disciples who were right witty.
They lowered him down in a basket sound,
All the way to level ground.
Then, after that, with his Christian brothers,
He freely spread God's word to many others.

This little pageant thus we end,
As we can, without much skill.
Of rhetoric, we little ken.
Overlook our faults, and love us still.
We commit you all to our Lord Jesus!
Heaven will rejoice with praises!

FINIS

APPENDIX D: TEXTS A and B of the Norwich Grocers' Play

THE NORWICH GROCERS' PLAY
Garden of Eden
Excerpts from Text A and Text B

CHARACTERS

God
Adam / Man
Eve / Woman
Serpent
Holy Spirit

SETTING

Garden of Eden

I. The Creation of Eve

Text A

[God creates woman from the rib of Adam.]

ADAM
O my Lord God Incomprehensible, without sin,
Ye thy high excellent magnificence,
this creature to me is *nunc ex ossibus meis*,
and *virago* I call her in thy presence.
Laud, honor, and glory to thee I make,
both father and mother, man shall for her forsake.

Text B

[God creates a Woman from the rib of the Man. Then Man and Woman both speak.]

MAN AND WOMAN
We thank thee, mighty God, and give thee honoration.

MAN
Oh, bone of my bones, and flesh of my flesh eke,[a]
Thou shalt be called woman because thou art of me.
O, gift of God, most goodly that has us made so alike.
Most loving spouse, I much do here rejoice of thee.

WOMAN
And I likewise, sweet lover, do much rejoice of thee.
God therefore be praised. Such comfort has us give,
That each of us with other, thus pleasantly do live.

MAN
To walk about this garden, my fancy me move,
I will thee leave alone till that I turn again.
Farewell, mine own sweet spouse. I leave ye to remain.

WOMAN
And farewell, my dear lover, whom my heart doth contain.

II. Expulsion from the Garden

Text A

[After Adam and Eve be drawn out of Paradise, they shall speak the following:]

ADAM
O with dolorous sorrow we may wail and weep.
Alas, alas, why were we so bold?

---

[a] also

By our foul presumption, we are cast full deep
From pleasure to pain, with cares many fold.

EVE
With wondrous woo, alas, it cannot be told,
From paradise to punishment and bondage full strong.
O wretches that we are, so ever we shall be enrolled.[a]
Therefore, our hands we may wring with most doleful song,
With dolorous sorrow, we may wail and weep both,
Night and day in sorrow, times full deep.

[And so they shall sing, walking together about the place, wringing their hands.]

Text B

[Then Man and Woman depart to the nether pit of the pageant, and then:]

MAN
Alack, mine own sweetheart how am I struck with fear,
That from God am exiled, and brought to pain and woe,
Oh, what have we lost? Why did we no more care?
And to what kind of place that we resort and go?

WOMAN
Indeed, into the world, now must we to and fro,
And where or how to rest, I cannot say at all.
I am even as ye are, whatsoever me befall.

[Then come Dolor and Misery and take Man by both arms.]

DOLOR
Come forth, O Man. Take hold of me,
Through envy hast lost thy heavenly light
By eating in bondage, from hence shall be,
Now must thou me, Dolor, have always in sight.

---

[a] Archaic: to enroll [something] in the courts of justice

MISERY

And also of me, Misery, thou must taste and bite,
Of hardness, and of cold and also infirmity.
According to deserts, thy portion is of right,
To enjoy that in me, which is without certainty.

ADAM

Thus troubled, now I enter into Dolor and Misery.
Now, Woman, must we learn our living to get,
With labor and with travail. There is no remedy,
Nor anything therefrom we see that may us let[a].

[Then cometh in the Holy Ghost, comforting Man:]

HOLY GHOST

Be of good cheer, Man, and sorrow no more.
This Dolor and Misery, that then thou has taste,
Is not in respect, laid up in store,
For the joys for thee that ever shalt last,
Thy God doth not this, thee away to cast,
But to try thee, as gold is tried in the fire,
In the end premonished,[b] shalt have thy desire.
Take out of the Gospel, that it thee require[s]
Faith in Christ Jesus and grace that ensue[s],
I will be thy Guide and pay thee thy hire,
For all thy good diligence and doings you do.
Give ear unto me, Man, and then it is true,
Thou shalt kill the feelings that by lust in thee reign,
And put Dolor and Misery and Envy to pain.
These arms are prepared, if thou wilt turn again
To fight with. Take to thee and reach[c] woman the same—
The Breastplate of Righteousness, St. Paul will thee retain;
The Shield of Faith to quench, thy fiery darts to tame;
The Helmet of Salvation, the devil's wrath shall lame,

---

[a] allow
[b] forewarned
[c] extend to

And, too, the Sword of thy spirit which is the Word of God.
All these are now thee offered, to ease thy pain and rood[a].

ADAM
Oh, praise to thee, most Holy, that has with me abode,
In misery forewarning by this thy Holy Spirit.
Now feel I such great comfort, my sins they be unloaded
And laid on Christ's back, which is my joy and light.
This Dolor and this Misery, I feel to me no weight,
No, death is overcome by fore predestination,
And we attained with Christ in heavenly consolation.
Therefore, my own sweet spouse, without cavalation[b],
Together let us sing and let our hearts rejoice
And glorify our God with mind, power, and voice.
Amen

[Music begins.]

With heart and voice, let us rejoice, and praise the Lord always, for this our joyful day to see from this God's majesty, who hath given himself to thee, over us to reign and to govern us. Let all our hearts rejoice together, and let us all lift up our voices, one of us with another.

---

[a] cross
[b] caviling

APPENDIX E: *Figures of Speech from Shakespeare*

Anastrophe (ă-NĂS-trō-fē) Inverting natural word order for emphasis, poetic meter, etc.

> SHYLOCK
> Hates any man the thing he would not kill? *(Merchant of Venice)*

Antanaclasis (ĂNT-ə-nə-CLĂS-əs) The repetition of a word in two different senses (a form of pun); the use of homonyms to create a special effect

> OTHELLO
> Put out the light, and then put out the light. *(Othello)*

Anthimeria (ăn-thə-MĔR-ē-ə) Using a word normally used as one part of speech (e.g., a noun) in the position of another part of speech (e.g., a verb)

> CLEOPATRA
> I'll unhair thy head. *(Antony and Cleopatra)*

Hyperbole (hī-PER-bə-lē) Exaggeration for effect

> MACBETH
> Will all great Neptune's ocean wash this blood
> Clean from my hand? No, this hand will rather
> The multitudinous seas incarnadine,
> Making the green one red. *(Macbeth)*

Irony (Ī-rə-nē; Ī-ər-nē) The use of words to represent the opposite of what is real

> RICHARD
> Because I cannot flatter and speak fair,
> Smile in men's faces, smooth, deceive and cog,
> Duck with French nods and apish courtesy,
> I must be held a rancorous enemy. *(Richard III)*

Litotes (LĪ-tə-tēz) Understatement by using a negative to mean a positive

> CASCA
> If the tag-rag people did not
> clap him and hiss him, according as he pleased and
> displeased them, as they use to do the players in
> the theatre, I am no true man. *(Julius Caesar)*

Meiosis (mī-Ō-sĭs) Understatement; the opposite of hyperbole

> BENVOLIO
> What, art thou hurt?
>
> MERCUTIO:
> Ay, ay, a scratch, a scratch; marry, 'tis enough.
> Where is my page? Go, villain, fetch a surgeon. *(Romeo and Juliet)*

Metonymy (mə-TŎN-ə-mē) Referring to a thing, group, place, etc., not by its own name, but by something with which it is associated.

> EXETER
> Thy father was a traitor to the crown. *(Henry VI, Part 3)*

Neologism (nē-ŎL-ə-jĭzm) A newly created word

> JAQUES
> And then he drew a dial from his poke,
> And, looking on it with lackluster eye,
> Says very wisely, "It is ten o'clock. . . ." *(As You Like It)*

Onomatopoeia (ŏn-ə-mät-ə-PĒ-ə) Use of a word that makes the sound of the thing or action described

> ARIEL
> Hark, hark! I hear
> The strain of strutting chanticleer
> Cry, "cock-a-diddle-dow!" *(The Tempest)*

Paronomasia (pĕ-rə-nō-MĀ-zh(ē)-ə) Creating a special effect by using two words that sound alike but have different meanings; a pun

> RICHARD, DUKE OF GLOUCESTER
> Now is the winter of our discontent
> Made glorious summer by this sun [son] of York. *(Richard III)*

Periphrasis (pĕ-RIF-rə-sis) A round-about way of saying something; circumlocution (sometimes employed for comic effect)

> NURSE
> Well, you have made a simple choice; you know not
> how to choose a man: Romeo! no, not he; though his
> face be better than any man's, yet his leg excels
> all men's; and for a hand, and a foot, and a body,
> though they be not to be talked on, yet they are
> past compare: he is not the flower of courtesy,
> but, I'll warrant him, as gentle as a lamb. Go thy
> ways, wench; serve God. What, have you dined at home?
>
> JULIET
> No, no: but all this did I know before.
> What says he of our marriage? what of that? *(Romeo and Juliet)*

Prosopopoeia (prō-sō-pə-PĒ-ə) Ascribing human qualities to animals or things; allowing animals or things to speak (also called *personification*)

> BRUTUS
> The present wars devour him. *(Coriolanus)*

Rhetorical Question (rĕ-TÔR-ĭ-kəl KWES-chən) Using a question, not to receive an answer, but to make a point

> MARC ANTONY
> I thrice presented him a kingly crown,
> Which he did thrice refuse: was this ambition? *(Julius Caesar)*

Synecdoche (sĭn-ĔK-də-kē) Using a part to represent the whole

> MACDUFF
> O horror, horror, horror! Tongue nor heart
> Cannot conceive nor name thee! *(Macbeth)*

Zeugma (ZŪG-mə) Allowing one word (usually a verb or an adjective) to govern more than one noun in logically different senses (Greek term for "yoking together")

> FLUELLEN
> Kill the boys and the luggage! 'tis expressly
> against the law of arms. *(Henry V)*

Zoomorphism (zō-ə-MŌRF-ĭz-əm) Ascribing animal characteristics to humans, things, or even spiritual beings (akin to prosopopoeia)

> LEONTES
>   methoughts I did recoil
> Twenty-three years, and saw myself unbreech'd,
> In my green velvet coat, my dagger muzzled,
> Lest it should bite its master. . . . *(The Winter's Tale)*

APPENDIX F: *Excerpt from* The Late Lancashire Witches

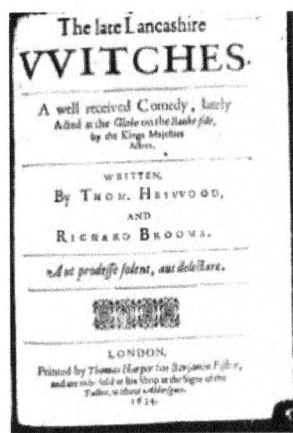

In scenes leading up to the excerpt that appears on the next few pages, Generous is presented as a man who does not believe that witches actually exist. He has argued with his friend about this several times. Unknown to him, his own wife is a witch, and she has been taking her husband's horse out at night to ride (sometimes to fly) to witches' meetings. Generous doesn't know why she's taking the horse, but he tells Robert (a boy who serves as a groom) not to let her take the horse anymore. He is fed up with her taking the horse and wearing him out.

When Mrs. Generous approaches Robert that evening, he tells her she is not allowed to take the horse. Angry, she turns Robert into a horse and rides him to her coven instead. Though he is in the form of a horse, Robert is aware of what is going on and now realizes that Mrs. Generous is a witch. When she tries to get on him to ride back home, he grabs the bewitched bridle and throws it over her. Now she is a horse, and he rides her home and places her in the stable with the other horses, getting even for what happened to him. At this point, Generous goes out to see if Robert has kept his promise and to find out if his horse is in good condition.

Excerpt from *The Late Lancashire Witches*
Act IV, Scene 2

CHARACTERS

Generous
Robert
Mrs. Generous

SETTING

Pendle, Lancashire, England

TIME

1634

> *[Enter GENEROUS]*
>
> ROBERT
> Have you found your gelding, sir?
>
> GENEROUS
> Yes, I have.
>
> ROBERT
> I hope not spurred, nor put into a sweat. You may see by his plump belly and sleek legs, he hath not been sore travailed.
>
> GENEROUS
> You're a saucy groom to receive horses
> Into my stable and not ask me leave.
> Is't for my profit to buy hay and oats
> For every stranger's jades?
>
> ROBERT
> I hope, sir, you find none feeding there but your own. If there be any you suspect, they have nothing to champ on but the bridle.

GENEROUS
Sirrah, whose jade is that tied to the rack?

ROBERT
The mare you mean, sir?

GENEROUS
Yes, that old mare.

ROBERT
Old, do you call her? You shall find the mark
Still in her mouth when the bridle is out of it!
I can assure you 'tis your own beast.

GENEROUS
A beast thou art to tell me so. Hath the wine
Not yet left working, not the Mitre wine,
That made thee to believe witchcraft? Prithee, 70
Persuade me to be a drunken sot
Like to thyself, and not to know mine own.

ROBERT
I'll not persuade you to anything. You will believe
nothing but what you see. I say the beast is your
own, and you have most right to keep her. She
hath cost you more the currying than all the
combs in your stable are worth. You have paid for
her provender this twenty years and upwards, and
furnished her with all the caparisons that she hath
worn, of my knowledge. And because she hath 80
been ridden hard the last night, do you now
renounce her?

GENEROUS
Sirrah, I fear some stolen jade of your own
That you would have me keep.

ROBERT
I am sure I found her no jade the last time I rid her. She carried me the best part of a hundred miles in less than a quarter of an hour.

GENEROUS
The devil she did!

ROBERT
Yes, so I say, either the devil or she did. An't[a] please you, walk in and take off her bridle, and then tell me who hath more right to her, you or I.   90

GENEROUS
Well, Robert, for this once I'll play the groom
And do your office for you. *[Exit]*

ROBERT
I pray do, sir, but take heed lest when the bridle is out of her mouth, she put it not into yours. If she do, you are a gone man if she but say once 'Horse, horse, see thou be.' Be you rid, if you please, for me.

[Enter GENEROUS and MISTRESS GENEROUS, he with a bridle]

GENEROUS
My blood is turn'd to ice, and all my vitals
Have ceas'd their working! Dull stupidity   100
Surpriseth me at once and hath arrested
That vigorous agitation which till now
Express'd a life within me. I, methinks,
Am a mere marble statue and no man.
Unweave my age, O Time, to my first thread;
Let me lose fifty years in ignorance spent,
That being made an infant once again

---

[a] If it

I may begin to know what, or where, am I
To be thus lost in wonder.

MRS GENEROUS
Sir—

GENEROUS
Amazement still pursues me: how am I chang'd,
Or brought ere I can understand myself
Into this new world?

ROBERT
You will believe no witches?

GENEROUS
This makes me believe all, ay anything,
And that myself am nothing. Prithee, Robin,
Lay me to myself open: what art thou,
Or this new transform'd creature?

ROBERT
I am Robin, and this your wife, my mistress.

GENEROUS
      Tell me the Earth
Shall leave its seat and mount to kiss the moon,
Or that the moon, enamour'd of the Earth,
Shall leave her sphere to stoop to us thus low.
What? What's this in my hand, that at an instant
Can from a four-legged creature make a thing
So like a wife?

ROBERT
A bridle, a jingling bridle, sir.

GENEROUS
A bridle? Hence enchantment!

[He casts it away. Robert takes it up.]

A viper were more safe within my hand
Than this charm'd engine. 130

ROBERT
Take heed, sir, what you do. If you cast it hence
and she catch it up, we that are here now may be
rid as far as the Indies within these few hours.
(To MISTRESS GENEROUS) Mistress, down
on your mare's bones, or your marrowbones,
whether you please, and confess yourself to be
what you are: and that's, in plain English, a witch,
a grand, notorious, witch!

GENEROUS
A witch? My wife a witch?

ROBERT
So it appears by the story. 140

GENEROUS
The more I strive to unwind
Myself from this meander, I the more
Therein am intricated. Prithee, woman,
Art thou a witch?

MRS GENEROUS
It cannot be denied, I am such a curs'd creature.

GENEROUS
Keep aloof,
And do not come too near me! Oh my trust,
Have I, since first I understood myself,
Been of my soul so chary (still to study
What best was for its health, to renounce all
The works of that black fiend with my best force) 150
And hath that serpent twin'd me so about
That I must lie so often and so long
With a devil in my bosom?

MRS GENEROUS
Pardon, sir—

GENEROUS
'Pardon'? Can such a thing as that be hop'd?
Lift up thine eyes, lost woman, to yon hills;
It must be thence expected. Look not down
Unto that horrid dwelling which thou hast sought
At such dear rate to purchase. Prithee, tell me,
For now I can believe, art thou a witch?

MRS GENEROUS
I am.

GENEROUS
With that word I am thunderstuck
And know not what to answer. Yet resolve me,
Hast thou made any contract with that fiend,
The enemy of mankind?

MRS GENEROUS
Oh, I have.

GENEROUS
What, and how far?

MRS GENEROUS
I have promis'd him my soul.

GENEROUS
Ten thousand times better thy body had
Been promis'd to the stake, ay and mine too,
To have suffer'd with thee in a hedge of flames,
Than such a compact ever had been made. Oh—

ROBERT
What cheer, sir? Show yourself a man, though 170
she appeared so late a beast. Mistress, confess all:
better here than in a worse place. Out with it!

GENEROUS
Resolve me, how far doth that contract stretch?

MRS GENEROUS
What interest in this soul myself could claim,
I freely gave him, but his part that made it,
I still reserve, not being mine to give.

GENEROUS
Oh, cunning devil! Foolish woman, know
Where he can claim but the least little part
He will usurp the whole. Thou'rt a lost woman.

MRS GENEROUS
I hope not so.

GENEROUS
Why, hast thou any hope? 180

MRS GENEROUS
Yes, sir, I have.

GENEROUS
Make it appear to me.

MRS GENEROUS
I hope I never bargain'd for that fire
Further than penitent tears have power to quench.

GENEROUS
I would see some of them!

MRS GENEROUS
You behold them now,
If you look on me with charitable eyes,
Tinctur'd in blood, blood issuing from the heart.
Sir, I am sorry. When I look towards heaven
I beg a gracious pardon; when on you,
Methinks your native goodness should not be

Less pitiful than they. 'Gainst both I have err'd; 190
From both I beg atonement.

GENEROUS
May I presume't?

MRS GENEROUS
I kneel to both your mercies.

[She kneels, crying]

GENEROUS
Know'st thou what a witch is?

MRS GENEROUS
Alas, none better,
Or after mature recollection can be
More sad to think on't.

GENEROUS
Tell me, are those tears
As full of true-hearted penitence
As mine of sorrow, to behold what state,
What desperate state, thou'rt fall'n in?

MRS GENEROUS
Sir, they are.

GENEROUS
Rise, and as I do, so heaven pardon me.
We all offend, but from such falling off 200
Defend us. *[She rises]* Well, I do remember wife,
When I first took thee 'twas for good and bad.
Oh, change thy bad to good that I may keep thee,
As then we passed our faiths, till death us sever.
I will not aggravate thy grief too much
By needless iteration. Robin, hereafter
Forget thou hast a tongue: if the least syllable

Of what hath pass'd be rumour'd, you lose me,
But if I find you faithful, you gain me ever.

ROBERT
A match, sir: you shall find me as mute as 210
If I had the bridle still in my mouth.

GENEROUS
Oh, woman, thou hadst need to weep thyself
Into a fountain, such a penitent spring
As may have power to quench invisible flames
In which my eyes shall aid. Too little, all;
If not too little, all's forgiven, forgot.
Only thus much remember: thou hadst extermin'd
Thyself out of the bless'd society
Of saints and angels, but on thy repentance
I take thee to my bosom, once again 220
My wife, sister, and daughter.
(To ROBERT) Saddle my gelding;
Some business that may hold me for two days
Calls me aside.

ROBERT
I shall, sir! Well, now my mistress hath promised
to give over her witchery, I hope, though I still
continue her man, yet she will make me no more
her journey-man. To prevent which, the first
thing I do shall be to burn the bridle, and then
away with the witch. *[Exit]*

[Exeunt GENEROUS and MISTRESS GENEROUS] [287]

IMAGE ATTRIBUTION

Ch. 1 Medieval Theatre

Notker the Stammerer (Notker Balbulus), c. 840–912. Medieval manuscript, St. Gall. PD.

Easter Sepulchre, 16th.c. Holcombe Burnell Church, Devon, north wall of chancel. PD.

Thurible. PD.

Frontispiece to Wynkyn de Worde's 1522 edition of the morality play *Mundus et Infans [The World and the Child]*. PD.

Feast of Fools by Peter Brueghel. *Wikimedia*. {{PD-old-70}}. 4 Oct. 2011. Web. 5 Sept. 2017.

Procession for Corpus Christi by the Master of James IV. PD. 11 Oct. 2012. Web. 5 Sept. 2017.

Medieval bakers' guild. PD.

Abbey Gate, Chester. *ChesterTourist.com*. *Wikimedia Commons*. CC-BY-SA 2.0. 7 Feb. 2004. Web. 5 Sept. 2017.

Chester, the Cross, and the Rows. Neil Kennedy. *Geograph.org.uk*. *Wikimedia Commons*. CC-BY-SA 2.0. 25 May 2006. Web. 5 Sept. 2017.

Alan Simkins, photog. St. Piran's Round [Plen an gwari]. Panoramic of the earthwork bank and ditch known as 'St. Piran's Round', northwest of Goonhavern, Cornwall. CC-SA 2.0. 21 Oct. 2005. Web. 1 May 2017.

Ch. 2 Rhetoric in Medieval Plays

Figures of Justice and Mercy by Alexander Mylne. Photog. Kim Traynor. *Wikimedia*. CC BY-SA 3.0. Unported. 29 Sept. 2013. Web. 1 May 2017.

Herod on His Throne. PD.

Cain Slays Abel with a Jawbone. {{PD-old-70}}.

The Ark of Noah and the Cosmic Covenant. PD.

Woodcut of the Fall of Lucifer. PD.

Christians of the 3rd Century. {{PD-1923}}

Roman soldier. PD.

Military code of conduct. PD.

Ch. 3 Medieval Plays

Everyman. {{PD-old-70}}.

"The Dragon Advances" in *St. George and the Dragon* by the St. Albans Mummers. *Wikimedia Commons*. CC By-SA 4.0. 26. Dec. 2015. Web. 16 Sept. 2016.

Ch. 4 Medieval Playwrights and Players

Roswitha of Gandersheim. {{PD-old-70}}.

Hildegard of Bingen. 14th-century manuscript. {{PD-old-70}}.

Medieval men in choir copes. {{PD-old-70}}.

Michał Radecki. St. Nicholas of Myra Monument. *Wikimedia Commons*. CC BY-SA 3.0.20 Nov. 2011. Web. 16 Sept. 2016.

Gilbertus. Fleury Abbey at Saint-Benoît-sur-Loir, France. *Wikimedia Commons*. CC BY-SA 3.0. 30 Oct. 2011. Web. 16 Sept. 2016.

The Dowry for the Three Virgins by Gentile da Fabriana. PD.

Medieval writer at desk. {{PD-old-70}}.

Ryal Rose Noble [coin] of Edward IV. *Wikimedia Commons*. CC BY-SA 3.0. Unported. 22 Apr. 2008. Web. 1 May 2017.

Medieval carpenter. {{PD-old-70}}.

Three Women at the Tomb (Visitatio Sepulchri) by Ferrer Bassa. PD.

Andreas Praefckge, Photog. Three-dimensional representation of the *Killing of the Innocents* in medieval costume. PD-US.

Medieval shoes with pikes. {{PD-old-70}}.

Medieval Court Entertainment. {{PD-old-70}}.

Ch. 5 Medieval Spectacle

The raising of Lazarus. PD.

Pilate's club. PD.

Battle of Gideon (Gideon and the Philistines). {{PD-old-70}}.

Hellmouth. PD.

Flanders crucifixion play. PD.

Bodkins. {{PD-old-70}}.

Cresset. PD.

Censer. CC BY-SA 2.0.

Brittany Diliberto, photog. Gill and the "baby" from *The Second Shepherd's Play*. Shakespeare Folger Consort. 2016. Web. 1 May 2017. CC BY-SA 4.0. International.

Three Peasants in Conversation by Albrecht Dürer. {{PD-old-70}}.

Clipart angel. PD.

Pageant wagon with fire cressets. *Le Théâtre en France I, du Moyen Âge à 1789*. *Wikimedia Commons*. {{PD-1923}}. 7 Nov. 2015. Web. 5 Sept. 2017.

Ch. 6 Medieval Theatre Tidbits from Primary Sources

Map of central London in 1666. *Wikimedia Commons*. CC BY-SA 4.0. Unported. 2008. Web. 1 May 2017.

Cheapside. PD.

Ludgate. PD.

Ray Blythe. The Gate at Temple Bar. *Fabulous Follies*. 2015. Web. 29 Sept. 2016. Used with permission.

Page from Wycliff Bible. {{PD-old-70}}.

Ch. 7 Theatre in the Renaissance

Lorenzo de'Medici. PD.

Siege of Constantinople, 1453. PD.

Lord Chamberlain's Men. Littrip. *Wikispaces*. CC-BY-SA 3.0. N.d. Web. 1 May 2017.

Sons of Edward IV in Yorkist livery. PD.

Midsummer Night's Dream frontispiece. {{PD-old-70}}.

The George Inn, Southwark. *Walks in London*. Ed. Augustus J. C. Hare. New York: Routledge, n. d. 462.

Globe drawing. PD.

C. Walter Hodges' imagined reconstruction of Shakespeare's *Merchant of Venice*, Act 1, Scene 3, being performed in an Elizabethan theatre. Drawn for *The Globe Restored*, published by Ernest Benn, 1953. Folger Shakespeare Library ART Box H688 no.3.1. *Wikimedia Commons*. CC-BY-SA 4.0 International. 9 Aug. 2014. Web. 7 Mar. 2017.

C. Walter Hodges' Conjectural Reconstruction of *The Merchant of Venice*, Act I, Scene 3. CC BY-SA 4.0. *Wikimedia Commons*. 9 Aug. 2014. Web. 19 Apr. 2017.

Erasmus of Rotterdam by Hans Holbein. PD.

Henry VIII by Hans Holbein. PD.

Robert Devereux, 2nd Earl of Essex by Marcus Gheeraerts the Younger. PD.

Elizabethan theatre illustration. "Elizabethan Theatre." *Wikispaces*. CC-BY-SA 3.0. N.d. Web. 7 Mar. 2017.

Anatomie of Abuses frontispiece. PD.

John Winthrop statue. PD.

Ch. 8 Elizabethan Playwrights

Christopher Marlowe. {{PD-old-70}}.

Tamburlaine the Great. PD.

Ianerc. Christopher Marlowe's memorial in the Churchyard at St Nicholas, Deptford. *Wikimedia Commons*. CC-BY-SA.3.0 Unported. 9 Feb. 2012. Web. 1 May 2017..

Postage stamp with Dr. Faustus and Mephistopholes. PD.

Ben Jonson. PD.

Ben Jonson's signature. PD.

William Shakespeare. {{PD-old-70}}.

J. L. C. Walker, photog. Shakespeare's birthplace in Stratford-on-Avon. *Wikimedia Commons*. CC BY-SA 2.0. 26 July 2007. Web. 1 May 2017.

Robert Green "suted in death's livery." {{PD-1923}}

Ch. 9 Elizabethan Players

Richard Tarlton. PD.
Will Kemp. PD.
Freeze tag images. PD.
Edward Alleyn. PD.
Richard Burbage. {{PD-old-70}}.

Ch. 10 Elizabethan and Jacobean Plays

Lars Jacob as Comedy and Tragedy. *Wikimedia Commons.* CC BY-SA 3.0. 14 July 2015. Web. 5 Sept. 2017.
Inigo Jones's design for *The Masque of Blackness.* {{PD-1923}}
Benedict Cumberbatch filming *Sherlock. Wikimedia Commons.* CC BY-2.0 Generic. 27 May 2011. Web. 1 May 2017.

Ch. 11 Why Shakespeare?

King James Bible, 1611. {{PD-1923}}.

Ch. 12 Subtext

Iceberg clipart. PD.
Girl in glasses. PD.
Old radio clipart. PD.
Shakespeare's letter to his patron. {{PD-old-70}}.
Prince Hal meets Falstaff. PD.
Richard III portrayed by Richard Mansfield. *Folger Shakespeare Library.* CC BY-SA 4.0. N.d. Web. 8 Mar. 2017.
Montagues and Capulets. Sir John Gilbert. c. 1873. PD-US.

Ch. 13 Spectacle on the Elizabethan Stage

Henry V frontispiece. {{PD-old-70}}.
17th-century Fencing School. PD.
Fencing positions. *Wikiwood.* CC-BY-SA 2.5 N.d. Web. 7 Mar. 2017.
Pikeman. PD.
Renaissance man fencing. PD.
The decollation of John Baptist. {{PD-1923}}.
John Dee. {{PD-old-70}}.
Alto sackbut. {{PD-1923}}.
Wire-flying system by Giacomo Torelli. PD. {{PD-1923}}.
Theatre machinery by Nicola Sabbatini. {{PD-old-70.}}

Ch. 14 Rhetoric in Elizabethan Plays

Marlon Brando as Marc Antony. {{PD-US-no-notice}}
Biblical illustrations by Jim Padgett, Sweet Publishing, Ft. Worth, TX, and Gospel Light, Ventura, CA. Copyright 1984. CC-BY-SA 3.0.

Ch. 15 Renaissance Theatre Tidbits from Primary Sources

New York Astor Place Opera House riots. {{PD-1923}}.
Paul's Conversion on the Damascus Road. Distant Shores Media/Sweet Publishing. *Wikimedia Commons.* CC BY-SA 3.0 Unported. 29 Mar. 2016. Web. 20 Apr. 2017.
Adam and Eve being sent out of the Garden. PD. {{PD-old-70}}.
Late Lancashire Witches frontispiece. PD.

ENDNOTES

[1] "The Theatre." *New Advent*. 2009. Web. 27 July 2016.
[2] "Council of Trullo." *New Advent*. 2016. Web. 27 July 2016.
[3] Karl Young. *Drama of the Medieval Church*. Oxford: Clarendon, 1933. *Google Books*. 1:249-50.
[4] William Tydeman. *The Theatre in the Middle Ages: Western European Stage Conditions, c. 800-1576*. Cambridge: Cambridge UP, 1978. 41. *Google Books*. 27 July 2016.
[5] "Subdeacon." *New Advent*. 2016. Web. 11 Aug. 2016.
[6] E. K. Chambers. *The Medieval Stage*. Oxford: Oxford UP, 1903 1:278. *Internet Archive*. 19 Sept. 2016.
[7] Chambers, 1:279, n. 1.
[8] Chambers, 1:294.
[9] Chambers, 2:100.
[10] F. J. Furnival. *The Digby Mysteries*. London, 1882. xviii-xix. *Internet Archive*. 19 Sept. 2016.
[11] Alexandra F. Johnston, ed. *The Proclamation. N-Town Plays*. CHASS. University of Toronto. N.d. Web. 11 Apr. 2017.
[12] Hugo Albert Rennert. *The Spanish Stage in the Time of Lope de Vega*. New York: Hispanic Society of America, 1909. 4-5. *Internet Archive*. 19 Sept. 2016.
[13] M. Lyle Spencer. *Corpus Christi Pageants in England*. NY: Baker, 1911. 62. *Internet Archive*. 19 Sept. 2016.
[14] Jeffrey L. Singman and Will McLean. *Daily Life in Chaucer's Time*. Westport, CT: Greenwood, 1995. 163. *Google Books*. 19 Sept. 2016.
[15] James Orchard Halliwell-Phillipps. *Outlines of the Life of Shakespeare*. 7th ed. London, 1887. 1:337. *Internet Archive*. 19 Sept. 2016.
[16] Will Coleman. "Dramatic Discovery at the Bodleian." *Oxford Today*. University of Oxford. 11 May 2015. Web. 19 Sept. 2016.
[17] Richard Carew. *Carew's Surveys of Cornwall*. Ed. Thomas Tonkin. London, 1811. 192. *Google Books*. 27 Sept. 2016.
[18] Virginia Crocheron Gildersleeve, ed. *Government Regulation of the Elizabethan Drama*. New York: Columbia, 1908. 24. *Haithi Trust Digital Library*. N.d. Web. 11 Apr. 2017.
[19] Alfred, Lord Tennyson. *Idylls of the King*. Ed. Joseph Villiers Denney. Chicago: Appleton, 1911. 124. *Internet Archive*. 11 Apr. 2017.
[20] Robert Frost. "Stopping by Woods on a Snowy Evening." *The Poetry Foundation*. N.d. Web 27 Sept. 2016.
[21] William Shakespeare. "Sonnet 18: Shall I Compare Thee to a Summer's Day?" *The Poetry Foundation*. N.d. Web 27 Sept. 2016.
[22] Knud Lyne Rahbek. "Introductory to Denmark: The Women of Denmark." Trans. William Sidney Walker. *Poems of Places: An Anthology in 31 Volumes: Scotland*. Ed. Henry Wadsworth Longfellow. Boston: James R. Osgood. 1876-79. *Bartleby*. 2011. Web. 27 Sept. 2016.
[23] William Cowper. "CLX. The Solitude of Alexander Selkirk." *The Golden Treasury*. Ed. Francis T. Palgrave. London, 1875. *Bartleby*. 1999. Web. 27 Sept. 2016.
[24] William Shakespeare. *Romeo and Juliet*. 1.1.24. *Open Source Shakespeare*. 2003-2016. Web. 26 Sept. 2016.
[25] William Shakespeare. *Julius Caesar*. *Open Source Shakespeare*. 2003-2016. Web. 26 Sept. 2016. 1.2.286.
[26] Robert Louis Stevenson. *A Child's Garden of Verses and Underwoods*. New York: Current Literature, 1906. *Bartleby*. 2000. Web. 27 Sept. 2016.
[27] W. and R. Chambers. *Chambers's National Reading-Books*. London, 1867. 49. *Internet Archive*. 27 Sept. 2016.
[28] A. C. Cawley, ed. *Everyman and Medieval Miracle Plays*. London: Dent, 1993. 30. Print.
[29] "The Battle of Brunanburh." *Loki.Stockton.edu*. Stockton University. N.d. Web. 27 Sept. 2016.
[30] Cawley, 27.
[31] *Joseph's Troubles about Mary. York Mystery Plays: A Selection in Modern Spelling*. Ed. Richard Beadle and Pamela M. King. Oxford: Oxford UP, 1999. 58. *Google Books*. 27 Sept. 2016.
[32] Beadle and King, *Herod and the Magi*. 70.
[33] Beadle and King, *Christ before Herod*. 182.
[34] Beadle and King, *The Crucifixion*. 218.
[35] Lucy Toulmin Smith. *York Plays: The Plays Performed by the Crafts or Mysteries of York, on the Day of Corpus Christi in the 14th, 15th, and 16th Centuries*. Oxford: Clarendon, 1885. 22. Web. 18 Dec. 2017.
[36] Alexandra F. Johnston and David M. Parry, eds. *The Castle of Perseverance. Computing in the Humanities and Social Sciences*. University of Toronto. 1999. Web. 27 Sept. 2016. 2986-3007.
[37] Stanley K. Stowers. *A Rereading of Romans*. New Haven: Yale, 1994. 1-41. Print.
[38] Johnston and Parry, 3407-3420.
[39] Beadle and King, *Christ before Pilate (2): The Judgement*. 198.
[40] Beadle and King, *Herod and the Magi*. 66.
[41] Beadle and King, *The Slaughter of the Innocents*. 89.
[42] Crawley, 87.

43 Beadle and King, *Christ before Annas and Caiaphas*. 148.

44 Beadle and King, *The Entry into Jerusalem*. 122.

45 David Bevington. *The Killing of Abel. Medieval Drama*. Boston: Houghton, 1975. 285. Print.

46 Cawley, *Everyman*. 212.

47 Beadle and King, *Herod and the Magi*. 68.

48 Bevington, *Noah*. 304.

49 Johnston and Parry, *Castle of Perseverance*. 3450-51.

50 Beadle and King, *Christ before Annas and Caiaphas*. 143.

51 Bevington, *Everyman*. 954.

52 Bevington, *Mary Magdalene*. 712.

53 Bevington, *Mary Magdalene*. 701.

54 Bevington, *Mary Magdalene*. 691.

55 Bevington, *Mankind*. 935.

56 Bevington, *Mary Magdalene*. 705.

57 J. S. Purvus, ed. *The York Cycle of Mystery Plays*. London: Society for Promoting Christian Knowledge, 1957. In *Religious Drama 2*. Ed. E. Martin Browne. New York: Meridian, 1958. Kindle loc. 327-28.

58 Purvus, Kindle loc. 336.

59 Purvus, Kindle loc. 336-37

60 Purvus, Kindle loc. 355-58.

61 Purvus, Kindle loc. 368

62 Purvus, Kindle loc. 370.

63 Purvus, Kindle loc. 373-80.

64 Purvus, Kindle loc. 427-28.

65 Roswitha of Gandersheim. *Gallicanus. The Plays of Roswitha*. Trans. Christopher St. John. London: Chatto, 1923. 18. Print.

66 Roswitha, 26-27.

67 Roswitha, 27.

68 Roswitha, 30.

69 United States Code of Military Justice. Section 892. Article 10. Failure to obey order or regulation. Legal Information Institute. Cornell University Law School. N.d. Web. 18 July 2016.

70 Roswitha, 30.

71 Roswitha, 30.

72 Clement A. Miles. *Christmas in Ritual and Tradition, Christian and Pagan*. London: T. Fisher Unwin, 1912. 83-84. *Internet Archive*. 7 Sept. 2017.

73 Montrose Jonas Moses, ed. *Everyman: A Morality Play*. New York: Kennerly, 1908. 103-106. *Internet Archive*. 7 Sept. 2017.

74 Bevington, 290.

75 Bevington, 302-303. [The medieval rendering and the single-bracketed stage directions are from Bevington; the gloss and the double-bracketed stage directions are ours.]

76 Catherine L. French. *The People of the Parish: Community Life in a Late Medieval English Diocese*. Philadelphia: U of Pennsylvania P, 2001. 130-34. *Google Books*. 7 Sept. 2017.

77 French, 133.

78 Robert Fortunaso. "The Dramatic Fragment." *Robin Hood: The Facts and the Fiction*. N.d. Web. 5 June 2016.

79 Jon Mills. "Depiction of Tyranny in the Cornish Miracle Plays: Tenor, Code Switching and Sociolinguistic Variables." Liam Mac Amhlaigh, ed. *Ilteangach, Ilseiftiúil: Féilscríbhinn in ómós do Nicholas Williams: A Festschrift in Honour of Nicholas Williams*. Dublin: Arlen House, 2012. 139. Print.

80 Mills, 78-83.

81 Mills, 152.

82 Katharina M. Wilson. *Medieval Women Writers*. Athens, GA: U of Georgia P, 1984. 31, 43. *Google Books*. 7 Sept. 2017.

83 Wilson, 30.

84 Roswitha. xiv.

85 Roswitha, 55.

86 Sabina Flanagan. *Hildegard of Bingen, 1098-1179: A Visionary Life*. 2nd ed. London: Routledge, 1998. 32. *Google Books*. 26 Sept. 2016.

87 *Ordo Virtutem*. Trans. Peter Dronke. *Oxford Girls Choir*. N.d. Web. 26 Sept. 2016.

88 William Hunt. "Geoffrey of Gorham." *Dictionary of National Biography*. London, 1885-1900 ed. *Wikisource*. 26 Sept. 2016.

89 Joseph Strutt. *The Sports and Pastimes of the People of England*. Kindle ed. London: Methuen, 1801. Loc. 4837-39.

90 Alfred William Pollard, ed. *English Miracle Plays, Moralities, and Interludes: Specimens of the Pre-Elizabethan Drama*. Oxford, 1890. 163. *Internet Archive*. 26 Sept. 2016.

91 Mary Harmon Del Villar. *The Saint's Play in Medieval England*. Dissertation. University of Arizona, 1970. Web. 26 Sept. 2016. 22-23.

92 George Raleigh Coffman. *A New Theory Concerning the Origin of the Miracle Play*. Dissertation. University of Chicago, 1914. 79. Web. 26 Sept. 2016.

93 C. Clifford Flanigan. "The Fleury 'Playbook' and the Traditions of Medieval Latin Drama." *Comparative Drama* 18.4 (1984): 365. *Jstor*. 26 Sept. 2016.

94 C. Flanigan, 361.

95 Bevington, 174.

96 Bevington, 176-77.

97 Bevington, 304.

98 E. Hamilton Moore. *English Miracle Plays and Moralities*. London: Sherratt, 1907. 62. *Internet Archive*. 26 Sept. 2017.

99 Kate Normington. *Gender and Medieval Drama*. Cambridge: Brewer, 2004. 36. *Google Books*. 7 Sept. 2017.

100 William Tydeman. *The Theatre in the Middle Ages: Western European Stage Conditions, c. 800-1576*. Cambridge: Cambridge UP, 1978. 248. *Google Books*. 16 Sept. 2017.

101 Alexandra F. Johnston and Margaret Rogerson, eds. *York 1: Introduction, the Record. Records of Early English Drama*. Toronto: U of Toronto, 1979. 1:99. *Internet Archive*. 7 Sept. 2017.

102 Johnston, 1:73.

103 Chambers, 2:248.

104 Mark Beeson. "Medieval Mystery Drama at Widecombe and Ashburton." *Dartmoor Resource*. 1. N.d. Web. 26 Sept. 2016.

105 Normington, 42.

106 Johnston, 188-89.

107 Furnival, 78-79.

108 William Shakespeare. *A Midsummer's Night Dream*. Open Source Shakespeare. 1.2.307. 2003-2016. Web. 26 Sept. 2016.

109 Paul Kuritz. *The Making of Theatre History*. Englewood Cliffs: Prentice, 1988. 145. *Google Books*. 26 Sept. 2016.

110 Lynette R. Muir. *The Biblical Drama of Medieval Europe*. Cambridge: Cambridge UP, 1995. 18. *Google Books*. 26 Sept. 2016.

111 John Heywood. *The Dramatic Writings of John Heywood*. Ed. John S. Farmer. London: Early English Text Society, 1905. 92. *Internet Archive*. 7 Sept. 2017.

112 "The Killing of the Innocents." Furnival. 11. [Spelling modernized.]

113 "The Killing," 13.

114 Normington, 43.

115 Frances Elizabeth Baldwin. *Sumptuary Legislation and Personal Regulation in England*. Dissertation. Johns Hopkins University. 1923. 123-24. N.d. Web. 6 Oct. 2016.

116 Baldwin, 125.

117 Paul Whitfield White. "Major English Acting Troupes to 1583." *Oxford Handbooks Online*. 2016. Web. 4 Oct. 2016.

118 Sidney W. Clarke. "The Miracle Play in England," qtd. in Carl H. Grabo, "The Stage for Which Shakespeare Wrote. I: The Mystery Plays." *The Chautauquan*. Vol. 44. Sept. 1906. 105. *Internet Archive*. Web. 28 Mar. 2017.

119 Paul Kuritz. *The Making of Theatre History*. Englewood Cliffs: Prentice, 1987. 146. *Google Books*. 11 Apr. 2017.

120 W. E. Urwick. "Medieval Drama in France before the Fourteenth Century." *Proceedings of the University of Durham Philosophical Society*. Vol. 2. 23 May 1901. 42-43. *Google Books*. 27 Mar. 2017.

121 Charles Mills Gayley. *Plays of Our Forefathers and Some of the Traditions upon Which They Were Founded*. New York: Duffield, 1907. 106. *Google Books*. 29 Mar. 2017.

122 Petts, David. *Pagan and Christian: Religious Change in Early Medieval Europe*. London: Bristol Classical, 2001. 61. *Academia*. 29 Mar. 2017.

123 William Henry Hudson. "English Religious Drama and Its Stage Arrangements." *The Antiquary*. Vol. 17. Jan. 1888. 64. *Google Books*. 29 Mar. 2017.

124 Clarke, 103-104.

125 Susan Crabtree and Peter Beudert. *Scenic Art for the Theatre: History, Tools, and Techniques*. Burlington, MA: Focal, 2005. 367. *Google Books*. 18 Apr. 2017.

126 Clarke, 103-104.

127 Clarke, 104.

128 David Mills. *The Chester Mystery Cycle: A New Edition with Modernised Spelling*. East Lansing: Colleagues, 1992. 6. *Google Books*. 29 Mar. 2017.

129 Thomas Sharp. *A Dissertation on the Pageants or Dramatic Mysteries Anciently Performed at Coventry*. Coventry, 1825. 73. *Google Books*. 29 Mar. 2017.

130 Hudson, 64.

131 Stephen K. Wright. The *Vengeance of Our Lord: Medieval Dramatizations of the Destruction of Jerusalem*. Toronto: Pontifical Institute of Medieval Studies, 1989. 203. *Google Books*. 29 Mar. 2017.

132 Beatrice Groves. *The Destruction of Jerusalem in Early Modern English Literature*. Cambridge: Cambridge UP, 2015. 61. *Google Books*. 29 Mar. 2017.

133 E. Martin Browne. *Religious Drama 2: Mystery and Morality Plays*. New York: Meridian, 1958. 25-26. *Internet Archive*. 30 Mar. 2017.

[134] Browne, 26.
[135] Peter Matthews, ed. *The Chester Plays*. London: Kegan Paul, 1916. 366-367. *Google Books*. 30 Mar. 2017.
[136] Johnston, 55.
[137] Browne, 251.
[138] Philip Butterworth. *Magic on the Early English Stage*. Cambridge: Cambridge UP, 2005. 148. Print.
[139] "The Cornish Mystery of the Crucifixion." *Everyman and Other Interludes*. London: Dent, 1909. 197. *Internet Archive*. 10 Apr. 2017.
[140] *The Scourging. The Towneley Plays. Corpus of Middle English Prose and Verse*. University of Michigan. 2006. Web. 10 Apr. 2017.
[141] *Everyman*. 194; Philip Butterworth and Kate Normington. *European Theatre Performance Practice, 1400-1580*. Farnham, SRY: Ashgate, 2014.Google Books. 11 Apr. 2017.
[142] *The Crucifixion. The Towneley Plays*.
[143] Johnston, 55.
[144] *The York Play of the Crucifixion*. W. W. Norton. N.d. PDF. Web. 10 Apr. 2017.
[145] *The York Play of the Crucifixion*.
[146] NeCastro, Gerard. *N-Town Cycle, Play XXXII: The Procession to Calvary and the Crucifixion of Christ. From Stage to Page - Medieval and Renaissance Drama*. 15 June 2011. Web. 7 Apr. 2017.
[147] Richard Beadle and Pamela M. King, eds. *The Death of Christ. York Mystery Plays: A Selection in Modern Spelling*. Oxford: Oxford UP, 1984. 232. Print.
[148] Ernest Rhys, ed. *Everyman with Other Interludes*. London: Dent, 1909. 204. *Internet Archive*. 11 Apr. 2017.
[149] M. D. Anderson. *Drama and Imagery in English Medieval Churches*. Cambridge: Cambridge UP, 1963. 160. *Google Books*. Web. 27 Mar. 2017.
[150] Charles Mills Gayley. *Plays of Our Forefathers and Some of the Traditions upon Which They Were Founded*. New York: Duffield, 1907. 107. *Google Books*. 29 Mar. 2017.
[151] Wright, Thomas, ed. *The Chester Plays*. Vol. 2. London: Shakespeare Society, 1847. 9. *Google Books*. 11 Apr. 2017.
[152] NeCastro, *The Chester Cycle VIII.: The Magi and Herod*.
[153] NeCastro, *VI: The Nativity*.
[154] NeCastro, *X: Slaughter of the Innocents*.
[155] *The Killing of Abel. The Towneley Plays*.
[156] Kuritz, 146.
[157] Will Geer and Ellen Geer. *Abraham and Isaac. YouTube*. Brome Version. Smithsonian Folkways Recordings. 30 May 2015. Web. 18 Apr. 2017.
[158] *The Brome Play of Abraham and Isaac*. W. W. Norton. N.d. PDF. Web. 11 Apr. 2017.
[159] Richard of Maidstone. "The Reconciliation of Richard II with the City of London." *Rerum Britannicarum Medii Ævi Scriptores, Or Chronicles and Memorials of Great Britain and Ireland during the Middle Ages*. Trans. Thomas Wright. London, 1859. 14: lxxv. *Google Books*. 23 Feb. 2017.
[160] Richard of Maidstone, lxxv-lxxiv.
[161] Furnival. Kindle location 341-43.
[162] John Wycliffe. *De Officio Pastorali. The English Works of Wycliffe Hitherto Unprinted*. Ed. F. D. Matthews. Early English Text Society. London, 1820. 429-30. *Corpus of Middle English Prose and Verse*. University of Michigan. N.d. Web. 23 Feb. 2017.
[163] Virginia Gildersleeve. *Government Regulation of the Elizabethan Drama*. New York: Columbia, 1908. 25. *Internet Archive*. 23 Feb. 2017.
[164] C. C. Stopes. *Burbage and Shakespeare's Stage*. London: Moring, 1913. 9. *Internet Archive*. 23 Feb. 2017.
[165] Kate Aughterson, ed. *The English Renaissance: An Anthology of Sources and Documents*. London: Routledge, 1998. 166. *Google Books*. 23 Feb. 2017.
[166] Sylvia Morris. 'Discussing the Evidence for Shakespeare's Theatre: Andrew Gurr, Stanley Wells and Reg Foakes." *The Shakespeare Blog*. 5 Dec.2012. Web. 26 Oct. 2016.
[167] John Raithby, ed. *The Statutes at Large of England and Great Britain from Magna Carta to the Union of the Kingdoms of Great Britain and Ireland*. 388. *Google Books*. 23 Feb. 2017.
[168] Tiffany Stern. *Rehearsal from Shakespeare to Sheridan*. Oxford: Clarendon, 2000. 92. *Google Books*. 23 Feb. 2017.
[169] Martha Fletcher Bellinger. "Restoration Drama." *A Short History of the Theatre*. New York: Holt, 1927. 249-59. *Theatre History*. Web. 23 Feb. 2017.
[170] Phillip Stubbes. *The Anatomy of Abuses*. London, 1583. 87-88. *The British Library*. N.d. Web. 23 Feb. 2017.
[171] Stubbes, 90.
[172] Stubbes, 90-91.
[173] Stubbes, 91-92.
[174] Michael O'Connell. *The Idolatrous Eye: Iconoclasm and Theater in Early-Modern England*. New York: Oxford UP, 2000. 30. *Google Books*. 23 Feb. 2017.
[175] John Winthrop. "A Model of Christian Charity." Ed. John Beardsley. *The Winthrop Society*. 2015. Web. 23 Feb. 2017.
[176] Gildersleeve, 226.

177 J. R. Mulryne and Margaret Shewring, eds. *Shakespeare's Globe Rebuilt*. Cambridge: Mulryne, 1997. 75-76. *Google Books*. 23 Feb. 2017.
178 "Marlowe's Education." *The Marlowe Society*. N.d. Web. 18 Nov. 2016.
179 William Shakespeare. *Henry VI, Part 3*. 3.2. Ed. Barbara Mowat and Paul Werstine. *Folger Digital Texts*. 138-39. Folger Shakespeare Library. 1 Mar. 2017.
180 Oliphant Smeaton, ed. *Return from Parnassus*. London: Dent, 1905. *Internet Archive*. 7 Apr. 2017.
181 "Faust (Literary Character)." *Encyclopedia Britannica*. 4 Aug. 2008. Web. 11 Apr. 2017.
182 Christopher Marlowe. *The Tragedie of Doctor Faustus (B Text)*. Ed. Hilary Binda. *The Perseus Digital Library*. Tufts University. N.d. Web. 11 Apr. 2017.
183 Thomas Kyd. *The Spanish Tragedy*. *Elizabethan Authors*. N.d. Web. 11 Apr. 2017.
184 Amnon Kabatchnik. *Blood on the Stage, 480 B.C. to 1600 A.D.: Milestone Plays of Murder, Mystery, and Mayhem: An Annotated Repertoire*. Lanham, MD: Rowman, 2014. 189. *Google Books*. 11 Apr. 2017.
185 William Gifford. *The Works of Ben Jonson with a Biographical Memoir*. London, 1838. 37. *Google Books*. 7 Apr. 2017.
186 Ben Jonson. "To the Memory of My Beloved the Author, Mr. William Shakespeare." *Poetry Foundation*. N.d. Web. 1 Mar. 2017.
187 Thomas P. Hughes. "Poets Laureate." *The University Magazine*. 7:6 (Dec. 1892) 457. *Google Books*. 7 Apr. 2017.
188 "Ben Jonson." *Westminster Abbey*. N.d. Web. 28 Aug. 2017.
189 "The Upstart Crow: Shakespeare's Feud with Robert Greene." *Hold That Thought*. 23 June 2015. Web. 10 Aug. 2017.
190 William Shakespeare. *Henry VI, Part 3*. *Folger*. 138-39.
191 James Halliwell-Phillipps. *Tarlton's Jests and News out of Purgatory*. London, 1844. ix. *Internet Archive*. 21 Apr. 2017.
192 Halliwell-Phillipps, ix.
193 Thomas Nashe. *The Works of Thomas Nashe*. Ed. Ronald B. McKerrow. London: Bullen, 1908. 114. *Internet Archive*. 24 Feb. 2017.
194 Edmund Bohun. *The Character of Queen Elizabeth*. London, 1693. 352-53. *Google Books*. 7 Apr. 2017.
195 William Shakespeare. *Hamlet*. *Folger*. 250-51.
196 "A Curious Case of Casting." *Utah Shakespeare Festival*. Southern Utah University. 26 August 2015. Web. 10 November 2016.
197 Shakespeare, *Hamlet*. *Folger*. 138.
198 William Kempe. *Kemp's Nine Daies Wonder*. *Luminarium*. 2000. Web. 10 Nov. 2016.
199 Christopher Marlowe. *Tamburlaine Parts 1 and 2*. Ed. Anthony B. Dawson. London: Bloomsbury, 2014. 151. *Google Books*. 24 Feb. 2017.
200 Christopher Marlowe. *The Tragedie of Doctor Faustus (B Text)*. Ed. Hilary Binda. *The Perseus Digital Library*. Tufts University. N.d. Web. 24 Feb. 2017.
201 Christopher Marlowe. *The Jew of Malta*. Mineola: Dover, 2003. 80. *Google Books*. 24 Feb. 2017.
202 Robert Greene. *Orlando Furioso*. *The Dramatic and Poetical Works of Robert Greene and George Peele*. Ed. Alexander Dyce. London, 1883. 98. *Google Books*. 24. Feb. 2017.
203 Shakespeare. *Henry VI, Part 3*. *Folger*. 51.
204 Edward Guilpin. "Epigram 43, Of Clodius." *Skialethia*. Ed. Alexander B. Grosart. Manchester, 1878.18. *Google Books*. 24 Feb. 2017.
205 "Alleyn, Edward." *The Biographical Dictionary for the Diffusion of Useful Knowledge*. Vol. 2. Part 1. London: 1843. 38. *Google Books*. 24 Feb. 2017.
206 J. Payne Collier, ed. *Memoirs of Edward Alleyn*. Shakespeare Society. London, 1841. 6. *Google Books*. 24 Feb. 2017.
207 Richard Corbet. *The Poems of Richard Corbet*. Ed. Octavius Gilchrist. London: 1807. 193-94. *Internet Archive*. 24 Feb. 2017.
208 William Shakespeare. *Richard III*. *Folger*. 299.
209 H. Schütz Wilson. "Phantom Puppets of the Stage of Shakespeare." *The Gentlemen's Magazine*. 293. July to December 1902. 468. Web. 27 Feb. 2017.
210 Richard Flecknoe. "A Short Discourse of the English Stage 1664." *Critical Essays of the Seventeenth Century*. Ed. J. E. Spingarn. Oxford: Clarendon, 1908. 95. *Internet Archive*. 27 Feb. 2017.*Archive*. 27 Feb. 2017.
211 Kyd. 4.1.
212 Dawn Powell. *The Diaries of Dawn Powell: 1931-1965*. Ed. Tim Page. South Royalton, VT: Steerforth, 1995. 194. Print.
213 Aristotle, 1.6.
214 Aristotle, 1.9.
215 Aristotle, 3.24.
216 Aristotle, 2.15.
217 Aristotle, 2.15.
218 Aristotle, 1.6.
219 Aristotle, 1.5.
220 Aristotle, 1.2.

221 Aristotle, 1.4.
222 Shakespeare. *Henry IV, Part 1. Folger.* 14.
223 Denton Jaques Snider. *The System of Shakespeare's Dramas.* St. Louis: Jones, 1877. *Shakespeare Online.* 20 Aug. 2009. Web. 1 Mar. 2017.
224 Dawn Lewcock. "The Masque of Blackness." *The Literary Encyclopedia.* 12 May 2007. Web.1 March 2017.
225 Ben Jonson. *The Masque of Blackness.* Ed. Simon Barker and Hilary Hinds. *The Routledge Anthology of Renaissance Drama.* London: Routledge, 2003. 226. *Google Books.* 1 May 2017.
226 James Stewart. *Daemonologie. Sacred Texts.* xiii. N.d. Web. 26 Jan. 2017.
227 Verena Theile and Andrew D. McCarthy, eds. *Staging the Superstitions of Early Modern Europe.* Farnham, SRY: Ashgate, 2013. Web. 7 Apr. 2017.
228 Shakespeare, *Hamlet. Folger.* 11.
229 Shakespeare, *Hamlet. Folger.* 90.
230 Shakespeare. *Hamlet. Open Source Shakespeare.* 2003-17. Web. 29 Aug. 2017.
231 Shakespeare, *Henry VI, Part 2. Folger.* 66.
232 *Looking for Richard.* Dir. Al Pacino. Perf. Al Pacino, Alec Baldwin, and Kevin Spacey. Fox Searchlight. 1996. Film; Shakespeare. *King John. Folger.* 149.
233 Shakespeare, *Romeo and Juliet. Folger.* 133.
234 Shakespeare, *The Tempest. Folger.* 13.
235 Jonathan D. Lewis. "If Cleopatra Were Alive Today, She Would Be Diagnosed as a Borderline Personality." *Hektoen International: A Journal of Medical Humanities.* Winter 2014. Web. 2 Dec. 2016.
236 "Depression (Major Depressive Disorder)." *Mayo Clinic.* 7 July 2016. Web. 1 Mar. 2017.
237 Shakespeare, *As You Like It. Folger.* 142.
238 Eric Altschuler. "Shakespeare Knew the Layered Clothing Sign of Schizophrenia." *BMJ.* 21 Aug. 1999. 319 (7208): 520. 1999. Web. 14 Dec. 2016.
239 Shakespeare, *King Lear. Folger.* 144.
240 Shakespeare, *Hamlet. Folger.* 46-47.
241 Bruce Hubbard. "Obsessive Thinking, Worry, and Cognitive Behavior Therapy." *Cognitive Health Group.* 2016. Web. 14 Dec. 2016.
242 Shakespeare, *Measure for Measure. Folger.* 35.
243 Daniel Freeman and Jason Freeman. *Paranoia: The 21st-century Fear.* Oxford: Oxford UP, 2008. 17-18, 23. *Google Books.* Web. 14 Dec. 2016.
244 Shakespeare, *A Winter's Tale. Folger.* 51.
245 Shakespeare, *Henry V. Folger.* 165.
246 Shakespeare, *Romeo. Folger.* 244.
247 Shakespeare, *Twelfth Night. Folger.* 62.
248 Shakespeare, *Henry IV, Part 2. Folger.* 111.
249 Shakespeare, *Henry V. Folger.* 147.
250 Shakespeare, *Merchant of Venice. Folger.* 155.
251 Shakespeare, *Merchant. Folger.* 98-99.
252 Shakespeare, *Merchant. Folger.* 7.
253 Shakespeare, *Midsummer Night's Dream. Folger.* 11.
254 Shakespeare. *King Lear. Folger. 61.*
255 Shakespeare, *Julius Caesar. Folger.* 26.
256 Shakespeare, *Henry VI, Part 1. Folger.* 170.
257 Shakespeare, *Othello. Folger.* 101.
258 Shakespeare, *Henry VI, Part 3. Folger.* 45-55.
259 Shakespeare, *Julius Caesar. Folger.* 21.
260 Shakespeare, *Comedy of Errors. Folger.* 19.
261 Shakespeare, *Julius Caesar. Folger.* 79-80.
262 Shakespeare, *Romeo. Folger.* 12-13.
263 Shakespeare, *Julius Caesar.* Ed. Albert Harris Tolman. New York: Globe School Book, 1901. xxv. *Google Books.* 22 Feb. 2017.
264 Shakespeare, *Julius Caesar.* Tolman. xxv-xxvi.
265 Shakespeare, *Julius Caesar.* Tolman. xxvi.
266 Aristotle, 2.6.
267 Shakespeare. *Henry V. Folger.* 23.
268 Shakespeare. *Romeo. Folger.* 92-93.
269 George Silver. *Paradoxes of Defence.* Ed. Cyrill G. R. Matthey. London: Bell, 1898. 65. *Internet Archive.* 22 Feb. 2017.
270 Silver, *Paradoxes.*

[271] Thomas Heywood. *The Four Prentices of London. A Selection of Old Plays*. Ed. R. Dodsley. London: 1825. 6:437-38. *Google Books*. 23 Feb. 2017.

[272] Reginald Scot. *The Discoverie of Witchcraft*. London, 1665. v. *Internet Archive*. 27 Apr. 2017.

[273] Scot, 286-87.

[274] Thomas Middleton. *Women Beware Women*. London: Bloomsbury Methuen, 1968. 110. *Internet Archive*. 22 Feb. 2017.

[275] "Special Effects." *Shakespeare's Globe*. 2014. Web. 22 Feb. 2017.

[276] Iain Wright. "Shakespeare's Smoke and Mirrors Tricks Solved." *Phys*. 15 Dec. 2005. Web. 23 Feb. 2017.

[277] G. H. Cowling. *Music on the Shakesperian [sic] Stage*. Cambridge: Cambridge UP, 1913. 3-4. *Hathi Trust Digital Library*. 23 Feb. 2017.

[278] Shakespeare, *Midsummer*. *Folger*. 169.

[279] Thomas Heywood and Richard Brome. *The Late Lancashire Witches*. Ed. Gabriel Egan. London: Nick Tern, 2002. 154. Web. 27 Apr. 2017.

[280] Kennedy, George Alexander. *Classical Rhetoric and Its Christian and Secular Tradition from Ancient to Modern Times*. Chapel Hill: U of North Carolina P, 1999. 247. Print.

[281] Shakespeare. *Henry VIII*. *Folger*. 231-32.

[282] Shakespeare. *Julius Caesar*. *Play Shakespeare*. N.d. Web. 27 Feb. 2017. In this section, all line numbers for *Julius Caesar* are from this edition.

[283] Tim Kirkjian. "It's Friday the Thirteenth: Be Afraid Amused." *ESPN*. 13 Sept. 2013. Web. 8 Aug. 2017.

[284] *Account of the Terrific and Fatal Riot at the New-York Astor Place Opera House, 1849*. New York: Ranney, 1849. 5-6. *Internet Archive*. 21 Feb. 2017.

[285] Heather Hill-Vásquez. *Sacred Players: The Politics of Response in the Middle English Religious Drama*. Washington, DC: Catholic U of America P, 2007. 51-74. *Google Books*. 12 Apr. 2017.

[286] Furnivall, *Digby*.

[287] Heywood and Brome. 50.

www.ingramcontent.com/pod-product-compliance
Lightning Source LLC
Chambersburg PA
CBHW081216170426
43198CB00017B/2630